Living
Prehistory

Living Prehistory

AN INTRODUCTION TO
PHYSICAL ANTHROPOLOGY
AND ARCHAEOLOGY

Sharon S. McKern
Thomas W. McKern

BENJAMIN/CUMMINGS PUBLISHING COMPANY
Menlo Park, California • Reading, Massachusetts
London • Amsterdam • Don Mills, Ontario • Sydney

illustrations and cover drawing by Darwen and Vally Hennings
cover design by Jaren Dahlstrom of Crow Quill Studios
book design by Paul Quinn

IN MEMORY OF
H. H. PATTERSON
AND FOR HIS
ROSIE, REID, AND LLOYD

PREFACE

With this volume we wish to bring the past to life—emphasizing not only bony remains and fragmentary artifacts but the depth and excitement of a prehistory which is alive. To know the prehistoric past is to wield pick and shovel, to lift rock and rubble, and to sift tons of ancient soil and other debris for bits of bones and cultural artifacts that serve as clues to our forgotten past. Although such excavation has been and still is the cornerstone upon which scientists reconstruct the past, it is now complemented by researchers pursuing highly original studies in "living prehistory." This term covers dozens of imaginative, new experiments in such areas as lithic technology, radiography, and primate art. In this text we combine basic principles of a number of disciplines that inquire in traditional ways into prehistory, and we also relate some of the newer, less conventional approaches.

With the emphasis on a "living prehistory" we present to students a concise but thorough coverage of the basic principles of physical anthropology and archaeology that is both lively and exciting. This text can be used effectively in Introductory General Anthropology classes as well as in one-term Physical Anthropology and Archaeology courses.

Part 1 introduces the study of prehistory, its relationship to other sciences, and its placement within the discipline of anthropology. A brief history of Western thought traces the scientific development of prehistory from Greco-Roman times to the present. A discussion of comparative anatomy and embryology introduces the field of physical anthropology. Here and throughout the text, definitions placed in the margins help emphasize and explain important terms and concepts.

Part 2, which concentrates on physical anthropology, begins

with the study of Mendelian genetics and concepts of evolution. A discussion of contemporary primates and studies in primatology prepares the student for an understanding of our primate heritage. The fossil record of the Primates through the Pliocene is followed by a detailed description of the fossil hominids through *Homo sapiens*. Numerous illustrations drawn especially for this volume clarify the relationships between monkeys, apes, and humans. These illustrations also help the student understand the nature of the hominid fossils and the reasons for the varying interpretations of the fossil record. The section concludes with a discussion of studies in human variation.

Part 3 is devoted to archaeology and presents a wide variety of methods employed to reconstruct the human past. Emphasis is on cultural prehistory—paleolithic industries, the development of agriculture and the rise of civilization in both the Old and New Worlds are covered. The section ends with some of the latest methods in "living prehistory."

We have drawn heavily upon advice and material generously extended by our friends and colleagues and we are grateful for their help. Our special thanks go to the members of the editorial and production staff of Cummings Publishing Company for their enthusiasm and invaluable assistance.

SHARON S. MCKERN
THOMAS W. MCKERN

VANCOUVER, B.C.
JANUARY, 1974.

CONTENTS

PART 3
STUDIES IN ARCHAEOLOGY 175

PART 1
INTRODUCTION

PART
INTRODUCTION

CHAPTER I

INTRODUCTION TO
THE STUDY OF PREHISTORY

It has not always been prudent to search the shadows of the distant past. For example, Giordano Bruno, a sixteenth-century Italian philosopher, merely suggested that fossils might represent the remains of once-living creatures. He was driven from his home, excommunicated from the Church, imprisoned for seven years, and, finally, burned at the stake. Bernard Palissy, a prominent French potter and glass-painter who collected fossils in his sparc time, made the mistake of writing a book about his collections. The 78-year-old artist was thrown into the Bastillc, where he died two years later of malnutrition and ill treatment.

FOS´ SIL
any hardened remains of past plant or animal life; any organic object that has been preserved in or transformed into stone, or one that has left an imprint in stone.

The penalties for original thinking were less severe three centuries later when Charles Darwin introduced his theory of organic evolution, suggesting that forms change, or modify, over vast periods of time. Nevertheless, Darwin, who realized his ideas would be unpopular in Victorian England, hesitated for more than twenty years before publishing *The Origin of Species* in 1859. And hesitate he might, for he was lampooned in newspapers around the world and ridiculed on every street corner. Some of his American followers were threatened with fines, imprisonment, and hanging. This single volume, so cautiously authored, triggered a storm of controversy that rages in some quarters even today.

EV´ O LU´ TION
the theory of organic or biological evolution postulates that all existing life forms have grown out of preceding life forms through a natural process of change and modification.

Those who do not fully understand Darwin's theory battle phantom issues. "We didn't crawl out from under any rocks!" "We never had tails!" "We didn't come from prehistoric monkeys!"

And we did not, of course; but then Darwin never claimed that we did. What he did suggest, in subsequent writings, was that man and the modern primates, including the monkeys and the apes, share a mutual animal ancestor that existed ten to

twenty million years ago. But few books have been as widely
misquoted as Darwin's *Origin of Species* and his *Descent of Man,*
published some twelve years later. And few disciplines have been
as widely misunderstood as the science of prehistory, the goal
of which is to reconstruct the development of man and his
primate relatives.

PRE HIS′ TO RY
the study of life
before the time
of recorded
history, usually
through the
combined
methodologies
of archaeology
and physical
anthropology.

    Prehistory is a unique scientific discipline. It takes its evidence
in large part from the dead—from ancient tombs, gravesites, and
scattered skeletons; but its aim is the illumination of the *living*
past. It is not enough to excavate the bones of prehistoric man
and display them as museum curiosities. Human nature has its
deepest origins in the ancient past, and in order to understand
modern human beings and their behavior, we must learn about
patterns of thought and action that were established millions
of years ago. Toward this end, prehistorians use the evidence
contained in stone and bone to reconstruct human origins, to
decipher man's relationships with other primates, to trace his
biological and his cultural development, and to answer a host
of questions that deal directly with man's past and present
nature:

    Who were the ancestors of modern humans?

    In what racial varieties did they appear?

    What did they look like?

    On what animals did they prey?

    Who were their enemies?

    How did they organize into social and economic groups?

    Which patterns of behavior accounted for their group survival?

    What attitudes and beliefs guided their daily actions?

    How did they choose their mates?

    In what ways did they distinguish between male and female
roles?

    What forces led them to discovery and invention?

    Which pressures shaped their earliest nature?

    What remains of that early nature to influence the tempera-
ment and behavior of modern human beings?

Prehistory as Anthropology

These questions and countless others like them fall into the province of *anthropology,* the broader science of which prehistory is an important part. Anthropology is the "science of man"—the only science which claims to investigate both man's physical and his cultural nature. In a sense, of course, all the social sciences are concerned with man; they differ only in emphasis or approach. Sociology, for example, deals with man as a member of a group in order to examine the dynamics of group behavior; psychology focuses on individual human behavior; history studies man on the basis of past human events; and economics deals with problems of human trade and commerce. Scientists in these fields and in numerous others have as a common goal a fuller understanding of human behavior. Each, however, selects a single aspect of behavior through which to approach his study. Collectively, anthropologists investigate man as an integrated whole. Essentially, they are synthesizers, drawing together knowledge gleaned from their own and dozens of other sciences in order to illuminate the whole of man's biological and social nature.

AN' THRO PO' LO GY the comparative study of mankind both past and present.

CUL' TURE the integrated sum of learned patterns of behavior characteristic of the members of a society; also, the material objects produced through such patterns of behavior.

Anthropology as a Unique Science

Man is first of all a physical organism subject to the same natural laws as other animals. But he is also a social animal, and a unique one at that, although social organization is known among numerous animals. Bee society, for example, is noted for its clear division of labor among drones, workers, and queens. For such animals, behavior is instinctive. Individuals carry out their life-roles without coaching from their parents or other adults. Behavior is genetically determined. For man, however, most behavior is learned. Man's uniqueness lies in his capacity for culture, the potential, born of a complex mental development unsurpassed in the animal kingdom, which enables man to manipulate the environment to suit his own desires and comfort.

Since man can be classified as neither a wholly biological nor a wholly social animal, anthropologists take into account man's dual nature, recognizing that he is subject to natural laws, yet studying him always with reference to the ways in which

he modifies or directs the course of his own destiny. This makes
for an infinitely complex science and inevitably generates a high
degree of specialization.

The Divisions of Anthropology

Generally, anthropology is divided into two main categories:
cultural anthropology and *physical anthropology*. Scientists in the
former field are concerned with the origin and development of
man's culture—his tools, languages, arts and crafts, politics, reli-
gions, courtship and mating behavior, and systems of kinship.
Even within this branch of anthropology, the mass of information
is clearly overwhelming, and so, although all anthropologists
receive generalized training in the varied divisions of anthropology, most choose one or two sub-disciplines on which to focus
their advanced training and their professional research. The

FIGURE 1. The disciplines of anthropology and their relationships to the social,
biological, and physical sciences. (© James D. Wilmeth and Darwen Hennings)

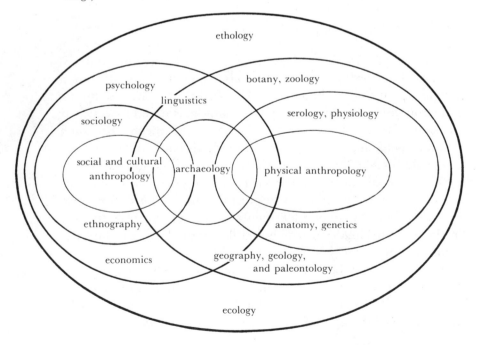

following are just a few of the sub-divisions in cultural anthropology:

ARCHAEOLOGY, the reconstruction of the human past, generally through analysis of cultural evidence left behind by ancient peoples;

ETHNOGRAPHY, the descriptive study of human societies;

ETHNOLOGY, the analysis and systematic interpretation of cultural information;

LINGUISTICS, the study of written and spoken languages;

SOCIAL ANTHROPOLOGY, the study of social structures, including kinship, political organization, religion, law, and economics.

Physical anthropologists concentrate on the development and current nature of human physical structure—but with constant reference to human cultural capacity. Among the fields of specialization within physical anthropology are the following:

PALEOANTHROPOLOGY, the study of fossil populations, including ancient human groups and the fossil apes;

PALEOPATHOLOGY, the study of disease and injury among prehistoric varieties of man;

PRIMATOLOGY, the study of man's living primate relatives, with emphasis on Old World monkeys and the four existing great apes (the gorilla, chimpanzee, orang-utan, and gibbon);

RACIAL STUDIES, the study of man's racial varieties;

OSTEOLOGY, the study of bone growth and bone structure;

ANTHROPOMETRY, the comparative measurement of human populations.

Because it is intended as an introduction to the study of prehistory, this text emphasizes the work of the physical anthropologist as a prehistorian, although his crucial role as a human biologist is not forgotten. Current studies in human biology are noted in later chapters, and the bibliography following Chapter VIII focuses on human genetics, biochemistry, and other biological data which provide a research framework within which investigations of past and present human nature may be pursued.

Prehistorians defy classification. Since their efforts are directed toward the total reconstruction of human life in the distant past, they straddle the division between cultural and physical anthropology, and draw their evidence from both. A prehistorian may take his training in archaeology or paleoanthropology, or be drawn into the study of prehistory through research in geology, genetics, anatomy, or zoology. In any case, he is ultimately interested not only in the ruins and relics left behind by early man but also in man's biological nature, his kinship with other groups, his social behavior, and his most remote life history.

Prehistorians apply the techniques and methodologies of archaeology in extracting cultural artifacts and skeletal remains from ancient sites. In interpreting the evidence they gather, they often utilize methods of physical anthropology and in addition borrow tools and techniques from dozens of related sciences. Even in relatively modest archaeological excavations the skills of diverse scientists are brought to bear on the over-all problem of reconstruction.

Students attending the 1969 and 1970 Canadian summer field schools sponsored by the Department of Archaeology at Simon Fraser University excavated a site known as Kwatna Bay, near Bella Coola in northern British Columbia. Their purpose was to learn more about the early Indian populations of the northwest coast, and they chose this particular site because it was once a popular Indian fishing location. Excavations were completed by the end of the summer of 1970, but analysis and interpretation go on even today.

One of the most productive areas of the Kwatna Bay site turned out to be the village dump, where refuse had been thrown by generations of Indian inhabitants—some dating back 2000 years. Lengths of cedar rope, animal bones and other food remnants, fish hooks, wooden wedges, and other implements were tossed into the dump as garbage. To the S.F.U. archaeologists it was priceless material from which to draw insights into the daily lives of vanished tribes.

Ancient refuse provides important information in any archaeological site, but at Kwatna Bay the dump was spectacularly productive. Here refuse was covered by silt each day by the outgoing tide, and perishable material—the sort normally subject

GE OL′ O GY
the science dealing with the formation and development of the earth's various layers, and the study of early life forms represented as fossils in the rocks.

GE NE′ TICS
that branch of biology that deals with heredity and variation in similar or related plants and animals.

A NAT′ O MY
the science of the morphology, or structure, of plants and animals.

ZO OL′ O GY
the division of biology that deals with the classification of animals and the study of animal life.

to rapid decay—was encased in wet mud and thus preserved.

The archaeologists at S.F.U. must sift through hundreds of bits of material taken from the Kwatna Bay excavation. Each bit must be catalogued, photographed, identified, and preserved. In most cases, identification is relatively simple. In classifying ancient evidence, archaeologists use what they call *ethnographic analogy;* that is, they compare excavated artifacts with objects of known function (usually items in use today by largely unacculterated peoples) and, based on similarity of shape and structure, make conclusive functional identifications. This was the case, for example, at Kwatna Bay when dozens of bone fish-hooks were unearthed from the refuse heap. The archaeologists had seen hundreds of similar implements in previous excavations, and they were familiar with similar bone hooks used by modern Eskimo fishermen.

This procedure also illustrates the inextricable bond that exists between archaeology and the other sub-disciplines of anthropology. Archaeologists draw constantly upon their knowledge of ethnography in making archaeological analogies, and if their knowledge is insufficient, they turn readily to their colleagues in cultural anthropology for assistance.

SPECIALISTS IN PREHISTORIC ANALYSIS

In every excavation, the archaeologist is in charge of all field investigations. He arranges financial support, selects student participants or hires outside labor, organizes the excavation, and supervises the work in progress. At any phase of excavation, however, he is likely to call upon the specialized skills of his colleagues both in and outside anthropology. For example, geologists often aid in the selection of the site. They might direct the archaeologist to the almost-invisible borders of an ancient, dried-up streambed where prehistoric hunters are likely to have camped. In the case of Kwatna Bay, however, historians rather than geologists pinpointed the target site: written records told of the existence at Kwatna Bay of an abandoned Indian village.

Surveyors and photographers map the general region of the site before excavation, often arranging for aerial photographs to be taken. In this way, archaeologists are assured of a detailed record of the site as it exists before its surface is obliterated by digging. As excavation begins, draftsmen and photographers document the exact position of each bone or artifact before removing it from the burial environment. Museum curators contribute methods and materials for preserving and cataloging excavated specimens.

Regardless of the effort involved in these preliminaries, the work has not really begun until evidence begins to emerge from the site. That is when the archaeologists begin their intensive analyses of excavated materials, often in consultation with experts from allied sciences. Artifacts made of stone—tools, implements, carvings, rock-work used in the building of ancient walls and houses—are given to geologists for examination; these scientists can readily identify stone which is not native to the region and which therefore indicates trade or importation by early man.

PAL′ Y NOL O GY the branch of science concerned with the study of spores and pollen for the purpose of determining prehistoric climatic conditions.

Soil samples are sent to chemists who, by microscopic analysis, determine the chemical composition of the samples and thus help to characterize the nature of the site's environment at the time of habitation. Samples are sent also to palynologists who analyze the soil for grains of fossil pollen in an attempt to determine which trees, shrubs, and other vegetation flourished at the site in ancient times. Archaeologists learn more in this way about the habitat and the diet of the people who once inhabited the site under excavation.

[1] See Chapter IX.

Samples of organic material are forwarded to physicists and chemists for laboratory dating techniques. There are numerous ways to determine the age of cultural or skeletal remains,[1] and one of the most common is the radiocarbon technique, often called *carbon-14*. Results of carbon-14 tests performed on objects taken from the site at Kwatna Bay indicate that the settlement had been occupied continuously since about 1000 A.D. It was abandoned, according to written records, about a century ago.

OR GAN′ IC derived from or having the characteristics of living organisms.

CAR′ BON *14* a radioactive isotope that provides the basis for a technique of archaeological dating.

Prehistorians and archaeologists are usually familiar with the fauna characteristic of the region under study and are able to identify animal remains without the aid of colleagues from other fields. This was the case at Kwatna Bay. However, when animal bones cannot easily be identified, they are sent to paleontologists or zoologists for analysis. Shells and fish bones are identified by marine biologists.

Human skeletal remains go to the physical anthropologist. The bones, interpreted through the techniques of osteology and osteometry, yield important information on the physical nature of the site's inhabitants and on possible kinships with inhabitants of nearby regions. Co-mingled remains (bones mixed in a burial) are first separated, and the physical anthropologist examines each skeleton for distinguishing features. Through an analysis of bone structure, he can determine age at the time of death, sex, race, living height, and approximate living weight. Often, he discovers traces of specific diseases or injuries suffered during life, and sometimes he is able to pinpoint the actual cause of death.[2]

Occasionally, cultural practices also leave their marks on a human skeleton. This was so at Kwatna Bay, where archaeologists recovered a human skull containing fifteen neatly drilled holes, some of which were fitted with bone pegs. The holes were

PA LE ON TOL′ O GY the branch of geology that deals with prehistoric life forms through the study of fossilized plants and animals.

OS TE O′ ME TRY the comparative measurement of skeletal remains.

[2] See Chapter IX.

FIGURE 2. Human skull found at Kwatna Bay, British Columbia, containing fifteen drilled holes, some fitted with pegs. Ethnographic studies suggest that the skull may have been utilized in tribal rites. (Photo courtesy Owen Beatty)

drilled or punched shortly after death, before the bone became brittle. Indians now living in the area recall no custom or ceremony connected with the piercing of human skull-bone, and no local literature exists which might explain the baffling find. But ethnographic studies of related tribes tell of the use of pegged skulls as tools of the magician's trade. Did the pegged skull come from an ancient medicine bag? No one knows, for in a science that takes its evidence from the distant past, there are always more questions than there are answers. And prehistorians get by with more than a little help from their friends.

Interdisciplinary Studies in Prehistory

Scholars in almost every field join with archaeologists and physical anthropologists in searching for the hidden facts of man's buried past, and few paths are left unexplored in the continuing quest for more and better answers. Geographers who trace the distribution of mankind over the globe are often able to reconstruct ancient migration routes, adding to the prehistorian's knowledge of past human movements and contacts. Sociologists who study modern human groups make important contributions to our growing knowledge of the nature and development of ancient cities and civilizations. Zoologists and primatologists observe and record every aspect of behavior among free-ranging monkeys and apes in the hope that prehistorians may one day be able to reconstruct the social life of our earliest ancestors. Anatomists study the human form, in an attempt to define man's true taxonomic position. Serologists trace kinships among modern groups of men and relationships between man and the non-human primates through similarities in blood chemistry. Embryologists venture to investigate the human egg, watching human development before birth occurs, and geneticists examine the cell nucleus itself, seeking the answers that eluded Darwin and his pioneering nineteenth-century colleagues.

Gone forever are the days in which prehistorians sought their answers with picks and shovels alone. This is not to say that excavation no longer plays an important role in prehistoric inquiry. But now, armed with new tools and refined techniques, prehistorians plot far-ranging investigations that are more ambi-

TAX ON´ O MY
the systematic
classification of
plants and
animals
according to
scientific
principles.

SE ROL´ O GY
the science that
deals with the
properties or use
of blood serums.

EM BRY O´ LO GY
the study of an
animal in all
prenatal stages
of development.

tious, productive, and imaginative than ever before. Archaeologists at the University of Pennsylvania, for example, are using a computer to aid in the reconstruction of an ancient Egyptian temple—one that has been dismantled, its pieces scattered, for more than 3300 years. About 35,000 relief-cut sandstone blocks from the destroyed temple had been located in museums and antiquity storehouses around the world, but the problems of actual, physical re-assembly were insurmountable. With the help of modern computer science, however, a pictorial reconstruction could be made. Each sandstone block was photographed and coded on IBM cards, which were fed into a master computer at Cairo. Investigators then set to work matching photos in the sequence ordered by computer. The government-financed study is designed to yield important new information on six "lost" years of Egyptian history—from 1367 to 1361 B.C.—and shed new light on the little-known reign of King Akhenaten, a time of enormous human activity, in which one of the greatest concentrations of building took place.

Prehistorians have also made productive liaisons with chemists and physicists. In 1970, Nobel Prize-winning physicist Luiz Alvarez used *muons*—high-energy particles from space—to scan the 4500-year-old Second Pyramid at Giza for hidden burial chambers. Alvarez believes that, by using his new detecting device much as a physician uses x-rays to scan body cavities, he can locate yet-unknown chambers in the inner pyramid.

Physicists, engineers, and archaeologists collaborated on the production of the *cesium magnometer,* an instrument designed to detect buried artifacts. University of Pennsylvania prehistorians utilized this sensitive new device in 1970 to locate the ancient city of Sybaris, which had been lost for more than 2500 years.

In addition, techniques of *thermal radiography* are used to pinpoint previously-undetected archaeological sites. Buried stone constructions absorb and retain heat from the sun to a greater degree than does surrounding soil or vegetation, and variations in heat retention show up in aerial photographs taken with infra-red film. So far, the method has been useful only for shallow sites, but improvements are expected. Even now aerial photographers can "map" vast geographic regions in a single afternoon. Resulting photos lead archaeologists directly to sites buried near the soil surface. A similar technique, *microwave radiometry,* has been used successfully in Central America to locate ancient Mayan sites hidden beneath the jungle canopy in dense tropical forests.

In 1960, archaeologists and physicists at Oxford University teamed up to test a new method of dating ancient pottery. Called *thermoluminescent dating,* this technique is based on the fact that most fired clay traps by absorption numbers of free electrons from the atmosphere and does so at a constant rate. When a clay object is heated to its original firing temperature, the electrons become energized and escape, emitting high-frequency light waves in the process. By measuring these tiny quantities of light, which are not visible to the human eye, scientists can date fragments of pottery unearthed from archaeological sites. In the first year of use, the test revealed nearly fifty forgeries in collections of prehistoric Turkish pottery housed in American and British museums.

Another way in which interdisciplinary cooperation yields significant results is in the examination of evidence from many points of view. In 1971, this method led prehistorians much closer to agreement that *Australopithecus africanus,* a fossil primate dating back some five million years, was indeed an ancestor to modern man. This near agreement, rare in a field noted for its controversies and baffling contradictions, was effected by paleontologists, biochemists, and primatologists collaborating to gather the most recent evidence for the nature of *Australopithecus.*

Increasingly, important supplementary investigations are conducted in the laboratory and among modern primate—both human and non-human—populations. Here, particularly in the fast-paced field of genetics, giant strides are taken in the race for new knowledge of early man. Prehistorians do not hesitate to seize upon tools and techniques developed by scientists in such related fields, but in addition they often formulate unique methods of their own in order to pursue some specific, individual research goal.

L. S. B. Leakey, until his death in October, 1972 one of the most diligent workers in the field of prehistory, provides us with an excellent example. Leakey began his researches at Olduvai Gorge in Tanzania, East Africa, nearly fifty years ago. Accompanied by his scientist-wife Mary, he has been responsible for some of the most exciting developments in paleoanthropology. Although Leakey is best known for his fossil discoveries, he never claimed human paleontology as his only field of interest. His contributions to geology are significant: at Olduvai, he succeeded in uncovering a continuous geologic sequence that spans more than two million years. Fossils recovered from successive geologic layers help to compose a fascinating panorama of life in ancient East Africa.

Like his imaginative colleagues, Leakey was not content to know only what early man looked like, or what sort of stone tools he favored. Instead, Leakey sought to reconstruct the total daily life of prehistoric man, and he did so by immersing himself in the problems that must have confronted our most remote ancestors.

Chief among these was food-getting. Leakey taught himself to make stone tools identical with those found buried with the bones of early man. By using these to butcher wild game (he could skin and butcher an antelope, with tools of his own making, in little more than an hour), Leakey learned how early hunters went about this necessary task. In other experiments, Leakey tried to duplicate prehistoric hunting techniques. With leafy branches tied to his belt in crude camouflage, Leakey stalked

FIGURE 3.   Louis S. B. Leakey. Here Dr. Leakey displays the broken molar of a dinotherium and, on his hat, a million-year-old elephant tooth discovered at Olduvai. (© National Geographic Society)

the animals of the African savanna—advancing slowly, freezing when the prey sensed movement, pouncing with one great flying tackle. He captured wild hares with his bare hands, and flung himself upon grazing antelope with speed and agility unique in a man in his sixties.

Leakey and others like him represent a remarkable new breed of prehistorian. They are scientists dedicated not to the study of the dead but of the living—past and present. They are responsible as well for the convergence of numerous separate disciplines in prehistory. Willing to cross traditional barriers, eager to borrow freely the tools and techniques of related sciences, and sufficiently imaginative to devise new and unorthodox methods of their own, they bring a special flair to an already dynamic science.

Prehistory, of course, is an exceptional discipline, and it is not surprising that it often demands exceptional treatment—even if it means stalking, like Leakey, a fleeing hare. Few other sciences attempt to delineate so wide and diverse a range of subject matter. Fewer still have had to work, from the very beginning, with such sparse and fragmentary evidence.

Like other scientists, prehistorians have had to contend with social and religious pressures which would at times have denied the expression of scientific observation. Unlike other scientists, however, prehistorians boast no long tradition of scientific development and expansion. As we shall see in the following pages, archaeology and physical anthropology have their roots in half a dozen nineteenth-century sciences on which they are still dependent. Nevertheless, prehistorians have managed in a relatively brief time to weave together the twin threads of prehistoric evidence—man's fossil remains and the artifacts he left behind —into a rough tapestry of past human achievement.

CHAPTER II

THE HISTORICAL PERSPECTIVE

There are sound, practical reasons for studying archaeology and physical anthropology. If we are to modify human behavior in ways that will help to improve the quality of modern life, then we must probe characteristic patterns of human thought and action. These were established in the distant past, at the very dawn of human existence.

Also, as in other sciences, "spin-off" benefits are common. Evidence from archaeology, for example, has led on more than one occasion to new directions in medical research. Several diseases previously assumed to be modern in origin (including arteriosclerosis, or hardening of the arteries, and cirrhosis of the liver) have been diagnosed in ancient Egyptian mummies. Such discoveries trigger new research into causative factors.

Physical anthropologists who specialize in anthropometry contribute invaluable knowledge to designers and manufacturers of machines, office equipment, home appliances, clothing, and facilities for aerospace exploration. Through studies of general and racial human variation, they have devised chromatic scales which measure quantitatively minute variations in skin color. Among other uses, such scales make possible the development and mass manufacture of cosmetics. Recently improved scales, together with instruments that measure light reflectance (reflectometers) have permitted the development and distribution of new cosmetics for black women. In numerous other ways, new knowledge of man's past and present nature is applied to the solution of both major and minor modern problems.

Even if this were not the case, scholars would nevertheless study fossil bones and ancient artifacts, for no subject so fascinates man as man himself. Man's natural curiosity, basic to any scientific endeavor, has played a crucial role in the development of the study of prehistory. The peoples of early societies were interested in knowing more about their immediate ancestors and about the ancestors of the peoples with whom they traded and waged war. They were puzzled by the curious objects they found in the ground—bones that could not belong to any living animal, artifacts whose purposes could not be deciphered, scattered ruins of civilizations long lost from human memory. They were excited by fantastic tales told by seafaring travelers, and intrigued by reports of wild alien peoples with hairy bodies and strange life-ways that bore little resemblance to those of known races of human beings.

The Classic Scholars

It is not surprising that the Greeks, pioneers in so many sciences, were the first to attempt a serious study of prehistory. The Greek classic period was an era of unprecedented physical and intellectual human activity. It was a dynamic time, when men traveled, recorded their observations, and pondered the significance of what they had learned. And much of their study centered on man and his origins.

No coordinated efforts were made in classical Greece to consolidate available facts bearing on the study of man, but information was collected and theories were advanced. The Greeks were devoted to the principle of careful observation and endowed with boundless curiosity. If their early theories contain obvious and seemingly naive errors, they are errors which have been corrected only in the recent past, and they should not lessen our admiration for the Greeks' efforts in the field of prehistory.

For example, Herodotus (484–425 B.C.) posed numerous questions that are familiar to modern physical anthropologists and archaeologists:

Is the human physique affected by habits of diet or life-style?

What effects does climate have on body form?

How long did it take for mankind to differentiate into separate races?

Do human customs arise independently, or must an historical connection account for similar life-ways?

Herodotus traveled widely and made copious notes. He anticipated future methods of research by carefully recording the
physical characteristics, customs, and habits of the diverse peoples he met on his voyages. And he chanced a few tentative
theories in the hope of explaining what he had seen. For example,
he noticed that the skulls of the Egyptians were thick compared
with those of the Persians, and he attributed the difference to
environment and custom. He noted that the Egyptians shaved
the heads of their children, letting them run hatless in the sun,
while the Persians covered their children's heads and kept them
from the light. In spite of his careful research, however, Herodotus never gained much favor among his contemporaries, and
his writings were generally ignored during his lifetime. Today,
however, he is known as the "father of anthropology," for he
succeeded in keeping alive a flickering spark of interest in the
diverse peoples who lived in different geographic regions.

The testimony of other travelers fanned this spark. Hanno,
for instance, a Carthaginian navigator of the fifth century B.C.,
was responsible for one of the earliest accounts of human variation. He was commissioned by his government to establish colonies in coastal Morocco, but this is of less interest to modern
scientists than his secondary chore of record-keeping.

In addition, sailing close to the African coast, Hanno sighted
"wild people," mostly "women with hairy bodies." Later in-
terpreters corrected Hanno's excited impressions, calling these
creatures gorillas or chimpanzees. And although he confused
them with humans in this early instance, Hanno gave us the
first indication of the presence of great apes in Africa.

The geographer Scylax traveled through the Mediterranean
area and to the Indus delta, making careful notes on the distinct
racial groups he encountered. Ctesias, physician to the king of
Persia, described the inhabitants of India, and numerous subsequent voyagers added to the growing stockpile of information
regarding diverse human populations. It was from such data
that Greek and Roman philosophers formulated their theories
to explain the origins and the diversity of mankind. And in
the sixth century B.C., Archelaus of Miletus offered an early
evolutionary theory for man, suggesting that man was derived
from a fish that came ashore to develop on land.

Empedocles (*ca.* 496–430 B.C.), both physician and philosopher, is best remembered for his fanciful account of organic evolution. He theorized that in the beginning different parts of humans and animals (heads, hands, arms, legs, eyes, and so forth) wandered about separately. Chance combinations of these parts was precipitated by love or some other mutual attraction and resulted not only in present life forms but in grotesque types of monsters as well.

Hippocrates (460–357 B.C.) sought more realistic factors in accounting for the present nature of man. He believed that physical and mental traits were subject to the effects of environment, and he urged that cities be located where ideal climates might favorably affect human physical development.

Aristotle (384–322 B.C.) was the first scientist before Linnaeus to set forth the belief that man must be classified with the animals. In addition, he rightfully classed bats with the mammals rather than with the birds, and whales with the mammals rather than with the fishes. Undoubtedly, he understood the difference between morphological similarities that arose from like function and those that arose from common ancestry. This distinction was not fully grasped by other scientists until after the Middle Ages.

MOR PHOL' O GY
the bodily
structure of an
organism.

The Roman Titus Lucretius Carus (98–55 B.C.) was among the first to set forth a theory of cultural development. He believed that civilization was the product of a long and complicated course of human development. In the beginning, Lucretius wrote, man lived much as other animals do. He had no knowledge of fire, clothing, agriculture, or law. He lived in caves, and government, marriage, and family life were unknown to him. He was a vulgar and a brutish beast.

In time, however, man began to build crude huts for shelter. He developed a primitive form of family life and took to wearing skin garments. A natural impulse led him to develop his ability for speech. He discovered fire accidentally, either from lightning or from a chance rubbing-together of dry twigs. At first, war was rare, for early man had to fight with only fists, boughs, and stones.

With the discovery of copper, however, man found more effective means for waging war and for tilling the soil, and the subsequent use of iron provided an even more efficient means of producing tools and weapons. Slowly man progressed to the civilized state.

However crude, Lucretius' theory is indeed a reflection of the development of civilization based upon philosophical speculation. Such early theories of man and society were filled with glaring errors and easy generalizations, and they were often based more firmly on imagination than observation. Nevertheless, they contained insights remarkable for their time.

The Greeks and Romans collected fossils and recognized them for what they were. They appreciated the vast extent of human variation, both physical and cultural. They had some notion of how environment might shape the course of human development, and they formulated a few tentative theories regarding the evolution of man and society.

The Middle Ages

With the coming of the Middle Ages, however, these extraordinary Greco-Roman insights were forgotten. The story of creation as set forth in Genesis replaced former speculations concerning the origins of earth and man. Fossils were no longer regarded as petrifactions of once-living organisms but as freaks of nature, products of a mysterious supernatural power that modeled in stone all sorts of strange and bizarre creatures.

This is not to say that scientific researches ceased entirely during the Middle Ages, for a few significant contributions were made in the field of accumulated knowledge. Thomas Aquinas (1226–1374 A.D.) developed a taxonomic classification of human beings, placing man midway between the angels and the lower animals. In addition, he recognized the importance of man's erect posture, noting that if man walked prone to the ground he would be forced to use his hands as forefeet, surrendering their utility for other purposes. Numerous travelers—Marco Polo, John Plano de Carpini, William de Rubruquis, and the adventurous Viking raiders—penetrated distant lands; their voyages furnished valuable additional information regarding the physical nature and customs of alien peoples. European universities began to evolve from guild-like associations of masters and students.

Medical schools were established. King Frederick II of Germany
(1194–1250) formulated elaborate regulations regarding medical
research, decreeing that each student must know human anatomy
and must witness the dissection of a human cadaver.[1]

Unfortunately, such advances were eclipsed by a stringent new
emphasis on religious scholasticism. Studies in all branches of
learning passed into the hands of the clergy, where they remained
for more than a thousand years. Theology was the order of the
day. Christian faith as revealed in scripture was regarded as
a matter of supreme interest, and scientific experimentation, if
it was permitted at all, took a back seat.

It was during the Middle Ages that the "deluge theory"—one
that would hamper all research in prehistory for generations
to come—was first formulated. Its chief architect was an Italian
naturalist named Ristoro d'Arezzo, who believed, during the
early part of his career, that fossils were products of the sun
and stars, whose rays beamed down upon the earth to make
whimsical impressions in the rocks. By 1282, he had changed
his mind, deciding that fossils represented petrifactions of once-
living organisms. Noting marine fossils in inland regions, he
insisted that the deluge described in the Bible had left obvious
traces on the earth. Seashells found near towering mountain
peaks, he said, proved that these same mountains were once
swept by the waves of the biblical flood. D'Arezzo's theory
blended nicely with the Old Testament account of the creation
and the biblical deluge. Yet, surprisingly, his work was ignored;
it was not reconsidered until more than four centuries later.

In the meantime, fossils continued to be regarded as inorganic
freaks and curiosities. Any other interpretation of the mysterious
"figure-stones" was held to run counter to the biblical story of
creation, and thus contrary to the interests of the Church. Indeed,
it became quite a risky business to regard fossils as objects of
organic origin. Understandably, most well-known scientists fell
silent on the subject of the "figure-stones." The public was free
to manufacture their own interpretations of the strange forms
they found etched in rock. And manufacture tales they did: soon

---

[1] Frederick was twice excommunicated from the Church for his trouble. The Papacy
steadfastly held that the opening of a human body constituted mortal sin.

ancient stories of dead giants, fanged demons, and fire-breathing dragons were revived and embellished throughout Europe.

THE RENAISSANCE

Then, with the beginning of the fifteenth century, came the Renaissance, and with it a revived interest in human history and prehistory. Early travelers' tales, revived from classical sources, provided much of the stimulus for the systematic collection of odd and exotic curiosities, including not only artifacts from the classical civilizations of Greece and Rome but fossil bones from earlier times as well.

The first impressive collections began to accumulate in the Vatican itself, as a succession of Popes collected dazzling antiquities for their own amusement. Lesser clergy and rich laymen quickly followed suit, furnishing their opulent villas with ancient art treasures. In the race to obtain rarer, more extraordinary prizes, the first private excavations were conducted in the Mediterranean region. Little if any attention was paid to the reconstruction of ancient cultures. Those who could afford to finance such expeditions were collectors rather than scientists, and they were motivated by collector's zeal, stripping their excavation sites of whatever treasures lay hidden within.

During the period between the sixteenth and eighteenth centuries, however, a different kind of antiquarianism developed in England. Here investigations were better organized and more sophisticated in scope and purpose, and they emphasized description and preservation rather than random collection.

AN TI QUAR' I AN ISM
an interest in the collection of ancient objects and artifacts.

John Leland, appointed King's Antiquary, must be considered the first state-supported archaeologist; it was his job to travel throughout England and Wales to inspect and describe known prehistoric sites. He was the only person ever to fill the post; but later, in 1572, a group of concerned subjects petitioned Queen Elizabeth for a charter to establish a society for the preservation of national antiquities.[2] Museum personnel and county historians began to scour the countryside for prehistoric

---

[2] The society was short-lived. After Elizabeth's death, James I abolished the society on the grounds that its aim was political.

ruins, initiating the first serious field studies in archaeology. Of these, John Aubrey is the best known. He investigated the curious stone structures at Stonehenge, on Salisbury Plain in England, and deduced that they must mark the site of ancient astronomical observances. Modern researchers agree.

Although observation was the rule at home, collecting abroad was encouraged. This period is known, in fact, as the "Age of Collectors." Charles I, stating that the study of antiquities was "serviceable and useful to the general good of the State and Commonwealth," used his admirals as collecting agents wherever they went. France's Napoleon I did the same.

The roots of modern archaeology lay in this early period of observation, description, and collection. Excavation was not common until the middle of the eighteenth century, when serious investigators in Europe began to dig for information about the buried past. Priceless artifacts and curious fossil bones began to accumulate in English and French storerooms and museums.

The Denial of Prehistory

For a long while, nothing was done with these excellent fossil specimens, nor with the strange and primitive stone tools found in caves or in the course of new construction. Few scholars viewed them for what they were: evidence of life on earth in ancient times. Even as recently as 150 years ago, many scientists refused to speculate on the mysteries of man's origins. In fact, for most of them, there were no mysteries. Scientists and laymen alike had been taught (and they believed) that God had created all living organisms, including man, separately and in their present forms. This doctrine of "special creation" lay outside the realm of scientific verification, and any attempt to supplant the biblical account of creation was viewed with alarm and hostility, not only by the clergy but also by the leading scholars of the time.

Numerous efforts were made to pinpoint the exact date of creation, and in 1654, the Archbishop Ussher arrived at a creation date of 4004 B.C. by calculating backwards the ages of the generations since Adam, as recorded in the Bible. Later, Dr. John Lightfoot, vice-chancellor of the University of Cambridge, was even more specific: he dated creation in the same

year but at precisely nine o'clock on the morning of October
23. In short, man had no prehistory.

But as in any age, a few doubting voices were raised; a few
determined men excavated prehistoric sites and reported their
findings. One of these was Father J. MacEnery, a Roman Catho-
lic priest who conducted excavations at Kent's Cavern in England from 1825 until his death in 1841. He found crude flint
implements together with the remains of extinct rhinoceros.
The implication was, of course, that man lived contemporaneously with animals of distant times. In 1828, Paul Tournal
reported his discoveries at the Grotte de Bize in southern France,
where he had found human bones in clear association with the
remains of extinct animals. And in 1833, Dr. P. C. Schmerling
published reports that, at Engis Cave in Belgium, he had excavated seven human skulls, primitive stone tools, and the bones
of extinct mammoth and rhino. "There can be no doubt," wrote
Schmerling, "that the human bones were buried at the same
time . . . as the other extinct species."[3] But Schmerling's work,
together with that of Tournal and MacEnery, was ignored.
The scientific world was not yet prepared to accept the fact
of man's great antiquity.

There was a reason for their reluctance. Early geologists had
noted that sedimentary rocks, acted on by the force of gravity,
form beds laid down on land or in water. These beds may be
composed of organic material, precipitates from water (e.g., salt),
or fragmented rock transported by air or water from other locales.
Whatever their origin, these beds exist collectively in layers called
strata (singular, *stratum*). The study of strata is termed *stratigraphy*
and provides a key to our understanding of geologic time. Even
the earliest geologists had some notion of how time might be
interpreted by the sequence of deposition. Generally, in undisturbed layers, any stratum is older than the strata above it, and
younger than the strata below.

Now the "special creation" theory held that all living organisms were created separately, *in their present forms,* by divine will;
and that none was subject to change. The discovery of lower

---

[3] Schmerling, P. C., *Recherches sur les Ossements Fossiles Decouverts dans les Cavernes
de la Province de Liège* (Liège, 1833–34), p. 59.

stratigraphic layers of extinct animal bones—so different from those of modern species—might have proved bothersome.

Geologists viewed the graded changes of fossil remains within the geologic stratigraphy and were forced to admit that change through time was evident. This admission, however, enhanced rather than damaged the doctrine of special creation, for d'Arezzo's "deluge" theory was plucked from the past, revised, and expanded. The author of this revision was the Baron Georges Cuvier (1769–1832), a highly-respected French paleontologist and one of the ablest proponents of the "special creation" theory. Cuvier hypothesized that the world had been subjected not to one but to a series of catastrophes, each of which had wiped out all creatures existing at the time. He insisted, further, that there had been a succession of special creations, one following each catastrophe. All living organisms dated from the last, the creation following the biblical deluge. Earlier forms reflected in the fossil record were products of previous creations, and man himself, according to Cuvier, did not exist before the biblical creation.

Most early nineteenth-century geologists were, like Cuvier, Catastrophists. They interpreted the earth's stratigraphy by hypothesizing a series of great catastrophes in the past, and they agreed with Cuvier that human beings could not have existed before the most recent creation. They denied that there could exist fossilized human bones of any great antiquity. When in 1823, Cuvier viewed a completely fossilized human skeleton unearthed from the banks of the Rhine River and associated with the bones of extinct animals, he rejected the find on the grounds that man had no prehistory. The skeleton, he said, must be intrusive, accidentally mixed with animal bones from an earlier deposit.

The Catastrophists continued to enjoy great popularity, arguing that the earth and all its life forms were static and immutable. But opposition had been growing, and, as early as 1785, a Scottish geologist, James Hutton (1726–1797), had insisted that the earth's strata could be interpreted in other ways. He explained carefully in his "Theory of the Earth," that the stratification of the rocks and landscape was due to on-going processes in the seas, rivers, and lakes. With this work, he sowed the seeds of the doctrine of Uniformitarianism, which was brought to full flower between 1830 and 1833 by the great anti-Catastrophist geologist Charles Lyell (1797–1875).

With the publication of his "Principles of Geology," Lyell argued that the earth had been shaped—and was still being shaped—by natural forces operating in a uniform way and at a uniform rate. What this meant, of course, was that human bones and artifacts buried under thick layers of earth must originally have been deposited a very long time ago. There was no reason to doubt the findings of such men as Tournal, Schmerling, and MacEnery. Indeed, the able geologist William "Strata" Smith (1769–1839) announced that geologic strata could be dated by noting their fossil contents. And so was born the "Law of Superposition": that is, fossils found in any given stratum are older than fossils found in strata above and younger than fossils found in strata below—at least in undisturbed layers. This single principle was crucial to the development of archaeology and paleoanthropology.

THE RISE OF DEVELOPMENTAL THEORY

As the industrial revolution grew in response to the nineteenth-century demand for more roads, buildings, mines, canals, and quarries, construction sites quite incidentally yielded numerous fossil remains, thus speeding the progress of geology. The time was ripe for progress in related fields as well, for the problem of man's prehistory no longer lay in the acquisition and stockpiling of evidence but rather in the assessment of such material as it appeared.

At this time, Charles Darwin (1809–1882) ventured to introduce his concept of organic evolution despite continued theological opposition. Darwin was an unlikely candidate for the role of intellectual reformer and completely unsuited for controversy. A shy, sickly, deeply religious man of wealth and social prominence, he lacked any appetite for fame. As we have mentioned, he hesitated for more than twenty years before being persuaded by friends and colleagues to publish his notes. And finally, in 1859, he released for publication his book, *On the Origin of Species by Means of Natural Selection.* Although he did not consider

human populations in this first volume, he nevertheless succeeded in unleashing a vigorous and undying interest in man's
origins and prehistory.

Darwin's concepts were not new; philosophers since the time
of the early Greeks had ventured repeatedly to suggest an evolutionary development for various life forms including man. Darwin's essential achievement, however, was to add something new
to developmental theory: he demonstrated a mechanism through
which organic evolution, or change, appeared to be taking place,
and that mechanism was natural selection.

Darwin was not alone in formulating that principle at this
time. Alfred Wallace, a biologist who had devoted some years
to the study of fauna in the East Indies, had perceived a selective
process that seemed to be operating among the animal populations he had observed. He wrote down thoughts and sent them
to Darwin, who was dumb-struck by the coincidence. At age
twenty-two, Darwin had accepted the post of naturalist on
board the H.M.S. Beagle, a ten-gun brig sent by the British
Admiralty on a surveying trip around the world. During the
five years of the voyage, he had made extensive notes on what
he had seen in Tierra del Fuego, Argentina, Brazil, Peru, Chili,
Tahiti, Australia, New Zealand, and the Galapagos Islands. Now
Wallace's notes seemed to echo his own, and in 1858, Darwin

FIGURE 1. Charles Darwin (1809-
1882) as a young man in the Galapagos Archipelago. (Culver Pictures)

and Wallace presented parallel papers at the same scientific meeting, each describing the biological principle of natural selection. Later, Darwin published his controversial book.

The thinking of both men had been shaped by a third, T. R. Malthus, whose writings had been published half a century before. In his *Essay on the Principle of Population,* Malthus had noted that human populations reproduce in geometric ratio, while space and available food supplies remain constant. In other words, human reproductive potential far exceeds the ability of natural resources to support an ever-increasing population. Malthus deduced that there must be some agent or agents— disease, war, drought, famine—that acted to keep down surplus population.

Influenced by Malthus' insights and by his years of personal observation, Darwin concluded that individual species had *not* been separately created as was so commonly believed. Species were mutable, or subject to change, and present-day groups must have evolved from earlier forms of life.

Darwin's Theory of Evolution

Darwin's theory rested on three observed facts and two deductions based upon these facts:

FACT 1   All organisms increase in geometric ratio; that is, they reproduce more than their own number.

FACT 2   Despite the tendency to multiply, the numbers of a given species remain relatively constant.

FACT 3   All living organisms vary: that is, organisms resemble but do not exactly duplicate their parents.

DEDUCTION 1   There occurs a universal struggle for existence, both among and within species.

DEDUCTION 2   Individuals with some advantage have the best chance for surviving and thus for reproducing their own kind.

Darwin noted that, in spite of the fact that more organisms are born into each generation than can possibly survive, each species appeared to have a natural, balanced population density appropriate for its environment. Since only a fraction of infants

born could live to become reproducing adults, and since the
survivors must compete for available space and food, they must
be the most fit.

Which individuals are the most fit? Darwin realized that they
need not always be the strongest or the most ferocious. It is, after
all, not the biggest cat that takes the lion's share of food but
the fastest, the best able to capture game, or the most able to
sniff it out and track it down. On the other hand, speed, claws,
and keen sense of smell are not important to the giant tortoise,
whose survival depends on the durability of its shell. The chameleon, able to blend with its surroundings by changing color, has
a better chance of escaping the notice of lurking predators than
does the common lizard, for which speed and agility count.

Fitness is ultimately measurable in survival rate. Survival rate
may be maintained or improved in two ways. One method, which
benefits organisms as diverse as oysters and rabbits, is a very
high fertility level, which means greater production of young
through increasing the number of progeny produced each time
and/or increasing the number of times that progeny are produced
in each year. The other method is in improving or maintaining
the percentage of progeny that survive to an age at which they
may reproduce. This is also accomplished in two ways. One
is extending the period of maternal and/or paternal care of
progeny. Primates, among others, employ this method in varying
degrees. Additionally or alternatively, organisms are altered in
ways which better suit them to survival in their environment.

The latter method is adaptation, and it is a process fundamental to evolution. In any species, those organisms which happen
to be best suited to their surroundings are also the most likely
to survive and to reproduce progeny with similar characteristics.

Extended parental care, production of large numbers of progeny and even cultural adaptations, such as wearing clothing
to protect against cold, are methods of adaptation. The term
is used most commonly, though, in reference to those random
alterations in an organism which happen to improve its ability
to cope with the environment. That is the sense in which we
are using the term here.

Organisms that survive and multiply with ease are those that
have most successfully adapted to their own environment. To

Darwin, modification in an organism generally meant greater adaptability; for new adaptations better equip the individual for survival in his own environment or enable him to exploit new environments and thus gain valuable access to new and expanded resources. In addition, any modification that increased the individual's chances to survive to sexual maturity would be preserved within the population; changes that decreased chances for survival would most likely be eliminated. Well-adapted individuals would survive to mate and reproduce, endowing their offspring with whatever traits helped to insure parental survival. The less fit—those individuals that are weak, slow, non-alert, or conspicuous to predators—would not survive. This is *natural selection,* the force Darwin deduced must operate to carry into action the processes of organic evolution.

For example, the survival value of color change, such as we discussed earlier in reference to the chameleon, is an example of moderate adaptation. Similarly, bears found in snowy habitats are white, while woodland bears are brown or black. These are the sorts of observations that led Charles Darwin to the formulation of his theory. Ironically, however, Darwin—who recorded hundreds of such adaptations from around the world—failed to notice the most striking color change ever witnessed by man, a change that occurred in his own country.

In Darwin's time, certain species of British moths were predominantly light in color, their characteristic coloration closely

FIGURE 2. Charles Darwin in 1871. (Culver Pictures)

matching that of the light-colored tree trunks and lichen-covered rocks against which they rested by day; thus they tended to escape the notice of moth-eating birds. But, also in Darwin's time, the industrial revolution began to cause a massive fall-out of smoke particles that dispersed over the countryside, polluting foliage and killing vegetative lichens on rocks and trees. Trees, rocks, and even the ground itself quickly darkened, and the light-colored moths were ruthlessly eliminated by hungry birds. Darker forms of the same species, their protective coloration better suited to the changed environment, increased, and soon these moth species were predominantly dark in color.[4] Similar color changes have characterized moth species in industrial areas in France, Germany, Czechoslovakia, Poland, Canada, and the United States as well.

In the 1950's, studies were conducted by H. B. D. Kettlewell of the University of Oxford in an attempt to discover how this

ME′ LAN ISM abnormal development of dark pigmentation.

phenomenon, called "industrial melanism," occurred. These studies led to three conclusions: first, that a sudden change in the environment led to the devastation of moths who could no longer blend with the environment; and second, that the melanistic variants (dark moths), formerly at a disadvantage, now had an increased survival rate. Finally, that one form (the dark) so quickly replaced another is an illustration of the speed with which selection can operate. Darwin, who could point to no visible example of evolution at work in nature, would have witnessed the confirmation of much of his life's work had he observed the phenomenon of industrial melanism that occurred within his lifetime.

Nature, of course, abounds with dramatic examples of adaptation. Desert plants store water in order to survive all but the most prolonged droughts. Other plants have assumed, through time, rock-like shapes that escape the eyes of grazing animals. The brilliant, multi-colored faces and red rumps of male mandrill baboons exert an irresistible attraction for female mandrills; and some birds, like the peacock, develop magnificent plumage with which to attract mates. Tiny insects called tree-hoppers, shaped

---

[4] Kettlewell, H. B. D., "Darwin's Missing Evidence," *Scientific American,* Vol. 200, March 1959, pp. 48–53.

like thorns, rest on the stems of rosebushes and escape the eyes of predatory birds. Animals like the skunk and porcupine have developed, through natural selection, protective means to discourage most attackers; so successful are these adaptations that today, when most wildlife populations are dwindling, the skunk and porcupine are spreading.

The foregoing are all examples of moderate adaptation; but other forms of adaptation may be extreme. This was the case when early four-footed mammals gave rise to bats and whales, enabling new species to reap the benefits of new environments while escaping the dangers of the old.

Modern scientists know the value of successful adaptations, but they have modified Darwin's theory to accommodate a new realization that it is *fertility* that most crucially determines survival. The form best able to reproduce itself in great numbers is most likely to endure, which is why man and the other mammals are so greatly outnumbered by the fish and the insects, which reproduce in great quantity. Compared with 3200 known species of living mammals, there are 20,000 species of fish—and more than 800,000 species of insects. Human beings, with their single rather than multiple births, would appear to be at a distinct disadvantage, but the compensation lies in the fact that humans do not have a restricted mating season. Like his hominid ancestors, *Homo sapiens* is able to reproduce year round, and most experts agree that this is one of the key factors in man's survival.

HO′ MI NID
a member of the taxonomic family of man, or Hominidae; having human or man-like characteristics.

EARLY STUDIES IN VARIATION

Darwin realized that variation was crucial to natural selection, and hence to the process of evolution itself, but he was at a loss to explain how variation occurred. Why do living things vary? How do the variations arise? For decades, this thorny riddle remained unsolved.

HO MI NOID′
a member of the taxonomic superfamily Hominoidea, including both man and the apes.

Among the first to attempt an explanation was a French scholar with the improbable name of Jean Baptiste Pierre Antoine de Monet, Chevalier de Lamarck (1744–1829). Lamarck, among the most prominent of France's professors of zoology, thoroughly understood the fact that evolution was an ongoing process, and he had carefully documented instances of past evolution. But he was accused of assuming that characteristics acquired *during the lifetime* of an individual were transmitted to the offspring. He believed that all animals adapted to meet the pressures of environmental elements—temperature, climate, altitude—through the use and development of traits and organs best suited to their surroundings. At the same time, he thought, those organs and traits not utilized in response to environmental pressures would atrophy or disappear. For this, Lamarck was discredited in his own lifetime and has been ridiculed ever since.

The German zoologist August Weissmann (1834–1914) wasted no time proving the absurdity of Lamarckian theory. He collected a vast array of rats, chopped off their tails, and bred them—then gleefully reported that no tailless rats appeared in succeeding generations. Weissmann conducted his experiment in a spirit of ostentatious ridicule, an attitude generally frowned upon by reputable scientists; but he succeeded in demolishing the use-disuse theory and demonstrated that structural changes induced during the lifetime of an individual are not normally transmittable to offspring. Thus attempts to improve upon nature in the adult do not result in permanent change.[5]

Numerous scientists continued to wrestle with the riddles of heredity, but for all their thoroughness, they could not decipher the pattern of inheritance that they felt certain must exist.

Though it would not be recognized by the scientific world for decades, the answer that eluded Darwin and his colleagues had been found in the gardens of an Augustinian monastery in Brunn. Here an obscure Austrian monk, Gregor Johann Mendel (1822–1884), had launched a series of experiments destined to prove that inheritance is not a matter of chance or random progression, but is instead the predictable result of natural law.

From his youth, Mendel had been fascinated by the study of botany, and in the monastery garden he was free, so long

---

[5] Lamarck's vulnerability on the point of acquired traits unfortunately overshadowed his other efforts. He was a careful scientist who may yet be partially vindicated. Twentieth-century neo-Lamarckists take some pleasure in reminding us that modern experiments with radiation have proven that permanent change may now be induced in certain adult cells and transmitted to succeeding generations.

as he continued his religious studies, to pursue his botanical interests. He began by experimenting with crosses in flowers, puzzling over the fact that with certain varieties the same traits appeared with surprising regularity. To find out why, he turned to numerous studies of hybridization by other researchers. But these studies were fruitless: they reported hybrid varieties that followed no pattern at all. Sizes, colors, and forms seemed to result from hybridization in mystifying variety.

HY BRID I ZA′ TION the crossing of different races, species, or varieties.

In Mendel's orderly mind, the published studies appeared to be inexcusably haphazard and incomplete. So far as he could tell, no scholar had yet attempted a systematic analysis of the results of hybridization, and no one had bred hybrids over successive generations under strictly controlled conditions, nor recorded exactly which individual traits appeared in each resulting plant. He hastened to fill the gap.

Mendel selected for his experiments twenty-two varieties of the common garden pea, a plant that ordinarily fertilizes itself and which can easily be protected against the intrusion of foreign pollen carried in with the breeze. Neatly side-stepping the pitfall of trying to compare plants in all observable aspects, he chose for study a very few easily compared sets of pea characteristics. Were the ripe seeds round or wrinkled? Were the peas green or yellow? Were the ripened pods inflated or constricted between the seeds? Were the flowers positioned along the stem or bunched at the top of the stem?

At first, he cross-fertilized yellow- and green-seeded garden peas, finding that in the first hybrid generation all the seeds were yellow. Anxious to explain the mysterious disappearance

FIGURE 3. Gregor Johann Mendel (1822-1884) at work in his garden. (Culver Pictures)

of the green color, Mendel proceeded to self-fertilize plants of this yellow-seeded generation. His results: a new generation consisting of both yellow- and green-seeded plants, but in a three-to-one ratio.

Similarly, he crossed plants bearing wrinkled seeds with plants bearing smooth ones. In his first hybrid generation, not a single plant bore wrinkled seeds. In the second generation, wrinkled seeds reappeared but were outnumbered three-to-one by plants with smooth seeds.

He crossed tall plants with short ones; plants that had inflated pods with plants that had constricted pods; and plants bearing gray-coated seeds with plants bearing white-coated seeds. In each first hybrid generation, one and only one trait appeared. Its alternative, a trait of fifty percent of the parent plants, disappeared. The alternative trait would reappear only in successive generations, and then in an exact three-to-one recurrence.

In all, Mendel fertilized seventy plants in some 287 hybridizations, and he concluded from these experiments that heredity is effected by the transmission of discrete particles. He lacked, of course, the microscopic means to explore the inner structure of his plants and to search out the physical units of heredity that he knew must exist. He had, then, no way of knowing exactly what had occurred within the plant cell at the time of reproduction. But his inferences were sound. We know today that, in sexual reproduction, genes (similar in principle to Mendel's "particles") provide the physical link between generations.

Each new individual, plant or animal, develops from the zygote (fertilized egg) produced by the fusion of male and female sex cells. Each parent cell contains more than 40,000 genes. If counted in terms of the DNA code, a human parent cell contains anywhere from 100,000 to several million sequences of instruction. Thus, it is possible for the fusion of just two microscopic cells to effect the transmission of at least thousands of observable physical characteristics.

Prior to reproduction, the parent sex cells—the sperm and ovum—undergo numerous changes, the most important of which is gene duplication. How, within the narrow confines of a single cell, can thousands of genes be duplicated in an orderly fashion? The answer lies in the physical arrangement of the genes.

Through microscopic studies undreamed of by Mendel, scientists have learned that genes do not exist as separate units, but are arranged along the lengths of thread-like bodies called *chromosomes,* which are housed within the cell nucleus. In human beings there are forty-six chromosomes, each composed of thousands of genes. With such an arrangement, the cell can handle the duplication and segregation of great numbers of genetic units.

MENDEL'S LAWS OF HEREDITY

Mendel, although he knew absolutely nothing of chromosomes and genes, correctly inferred that each parent contributes hereditary units to the offspring, and that there must exist alternate or contrasting (tall-short, yellow-green, wrinkled-round) forms of these units. Modern geneticists call these contrasting forms *alleles* and recognize that each gene occupies a particular *locus,* or position, on a particular chromosome. Hereditary potentialities are inherited as discrete units, as Mendel deduced. They may be masked or hidden in the presence of contrasting ones, but they are not lost; and they may reappear in later generations.

AL′ LELE alternative form of a given gene. Any gene may have from one to several forms.

Consider, for example, Mendel's yellow-green experiments. The parent generation contributed alleles for yellow and for green, and in the first hybrid generation, yellow was expressed or, in other words, was visibly present. Alleles, or alternate forms, are segregated during the preparation of the reproductive cells. This is Mendel's first law, the *Law of Segregation,* which means that, if an individual has received contrasting factors, or alleles, from his parents, these factors will be segregated from each other in the preparation of his reproductive cells.

GE′ NO TYPE the set of alleles (genetic instructions) present in the cells of an organism as contrasted with the characteristics finally manifested by the organism.

But what determines which allele will be expressed and which will not? Mendel found that one allele may be *dominant* over another. This was the case in the yellow- and green-seeded pea experiment, in which yellow *dominated* over green and was expressed in the phenotype of the offspring individuals. The green, however, was not lost. It was *recessive,* and it continued to be carried in the genotype of the individual. The recessive trait is expressed in the phenotype only when recessive alleles are inherited from both parents. That is, the recessive is expressed only in the absence of a dominant allele.

PHE′ NO TYPE physical appearance; the physically apparent expression of the interaction of heredity and environment.

FIGURE 4. Landsteiner ABO system: diagram illustrating genotypes and phenotypes of blood groups. (I = dominant allele; i = recessive allele) (a) Parents both with blood Types AB (homozygous alleles I^AI^A and I^BI^B) produce offspring with blood Types A, B, and AB since neither I^A or I^B is dominant over the other. (b) Parents both with blood Types O [homozygous alleles ii (I^0)] produce offspring all with blood Type O. (c) Parents with blood Types AB and O (heterozygous alleles I^AI^B and homozygous ii) produce offspring with blood Types A and B, since O is recessive to both A and B. (d) Parents with blood Types A and O (homozygous alleles I^AI^A and ii) produce offspring with blood Type A, again since O is recessive. (e) Parents with blood Types A and O but with alleles I^Ai and ii produce offspring with blood Types A and O. (f) Parents with blood Types B and O (alleles I^Bi and ii similarly produce offspring with blood Types B and O.

(a)

(b)

(c)

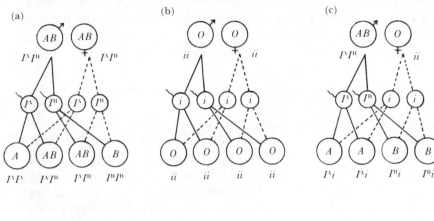

(d)

(e)

(f)

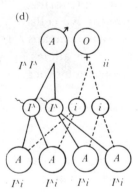
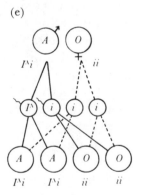
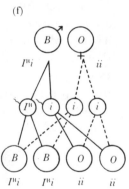

For any given trait, or at any given locus, an individual can have no more than two alleles, one from each parent. But sometimes there are three, four, or even more alternative forms, of which only one is totally recessive; so that if an individual's two alleles do not include the totally recessive one, neither of the two will be completely dominant. Among the blood groups discovered at the turn of the century, for example, three alleles exist: I^A, I^B, and I^O. I^O is recessive to both I^A and I^B, though neither of the latter is dominant over the other. Hence human blood may be of Type O, Type A, Type B, *or* Type AB. (See Figure 4.)

It might be wise at this point to retrace Mendel's steps, taking a closer look at what happened when he crossed yellow-seeded with green-seeded garden pea plants. For our purposes, we will assume that we are dealing with two "pure," or homozygous, parents, one yellow-seeded and one green-seeded. We will represent the parents by symbols indicating their genetic make-up: YY for dominant yellow, gg for recessive green. When these two individuals are cross-fertilized, the Hybrid-1 generation consists of four individuals. They are phenotypically yellow (that is, they will bear yellow seeds) because the allele for yellow is dominant over the allele for green. But the Hybrid-1 plants are genotypically heterozygous since the potential for bearing green seeds has not been lost to the plant population. Each individual has received contrasting genes from its parents. The capacity for bearing green seeds, masked by the dominant yellow and therefore not possible in the phenotype, is retained in the genotype. In genetic shorthand, we can write:

$$(YY) \ (gg) = (Yg) + (Yg) + (Yg) + (Yg)$$

Now we will self-fertilize one member of the Hybrid-1 generation. The resulting Hybrid-2 generation is composed of four individuals as follows:

1. ONE YY INDIVIDUAL. YY is both phenotypically and genotypically yellow. It has inherited no genetic potential for bearing green seeds because it received, one from each parent, two alleles for yellow and is therefore homozygous.

2. Two Yg INDIVIDUALS. These two are phenotypically yellow and therefore do not differ *visibly* from the YY individual above: like the YY plant, it will bear yellow seeds. But YY and Yg individuals do differ genotypically. The latter are heterozygous, carrying not only the dominant Y gene expressed but also the recessive g gene, which is masked.

3. ONE gg INDIVIDUAL. The fourth member of the Hybrid-2 generation is both phenotypically and genotypically green. It will bear green seeds. It received no potential for yellow seeds, having taken from each parent the allele for green. It is what geneticists call *homozygous recessive*. The recessive green is expressed only because the dominant yellow allele is absent.

In genetic shorthand, our Hybrid-2 generation looks like this:

$$(Yg) (Yg) = (YY) + (Yg) + (Yg) + (gg)$$

But there is more to an individual than color. An organism has form, shape, height, weight, and dozens of other traits which are influenced by hereditary potential. A garden pea may have seeds that are green and smooth, green and wrinkled, yellow and smooth, or yellow and wrinkled. Traits for other characters must be transmitted in the same way and at the same time as those for color. Mendel, working patiently in his monastery, experimented to find out how differing pairs of potentialities are inherited. He crossed plants with seeds that were yellow and round with plants bearing green, wrinkled seeds. The first hybrid generation consisted entirely of plants that bore round, yellow seeds. Mendel continued, self-fertilizing this generation to produce plants bearing seeds of all descriptions: round green, round yellow, wrinkled green, and wrinkled yellow. He concluded that the potential for seed shape was not connected with the potential for seed color. These characters were inherited independently of one another. This principle is known as Mendel's second law, the *Law of Independent Assortment*.

We know today that heredity is governed by many more complex principles than elucidated in Mendel's two laws, and we shall deal with modern genetics in a later chapter. For the time being, we need only to recognize that Mendel's experiments were sound, and that his discoveries ultimately formed the basis for modern genetic studies. He showed that variations arise through the transmission of discrete hereditary units, and he noted that characters may be inherited independently of one another. However, it was not until the early part of the twentieth century that Mendel's investigative notes were rediscovered and applied. Only then could genetics assume its present position of importance among the scientific disciplines that today form the foundation of modern evolutionary theory.

While Mendel's pioneering efforts went unrecognized, Darwin—who failed to consider human beings at all in his first book—published *The Descent of Man* in 1871. Here he presented his view that man was derived from an earlier primate form. He did not imply, though many assumed it, that man had evolved from a creature similar to any modern ape or monkey. Indeed, of the four genera of great apes and the innumerable varieties of monkeys living today, none ever could have provided an ancestral base for man. Darwin merely suggested that there had existed in the distant past an ancestor common to all primate forms, including *Homo sapiens*. Not being familiar with genetics, he never made use of any of Mendel's work.

Darwin reached his conclusions primarily through a thorough consideration of anatomy. He compared bodily structures, recognizing in the bones, muscles, nerves, and blood vessels striking similarities between man and his nearest animal relatives. Darwin decided that the mechanism of evolution must act upon humans as it did upon other life forms. He was convinced that there was no other feasible explanation for the observed similarities.

But Darwin never utilized the human fossil evidence that would, in his own lifetime, lend credence to his evolutionary theory. Thus, he ignored two of the most important areas of evidence in support of his views: genetics and paleoanthropology. Yet these and more recently developed studies have yielded irrefutable proof of ongoing evolutionary processes.

We no longer speak of the "theory of evolution." Instead, we talk about "evolutionary theory," and we continue to search for the ways in which human beings and human society have evolved since prehistoric times.

In the years since Darwin's lifetime, immense progress has been made in the search for human origins. People no longer rage at the suggestion that they live in kinship with others of the animal kingdom. Exciting new fossil discoveries from all parts of the world provide evidence of man's long history on earth. With the appearance of documented fossil specimens—and the development of tools and techniques with which to analyze these—the Catastrophist view was doomed. The clergy surrendered its long-held grip on scientific research, and the quest for man's past proceeded unhindered.

FURTHER READINGS

Bell, P. R. (ed.). *Darwin's Biological Work: Some Aspects Reconsidered.* New York: John Wiley & Sons, 1964.

Cary, Max and Eric Herbert Warmington. *The Ancient Explorers.* Baltimore: Penguin Books, 1963.

DeCamp, L. Sprague. *The Great Monkey Trial.* Garden City: Doubleday & Co., 1968.

Eiseley, Loren. *Darwin's Century: Evolution and the Men Who Discovered It.* Garden City: Doubleday & Co., 1958.

Gillispie, Charles Coulston. *Genesis and Geology: the Impact of Scientific Discoveries upon Religious Beliefs in the Decades before Darwin.* New York: Harper & Row, 1959.

Haddon, Alfred Cort. *History of Anthropology.* New York: G. P. Putnam's Sons, 1910.

Kluckhohn, Clyde. *Anthropology and the Classics.* Providence: Brown University Press, 1961.

Moorhead, Alan. *Darwin and the Beagle.* New York: Harper & Row, 1969.

Myres, John L. *Herodotus: Father of History.* Oxford: Clarendon Press, 1953.

Penniman, Thomas Kenneth. *A Hundred Years of Anthropology.* London: Gerald Duckworth & Co., 1952.

Rowe, John Howland. "The Renaissance Foundations of Anthropology," *American Anthropologist,* Vol. 67, No. 1. Menasha: American Anthropological Association, 1956.

CHAPTER III

INTRODUCTION TO
PHYSICAL ANTHROPOLOGY

Physical anthropology, that branch of anthropology dedicated to the study of man as a biological organism, is sometimes called *human biology*. Some of its practitioners consider this an accurate and acceptable label; others find it narrow and unnecessarily restrictive. While it is true that physical anthropologists are concerned primarily with reaching an exact understanding of human biological characteristics, and that it is toward this end that they have amassed a vast body of knowledge regarding ancient and modern human populations, they could not have done so had they limited themselves to investigations dealing solely with human biology. Man, however unique, is a member of the animal kingdom, and he must be viewed both within this context and simultaneously with reference to his cultural capacity. The study of mankind entails a brace of dynamic and highly diversified methods of research and investigation, which are drawn from dozens of scientific fields outside the realm of biology.

Physical anthropology was founded, in fact, on knowledge gleaned from a half-dozen eighteenth- and nineteenth-century sciences. It got off to rather a late start as a separate scientific discipline, chiefly because few of its earliest practitioners thought of themselves as physical anthropologists. Some were spirited amateurs endowed with sufficient financial means to indulge their passion for learning. Most were experts in older, better-established fields such as natural history, anatomy, geography, medicine, biology, and geology. They happened to share an interest in human biological nature, but they had their own research interests, contact with their own colleagues, and their own professional organizations. For a long time, they failed to band together in ways that would promote the free exchange of ideas and research results relevant to a comprehensive study of mankind.

It was not until 1918 that the *American Journal of Physical Anthropology* was founded by Aleš Hrdlička, a man who began his career in medicine. And it was not until 1930 that the American Association of Physical Anthropologists was formed in support of the *Journal*. Regardless of this late "official" start, however, scientists from the eighteenth century onward had been conducting investigations into the biological nature of man. They developed many of the tools and techniques upon which rest the foundations of modern physical anthropology. More importantly, they began to define specific "problem areas"—primary targets for investigation—that occupy the attention of modern scholars in this still-expanding field.

Among these problems, of course, was the matter of the origin and evolution of human beings. Charles Darwin has been accorded a position of eminence approached by no other scientist of the nineteenth century, yet he was careful to recognize and demonstrate the influence of earlier theories regarding evolution. In fact, a general knowledge of organic change was comparatively widespread among nineteenth-century scientists, and interest in the deliberate modification of plant and animal forms was intensified at this time by a concentrated program of experimentation in scientific breeding. By Darwin's time, cattlemen in Great Britain had documented the existence of a short-horned type of cattle on Yorkshire estates for more than 200 years. The subsequent development of the Durham, or short-horn, and the Hereford breeds of cattle provided Darwin with information that was of some assistance in the formulation of his evolutionary principles.

Numerous scientists, both before and during Darwin's lifetime, provided essential groundwork for the development of evolutionary theory. John Hunter (1728–1793), the Scottish anatomist, looked upon the gradation of animals one to the other as evidence of an "original" species. He believed that monkeys, half beast and half human, represented a middle stage in the development of mankind. And he suggested that carnivorous animals serve as "correctors of quantity," helping to maintain a population balance in the natural world.

Georges Louis Leclerc Buffon (1707–1788) managed, in a work published in 1749, to mention every essential ingredient later included in Darwin's *Origin of Species*: he noted a tendency for life to multiply faster than its food supply, thus promoting a struggle for existence among living populations; he recognized the wide range of variation inherent in all living species; and he noted the underlying similarity of structure among different animals, presupposing possible ancestral relationships in the fossil past.

Lamarck (1744–1829), mentioned earlier for his erroneous belief that characteristics acquired during the lifetime of the individual are transmitted to the offspring, did express sound beliefs concerning the origin of man. By a doctrine he termed *transformism,* Lamarck proposed that external circumstances modify ways of life which, in turn, bring about changes in the structure of bodily organs. Species, he thought, must develop one from the other by a multitude of transitions. And man was no exception to this law of progressive development.

Lamarck, first to chart the members of the animal kingdom in the form of a genealogical tree, hinted as early as 1809 at an anthropoid origin for man. He conceived of a "life power" which operated to shape a true progression of plant and animal development. And he recognized two primary causes of variability: environment and the passage of time. In short, Lamarck proposed that environmental pressures, acting through time, modify the structures of plants and animals.

AN′ THRO POID derived from or resembling ape-like forms.

Etienne Geoffroy Saint-Hilaire (1772–1844), who served as zoologist on Napoleon's scientific expedition to Egypt, was a supporter of the Lamarckian theory of transformism. He was not convinced that existing species are subject to ongoing evolution, but he recognized the extent of past change.

Saint-Hilaire, Lamarck, and Georges Cuvier were colleagues at the Paris Museum of Natural History. Although they shared an avid interest in the origin of man, their individual interpretations of the meager available evidence clashed violently: Lamarck and Saint-Hilaire believed that animal species formed a linear scale of evolutionary development, while Cuvier, a prominent geologist and impassioned Catastrophist, believed that animal species were divergent modifications of distinct structural types, and that they remained ever fixed in their original forms. And Lamarck and Saint-Hilaire diverged in that, to Lamarck, evolution was the gradual and continuous result of constant adaptation to changing environmental pressures, while Saint-Hilaire remained unconvinced that variations in organs resulted from responses to environmental changes.

Ironically, the two men who most effectively set the stage for the acceptance of evolutionary theory were fervent advocates of the special creation doctrine. Cuvier held that each species was created for a different purpose, and that each organ existed to fulfill a specific function. He believed that different species were created independently of one another, and that no evolutionary connection could be shown to exist between them. Nevertheless, he emphasized the fact that, in geologic deposits, the deeper and older a fossil might be, the more it differed from existing forms. And thus he provided a strong basis for the evolutionary theory to which he was so strenuously opposed. As a zealous and competent geologist, he extended biological investigations into the distant past and assisted in the formation of modern paleontology. He helped, in fact, to develop the tools necessary for gathering fossil evidence that would lead in time to the collapse of the catastrophic theory and to the decline of the special creation doctrine.

Carolus Linnaeus (1707–1778), best known for his exact and faithful method of classification, fixed man's place in nature as one of the animals. A firm believer in the doctrine of special creation, Linnaeus proposed a great chain of being rather than a doctrine of evolution, but his system of classification, grouping like animals together, laid firm foundations for the development of evolutionary theory.

COMPARATIVE ANATOMY AND TAXONOMY

The process of evolution is often defined as "descent with modification." Descent, of course, refers to heredity, and modification, as defined by Darwin, refers to adaptive variation, or change through time in response to environmental pressures. In short, evolution means that all life forms are derived from preceding life forms through a natural process of modification.

Early efforts in physical anthropology were directed toward the documentation of the evolutionary process. Since there is no way to prove events of the distant past, the evidence for human evolution must be based on inference, and it is not surprising that the first physical anthropologists sought that evidence in known scientific fields. For example, we have seen that Charles Darwin based many of his conclusions on his knowledge of comparative anatomy. Once scientists recognized the fact that all animals are related, it followed logically that the most closely related animals are those descended most recently from a common animal ancestor. In other words, anatomists and physical anthropologists could determine degrees of kinship by assessing anatomical similarities. When they compared, for example, the anatomy of modern human beings with the anatomy of other primates, they soon focused their attention upon the great apes, for of all the primates, the apes are most similar to man in overall body structure and in individual bodily organs.

COM PAR′ A TIVE A NAT′ O MY the study of morphological similarities between different classes of organisms, with emphasis on their structural relationships to one another and to man.

Just as kinship among living groups can be determined in this way, so can relationships be determined among fossil forms and between fossil and modern populations. It is through the principles of comparative anatomy that we are able to hypothesize what the ancestors of modern species looked like.

In assessing or proposing phylogenetic relationships, experts bear in mind that noted similarities may or may not have evolutionary significance. They are not surprised when they find that animals living in the same environment and/or having similar methods of locomotion resemble one another. Both whales and fishes live in the water; both have streamlined bodies and propel themselves by thrusting their powerful tails. Similarly, both birds and bats fly through the air; both have wings which support the body in flight and serve as the means of propulsion. Similarity of body structure arising from similarity of function is termed *analogy.* The wings of birds and bats, then, are *analogous.* Analogous similarities are superficial and do not indicate common ancestry.

PHY′ LO GE NE′ TIC having to do with the evolutionary development of any plant or animal species.

Homologous structures are those which in different animals have the same basic morphology, whether or not they are used for similar purposes. The foot of man is homologous to the foot of an ape, although they are functionally dissimilar: man's foot is designed to carry weight, while the ape's foot is a grasping, prehensile organ. Structurally, though, they are remarkably similar. Homologous similarities result from common ancestry, and these are the resemblances that demonstrate degrees of kinship. Another example is seen in the forelimbs of gorillas. While man's hand is primarily an unspecialized grasping instrument, several bone structures in the hand of the gorilla have evolved in the direction of increasing its ability to walk comfortably on its knuckles. Russell Tuttle (University of Chicago) has done much toward giving us a better understanding of the structure and evolution of these hand structures in gorillas.

Special note is taken when an entire part of an animal is fundamentally similar to another part of the same animal. Such similarities are termed *serial homologies,* good examples of which are human arms and legs. The portion of each that is attached to the trunk features a single bone as skeletal support (in the arm, this bone is called the *humerus;* in the leg, it is the *femur*). In the succeeding portion of both arm and leg there are two bones (the *radius* and *ulna* in the arm; the *tibia* and *fibula* in the leg). Next are a group of wrist and ankle bones, respectively the carpals and the tarsals, and following these are the metacarpals, the bones of the palm of the hand, and the metatarsals, the bones of the sole of the foot. Finally, there are phalanges, or the bones of the fingers and toes.

Obviously, man's arms and legs are modifications of a single fundamental pattern: the arms are modified for grasping and handling; the legs for locomotion in upright posture. The same fundamental pattern is seen in the limbs of the great apes, although they are modified to suit a different environment. Like homology in general, serial homology is explained most reasonably in a theory of evolution, or descent with modification. Such similarities cannot be explained rationally on the basis of special creation.

TAX ON' O MY
the science of
classification;
laws and
principles used
to classify plants
and animals.

The result, then, of the nineteenth-century researches in comparative anatomy was a taxonomic system based on proven animal relationships. In this system can be seen a phylogenetic history of life forms across the globe. This was a giant step beyond previous attempts to classify the world's living organisms.

For the earliest naturalists, taxonomy was an end in itself.

They took a *typological* approach, classifying life forms on the basis of their similarity to a model—that is, to the "ideal" or "average" member of a given population. However, this approach failed to take into account the variability inherent in all populations: no single representative can be termed "ideal," and no "average" individuals exist, for an average is no more than a statistical abstract. It is no easier to find an "average" orang-utan than it is to locate an "average" American family.

The goal of modern taxonomy is to refine the grouping system so that it not only records groupings of life forms but also reflects relationships among these forms. Through a phylogenetic approach, taxonomists seek to demonstrate evolutionary relationships. In fact, the degree to which such relationships, proven through other areas of investigation, correlate with established taxonomic classifications provides evidence of its own for the workings of the evolutionary process.

Another early accomplishment of comparative anatomists was the explanation of such phenomena as *vestigial organs*. These are parts of the body that are small in size, serve little if any ascertainable purpose, and appear to be remnants of structures that were useful in ancient times. The dissected body of a whale, for example, reveals the presence of rudimentary hind limbs. Totally adapted to its aquatic environment, the whale has no use for legs; their presence in vestigial form points to an earlier land ancestry. The python has similar rudimentary legs.

Vestigial organs, then, are those which have lost their original function or become totally functionless, as in the case of the vermiform appendix in humans. This organ serves no apparent function today, although in various herbivorous (plant-eating) animals it acts as an aid to digestion. Apparently, man inherited his appendix from some remote ancestor whose diet necessitated this digestive adjunct. When dietary habits changed in descendant forms, the appendix was gradually reduced in size and eventually lost its original function.

Human beings retain a number of other vestigial organs; for example, we all possess muscles for moving the scalp and ears, but few individuals are able to use them. Man also has muscles for twitching his skin, much as a horse does to flick away flies, but has lost the ability to use them. Tail bones provide yet

another example. In humans, they are present only in rudimentary form, fused together to form the *coccyx*, a bony structure
which helps to support the pelvic organs. The coccyx is homologous to a chain of reduced tail vertebrae.

VER´ TE BRAE
(singular
vertebra);
the bones or
elements of the
spinal column,
or "backbone."

Techniques of comparative anatomy were crucial to the development of taxonomy and proved invaluable in the phylogenetic
assessment of fossil specimens when they began to be recovered
through archaeological or paleontological excavation. It is hardly
surprising that early physical anthropologists relied heavily upon

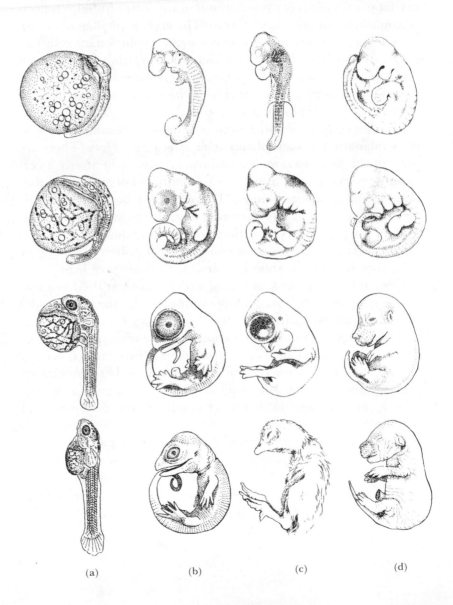

(a)   (b)   (c)   (d)

this field in attempting to interpret man's fossil history and to trace his relationships with other primates.

EMBRYOLOGY

Homologies are found not only in the adult structures of diverse animals but also in their embryonic development. All complex animals develop from a single fertilized egg, and it was by observing the growth and development of such simple cells that

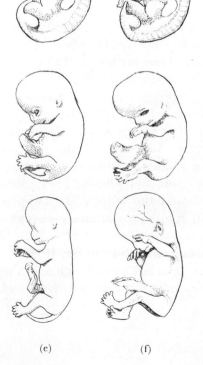

FIGURE 1. Comparative embryological development in (a) killifish, (b) lizard, (c) chicken, (d) mouse, (e) monkey, and (f) human.

(e)   (f)

physical anthropologists first viewed what they had inferred from their studies in comparative anatomy: that is, the ways in which complex forms arise from simple ones. Embryonic development is the process by which adult structures are attained. It is only reasonable to expect that similar results are achieved through similar developmental processes.

Among the first to record the facts of homology in embryonic development was K. E. von Baer. In 1828, von Baer reported a remarkable similarity among embryonic vertebrates which, once developed to the adult state, differed from one another. As is apparent in the accompanying diagram, embryos of diverse animals often are so similar that they can be distinguished only by experts. In the earliest stages of development, each embryo conforms to a common pattern; detailed similarities are obvious in the early developmental sequence. Gradually, each embryo progresses from this common pattern to assume the identifying characteristics of its eventual adult morphology. The embryos of closely related animals can be readily distinguished only in the later stages of development. The closer the kinship, the longer and more pronounced are the embryonic similarities, implying that similarities in development during the embryonic phase result from inheritance, or descent from a common ancestor.

In 1874, the noted biologist Ernst Haeckel (1834–1919) modified von Baer's observations into a biogenetic law, often referred to as the "theory of recapitulation." Haeckel believed that "ontogeny recapitulates phylogeny"; that is, that the developmental stages of the embryonic individual repeat or review the evolutionary history of the species as a whole. In other words, man climbs his own family tree, repeating in the womb the evolutionary development of his species. Advocates of the recapitulation theory pointed to certain phases in human embryonic growth in an attempt to prove their hypothesis. They cited embryonic neck grooves, the tail, and the lanugo as examples of features representing stages in man's evolutionary development.

The recapitulationists, of course, went a bit too far. It is true that the human embryo develops pouches in the region of the throat as well as corresponding furrows on the neck surface, and

VER' TE BRATE
a member of the division of animals that possess internal segmented skeletons, or spinal columns.

LA NU' GO
a hairy covering that envelops the human fetus at six to eight months' gestation.

that these occupy the same position as do gill pouches in fish. But in the human embryo, the pouches do not open, nor do they assume the gill-slit function or structure of an adult fish. On the contrary, they develop into other structures.

In the light of modern biological knowledge, scientists do not accept Haeckel's Law. As Simpson has pointed out (in *The Meaning of Evolution*), many animal *embryos* tend to resemble each other because cells divide and differentiate in a very old and established pattern. Evolutionary changes determine the *development* of the fetal cell-mass. Thus, the further development progresses, the less similar fetal animals of different species will become because the genetic code will have had that much more time for expression from the time that the division and differentiation process began*. Modern prehistorians warn against utilizing comparative ontogeny to determine the affinity between two groups of animals. Still, the more similar the ontogeny, and the later in embryonic development two animals diverge from a common pattern, the more related they are phylogenetically. *Chapter IV.

For the most part, studies in comparative ontogeny no longer play an important role in reconstructing human prehistoric development. Investigators in experimental embryology have turned their attention from observation and description to the isolation of factors in growth and differentiation. Armed with new knowledge gleaned from the field of biochemistry, they hope to determine how such factors as metabolism and differentiation are controlled in living organisms. They are also concerned with studies in regeneration, attempting to learn why some animals are able to regenerate missing parts while others cannot.

Nevertheless, investigations in comparative embryology still make occasional contributions to physical anthropology. Bertram S. Kraus, a noted physical anthropologist, found in comparing molar-tooth development in man and in the rhesus monkey, that he could distinguish between the two at the interval of initial molar calcification. Human racial differences (the distinctions among negroid, caucasoid, and mongoloid) could not be discerned at this early stage of development. Results of his study confirmed the early evolutionary divergence of man and monkey.

Kraus proved, then, that embryology can continue to play a role in offering supportive evidence of evolution; but in recent

FIGURE 2.   Ernest Haeckel's (1834–1919) theory of evolution from the very simplest of organisms to human beings. (Culver Pictures)

years more sophisticated techniques have been developed in the field of biochemistry. Numerous attempts have been made to formulate an "evolutionary clock" which might help to pinpoint the times at which new life forms arose in prehistory, and biochemists believe that they may have succeeded in basing such a system on a complex theory of protein-sequencing.

Proteins, of course, are large molecules composed of amino acids arranged in a sequence characteristic of each species. Biochemists believe that variations in protein sequences represent evolutionary changes, and that the greater the number of variations, the more distantly related are the species whose proteins are being analyzed. They count, for example, 42 variations between the red blood cells of a horse and those of a man, but only 12 variations between man and monkey. By charting in the laboratory the average rate of genetic change (the intervals between alterations in protein sequences), scientists can count backward and estimate the number of years required for variations to have taken place in the distant past. At the University of California, in fact, Vincent Sarich and other physical anthropologists have estimated with their new "protein clock" that man and ape diverged, and a truly pre-human form first emerged, three to six million years ago.[1] This date is not compatible with dates derived from radioactive dating techniques for the fossil population known as *Australopithecus,* believed to have lived slightly earlier. But both the "protein clock" and the various radioactive dating methods are now being analyzed for possible error, and results of current investigations may account for the discrepancy. In any case, physical anthropologists welcome new dating methods that may confirm or correct the results of those commonly in use today.

The earliest prehistorians were intrigued not only by human evolution but by human variation as well. Many of their initial efforts were directed toward the measurement and classification of diverse human types—so much so that early physical anthropologists were scorned by their colleagues as "caliper anthropologists." No apologies are necessary, however, for the use of

---

[1] Sarich, V. M. and P. Dolhinow. "A Molecular Approach to the Question of Human Origins," *Background to Man,* Boston: Little-Brown, 1971.

observation, measurement, description, and statistical analysis. These are fundamental to the development of any science, and they are indispensable to physical anthropology today.

THE NEW PHYSICAL ANTHROPOLOGY

It soon became apparent, however, that theories could not always be proven through the use of purely descriptive data; and by 1943, prominent physical anthropologists began to widen their scientific horizons. In that year, Sherwood Washburn and S. R. Detwiler urged physical anthropologists to adopt experimental methods.[2] Their proposal was a challenging one; it is not easy to conduct experimental research with human beings. But if the obstacles might be overcome, Washburn and Detwiler would succeed in stimulating new research procedures and priorities. More than that, they would generate new ways of approaching the basic problem areas of physical anthropology.

In the same year, W. W. Howells, one of the foremost physical anthropologists in the United States, called for the more efficient and imaginative use of existing methods.[3] He envisioned physical anthropology as a technique that might aid in the solving of modern social problems, and, accordingly, he suggested intensive research into the complex question of human race, as well as nationwide studies of the various factors that affect physical form.

The science itself was gradually changing direction. There was a new emphasis on directing the efforts of the physical anthropologist toward the study of modern social questions, and a new willingness to expand upon traditional research methods.

In great part, this reorientation was shaped by a new reliance upon genetic principles and theory. Discoveries in the dynamic science of genetics made new tools and techniques available for the study of man, and physical anthropologists were quick to seize upon them. In 1950,[4] a highly respected geneticist,

---

[2] Washburn, S. L. and S. R. Detwiler. "An Experiment Bearing on the Problems of Physical Anthropology," *American Journal of Physical Anthropology*, n.s. 1:171–190.

[3] Howells, W. W. "Physical Anthropology as a Technique," *American Journal of Physical Anthropology*, n.s. 1:355–361.

[4] Boyd, W. C. *Genetics and the Races of Man*. Boston: D. C. Heath & Company, 1950.

William C. Boyd, presented an appraisal of the ways in which genetics might contribute to a fuller understanding of man. His appraisal was most enthusiastically received.

The development of modern genetics offered a great new potential for isolating the processes of human evolution and for pinpointing the probable origins of human races. A few physical anthropologists, eager to get on with the utilization of new research techniques, broke completely with traditional methods; others, while equally receptive to innovative methods, argued that the new need not necessarily chase out the old. In studying human races, for example, one considers not only the genetic composition of a human population but also the morphological characteristics of its members. Comparative anatomy, long a valuable tool in physical anthropology, is still useful combined in a sensible balance with newer techniques gleaned from modern genetics and from other fields of scientific inquiry.

On the other hand, traditional methods must not be permitted to hinder the development of new anthropological theory. This was the essential point of Sherwood Washburn's 1951 paper on "the new physical anthropology,"[5] in which he complained that in the past physical anthropologists had depended too heavily on measurement, classification, and correlation, and had paid too little heed to the development of theory. He urged his colleagues to develop a "new" physical anthropology—one that would stop its endless sorting of the *results* of evolution and start focusing once again on the *processes* of evolution. What Washburn was suggesting was a return to Darwinism—with investigations into such evolutionary factors as selection, mutation, genetic drift, and human migrations—but with an added element. That element, of course, was genetics. The goal of the "new physical anthropology" would be to seek a firmer understanding of evolutionary processes.

Washburn's paper caused a good deal of controversy among physical anthropologists. At first, he was condemned for his tactless and aggressive criticism of past methods utilized by his colleagues. Later, he was praised for having triggered a new

---

[5] Washburn, S. L. "The New Physical Anthropology," *Transactions of the New York Academy of Sciences,* Ser. II, Vol. 13, pp. 298–304.

turn in anthropological thinking. The fact is, that Washburn served, not as the force behind the development of modern physical anthropology, but as a chronicler of natural change. Observation, measurement, and description are fundamental to the development of any science. It is only when information is gathered through these techniques that theories can be formulated and hypotheses tested.

Information must still be gathered, and the earliest techniques of physical anthropology—comparative anatomy, embryology, systematics and classification—continue to be useful tools in an ever-expanding science. But current emphasis is on building a theoretical foundation on which to base a modern understanding of man. Toward this end are directed unique and energetic studies in primatology, fossil behavior, genetics, and human variation.

New tools and techniques are only part of this reorientation, for with the growth of the science new problems emerged as well. Today's physical anthropologists venture into areas previously neglected or ignored: the mind of prehistoric man; the origins of human art; the beginnings of social organization; the vestiges of early behavior that persist in modern man.

In the past, problem areas in physical anthropology were largely historical and descriptive. Now they are questions that demand dynamic new analytical procedures as diverse as the subject matter is vast. Even today, techniques of inquiry must often be specially designed to suit the research at hand. If physical anthropologists are to solve riddles never before even asked, then they must devise wholly new techniques. Experimentation—in methods of exploration as well as in subject matter—is the rule rather than the exception.

FURTHER READINGS

Harrison, Richard J. and William Montagna. *Man.* New York: Appleton-Century-Crofts, 1969.

McKern, Thomas W. and Sharon McKern. *Human Origins.* Englewood Cliffs: Prentice-Hall, Inc., 1969.

Napier, John. *The Roots of Mankind.* Washington: Smithsonian Institution Press, 1970.

PART 2

STUDIES IN
PHYSICAL ANTHROPOLOGY

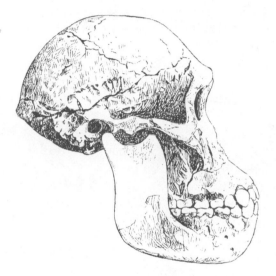

CHAPTER IV

EVOLUTION IN ACTION

How did the primates arise from simpler mammalian forms? How did they diverge into their present species? How do they relate, individually and collectively, to ancient and modern varieties of human beings? How in fact does any species come into being through a gradual process of evolutionary change?

Darwin, who so ably demonstrated the importance of variation in natural selection (and hence in the basic processes of evolution), was at a loss to explain the phenomenon of variation itself. The answers that eluded him are found in Mendelian genetics —and in complex new studies in biology and biochemistry.

Cellular Reproduction

Until a century ago, most people assumed that simple forms of life arose through a process of spontaneous generation. The use of improved microscopes proved otherwise and led to the first real comprehension of the function of cells in the architecture of living matter. In 1824, Henri Joachim Dutrocher stressed the importance of the cell as the basic structural unit in both plants and animals and noted that growth depends upon the formation and expansion of new cells. Some thirty years later, the Berlin pathologist Rudolf Virchow (1821–1902) pointed out that all organisms represent *communities* of cells and that each cell is the offspring of preceding cells. And in the years since, rapid advances in cytological techniques have enabled scientists to penetrate the cell itself, observing not only its structural organization but also the biochemical activities taking place within each cellular component and at each stage of cellular development. At last biologists could view the mechanics of reproduction and account for the variation that is crucial to evolutionary change.

CY TOL' O GY the study of cells and cellular processes.

Cellular reproduction, of course, may be *asexual,* involving one parent, or *sexual,* involving two. Because primates reproduce in the latter manner, we are concerned here only with sexual reproduction.

Like unicellular organisms, a multicellular organism commonly begins its life cycle as a single cell. In multicellular organisms, however, this single cell grows and divides to form two cells, each of which divides to form four, and so on. Continued cell divisions produce all the cells of the adult organism. It has been estimated that the mature human body contains on the order of 10^{14} cells, all organized in an integrated system. Each of these trillions of cells is the product of repeated reproduction of a single pair of *gametes,* or sex cells.

As we have mentioned in an earlier chapter, the fusion of a male gamete, or sperm, with a female gamete, or ovum, produces the zygote, or fertilized egg. It is at this early point in the organism's history that it receives its genetic inheritance—all the hereditary materials that will determine the molecular structure of its subsequent cell development. The organism itself grows through multiplication of additional cells through cell division. Once a cell is formed in a multicellular organism, of course, it does not necessarily live as long as the organism of which it is a part. Some cells, such as those comprising the lining of the digestive tract in high animals, have brief individual lives and must continuously be replaced by cell divisions. Cells of other types are replaced at different rates, according to the needs of the organism, and a very few cells, including some nerve cells, live as long as the organism itself endures.

In multicellular organisms, each cell contains a nucleus which in turn contains genetic materials in a substance called *chromatin.* From the chromatin are derived the distinctively shaped chromosomes. In man, each cell contains forty-six chromosomes, or twenty-three pair.

There are two important types of cell reproduction, of which *mitosis* is the more common. It is a complex process involving the division of both the cell nucleus and the surrounding cytoplasm. Repeated again and again, mitotic divisions assure that each daughter cell receives the same number of chromosomes as its mother cell. It is through mitosis, then, that each chromo-

MI TO′ SIS
a form of cell division during which chromosomes are duplicated.

CY′ TO PLASM
the protoplasm of a cell, exclusive of the nucleus; a semi-transparent material that is an aggregate of proteins, lipids, carbohydrates, and inorganic substances including water.

FIGURE 1. Mitosis. (a) Nucleus in EARLY PROPHASE: chromosomes have duplicated during interphase and have begun to shorten by coiling. (b) LATE PRO-
PHASE: *nucleolus* begins to disintegrate; centriole begins to migrate and spindle
fibers begin to form. (c) METAPHASE: paired chromosomes line up at equator
of nucleus attached by centromere to spindle fibers; nuclear membrane disin-
tegrates. (d) ANAPHASE: chromosomes divide and migrate toward opposite
centrioles. (e) EARLY TELOPHASE: chromosomes group at opposite poles; spindle
fibers dissolve and new cell wall or membrane begins to form between the
new nuclei. (f) LATE TELOPHASE: chromosomes uncoil; nucleoli reform and
new cell membranes firm.

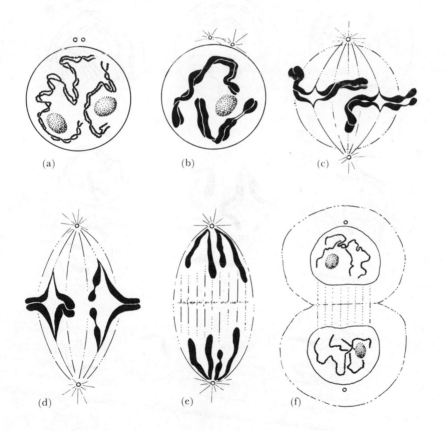

(a)　　　　　　(b)　　　　　　(c)

(d)　　　　　　(e)　　　　　　(f)

FIGURE 2.   Meiosis. (a) INTERPHASE: single unpaired chromosomes. (b) EARLY
PROPHASE: chromosomes duplicate (replicate, shaded; original, black). (c) DIP-
LOTENE PROPHASE: crossing over has occurred. If new mutations occurred during
DNA replication, they may recombine with unmutated chromosomes at this
point. (d) LATE PROPHASE: chromosomes shortened by coiling. (e) ANAPHASE
I: beginning of first reduction division. (f) TELOPHASE I: one tetraploid (4N)
nucleus has become two diploid (2N) nuclei with two new gene recombinations.
(g) ANAPHASE II: equivalent to a mitotic division, the paired chromosomes
separate during the second reduction division. (h) TELOPHASE II: four gametic
nuclei, each with a different gene complement. If the organism is male, all
four develop into sperm nuclei; if it is a female, one takes the bulk of the
original cell's cytoplasm and becomes an ovum, the other three are shed as
polar bodies.

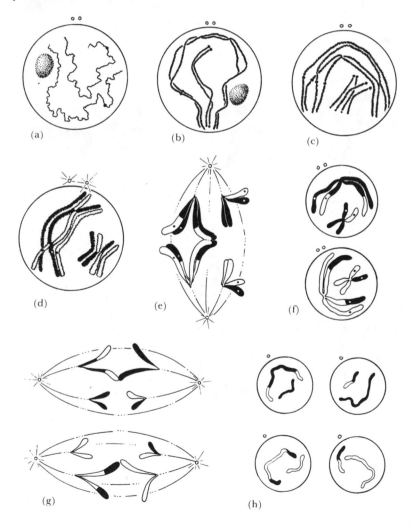

some produces an exact replica of itself. Repeated mitotic divisions produce the multitude of cells (with the exception of the sex cells) that make up the mature organism. Gametes are subject to a different process of self-reproduction called *meiosis.*

Meiosis is a specialized type of cell division by which reproductive cells are formed in organisms that reproduce sexually. In meiosis, the chromosome number is reduced to half that found in most body cells. Body cells, called somatic cells, are said to be *diploid;* that is, they have the diploid chromosome number (46 in humans). Mature gametes are said to be *haploid* (23 in humans), or have half the number of chromosomes typical for the species. The union of two haploid gametes, which occurs at the fertilization of an egg by a sperm, restores the diploid chromosome number. It is a tidy arrangement: obviously, if the gametes were diploid, the chromosome number would double with each new generation.

MEI O´ SIS the process of self-reproduction whereby the number of chromosomes in a gamete is reduced by half to compensate for the doubling effect of fertilization.

To sum up: mitosis produces exact cell replicas and lends hereditary stability; meiosis mixes chromosomes from both parents and injects an element of variation among offspring. And, as Darwin noted, it is variation that is the key to evolutionary change.

Mendel, who did not work with a microscope, hypothesized that heredity is effected through the transmission of discrete "particles." He knew nothing of the microscopic chromosomes, but his "particles" are similar in principle to the genes which in undetermined number constitute the chromosomes. Genes in turn are made up of combinations of deoxyribonucleic acid, called DNA, and several proteins. The evidence implies that DNA is the primary genetic material. The implication was supported in a classic study conducted in 1944 with pneumococcus, in which scientists demonstrated that DNA can induce permanent gene change. Cells of a rough, non-encapsulated strain of pneumococcus were transformed into cells of a smooth encapsulated strain simply by incubating the rough cells in an extract of DNA obtained from smooth cells. After the transformation occurred, cells continued to exist in the smooth encapsulated form for many generations. Obviously, a permanent gene change was effected.

A DNA molecule is believed to consist of intertwined sugar-phosphate strands in a shape similar to that of a spiral staircase, with nitrogenous bases—adenine, guanine, cytosine, and thymine—forming "steps" or internal links.[1] Apparently the DNA of all forms of plant and animal life has this same structure, but coding—variations in the four types of internal links—lends great variety.

In addition to DNA, plant and animal cells contain a similar substance called ribonucleic acid, or RNA, which contains a sugar called ribose, but which lacks the capacity of conferring change. DNA is found in the cell nucleus, RNA in the cytoplasm. Chemical instructions concerning protein manufacture are issued within the cell nucleus by the DNA, and then passed in cryptic chemical form by the DNA to the various forms of RNA, called "messenger RNA." Thus the actual determination of heredity and the manufacture of proteins necessary for life are carried out by the messenger molecules. Hence genes, with their DNA composition, play a crucial role in heredity. When the DNA code, or molecular structure, changes or mutates, the altered gene affects just one trait of a cell.

Mendel's *Law of Segregation* and his *Law of Independent Assortment* assure continued variation. The first law notes that genes pass intact from one generation to the next (although they do not necessarily produce visible traits), and that they segregate at random, producing predictable ratios of traits in the offspring (see Chapter 2). Mendel's second law holds that inherited gene pairs for a given trait are not influenced by the inheritance (or lack of inheritance) of any other specific gene, and it explains how it is that each individual (except in the case of identical twins) may receive a unique total of inherited traits.

The principle we know as Mendel's third law was discovered, not by Mendel, but by an early geneticist, T. H. Morgan (1866–1945). Morgan noted that the genes for specific traits are located in regular sequences along the length of a chromosome,

---

[1] Though hundreds of scientists working in laboratories around the world sought to demonstrate the molecular structure of DNA, F. H. C. Crick and James D. Watson of Cambridge were the first to portray DNA in the form of a helix. They were awarded a Nobel Prize for their work.

and that since they are linked together in chemical bond, they are normally inherited as a chromosome group. Ordinarily, when chromosomes inherited from the father match up in the fertilized egg with those from the mother, they come together in parallel strands. Occasionally, however, these strands twist across one another, and when this happens, a segment of each chromosome may become detached and join the chromosome of its opposite number. The result is an exchange of chromosome segments and an alteration in the genetic code of each chromosome in the pair. Crossing over changes the proximity of specific genes; and since genes can influence the effects of the other genes nearest them in the development of traits, their relative positions on the chromosomes are often significant. Crossing over, then, can alter the combined effect of the genes involved and so modify cell structure. This process, called the *Law of Lineal Order of Genes,* produces yet another source of variation among offspring.

MUTATION

Still other possibilities exist for even greater variation, which do not have to do with sexual recombinations of genes but rather with internal changes in the molecular structure of the genes themselves. When a failure occurs in the DNA coding process, or when there is an alteration of the molecular structure of DNA, and when such changes are sufficiently stable to be inherited by the offspring, mutations result. Genes are, on the whole, remarkably stable; they are capable of replicating themselves for generations. Occasionally, however, an inheritable change takes place, and, in effect, a new allele appears which may be responsible for dramatic changes in the organism.

MU TA′ TION a spontaneous change in the genetic composition of an organism.

Mutations occur with some regularity in all species, and the rates of mutations may be increased by exposure to radiation, to heat, and to various chemicals. Some mutations are favorable, such as the one that resulted in the increase in dark-colored moths in industrial England (see Chapter 2). More frequently (because natural selection has heightened the adaptability of the organism and rendered abrupt change undesirable) mutations are harmful in that they reduce the organism's potential to survive and breed. Ordinarily, harmful genes do not have great impact on the breeding population since the carrier is likely to die and/or fail to reproduce. Thus, lethal genes, unless they are linked to other genes, are seldom passed on to offspring. If the mutant gene is recessive, however, there is no visible effect in the generation in which the mutation occurs, though its effects will be revealed in homozygous genotypes of later generations.

Gene Pools

The smaller the population, the greater are the effects of mutations. A breeding population, of course, is a localized group of a given species, the members of which breed primarily among themselves. All the genes possessed by all members of the population make up its *gene pool,* the reservoir of genetic material available to be inherited by the next generation. Most gene pools are stable; they remain relatively unchanged from generation to generation. But changes do occur, often through mutation. (Other factors responsible for upsetting genetic equilibrium are natural selection, population mixture, and genetic drift. See Chapter VIII.)

As we have seen, natural selection consists of the operation of environmental factors upon genetic variations that result in differential reproduction. Variant individuals which reproduce and survive in the greatest number are those which are best suited to their environment. From generation to generation these are the individuals which contribute a progressively larger proportion of descendants. Eventually, their genes may come to dominate the population. And, since they are the best suited individuals, the entire population tends to become better adapted to its environment.

Obviously, a mutation must offer selective advantage and must occur with significant frequency in order to influence a population. Specialists in the study of gene frequencies and reproductive potential are called *population geneticists.* Population genetics plays a crucial role today in the study of human races. We shall discuss this further in Chapter VIII.

The degree to which mutations have selective advantage depends upon the specific environment in which the population lives. One example is the occurrence of *sickle-cell anemia,* a serious condition, usually fatal before maturity for the afflicted individual. Investigators have noted a highly variable distribution (from zero to forty percent of populations under study) of the disease in Africa and have found that the highest incidence of sickle-cell anemia occurs in areas where malaria is most common. Heterozygous individuals (those with genes both for normal and for sickling corpuscles) are more immune to malaria than are homozygous normals. This, then, is a case of double selection: against homozygous sicklers (doomed to serious and probably fatal anemia) and against homozygous normals (lacking immunity to malaria). The biological price of maintaining a heterozygous population is the birth of both kinds of homozygotes (normal and sicklers) in each generation. In a malaria-ridden environment, it is advantageous for the population to have the sickle-cell mutant in the gene pool even though it means that every child born a homozygous sickler is doomed to early death.

Evolutionary change is also fostered through geographic and reproductive isolation. When a species is splintered—with groups occupying many kinds of environments and undergoing different adaptations to these environments—it may become a polytypic species characterized by diverse races or subspecies. Lack of interbreeding among the varied groups prevents the exchange of genes and may lead to the formation of separate species.

Population mixture is yet another factor in genetic variation. When two populations meet and mate, they combine their respective gene pools, producing a new one. New phenotypes appear which sometimes become characteristic of the new population, as when hybridization continues over a long time or when the hybrids are better able to survive and reproduce. Occasionally, prolonged population mixture produces new taxonomic types. This has been the case in the continental United States with the American Negro population and, in the Pacific, with the Hawaiian population, both of which have interbred with other races.

But genetic change need not be triggered by outside factors. It is possible for an isolated population to experience a substantial change in its original genetic composition, independent of mutation or natural selection. This is the result of *genetic drift,* or the Sewall Wright effect, as it is also known. Genetic drift occurs most commonly, among human populations, in small groups with the accidental increase or decrease of genetic elements. One example is the departure of splinter groups, which may reduce the gene frequency for a given trait. Genetic drift may occur, in fact, whenever a relatively large group splits and the resulting smaller groups inbreed.

SPECIATION

We have referred to subspecies or races formed when one or more groups become isolated from their original population and adapt in different ways to their separate environments. Speciation—the formation of a new species—occurs when such sub-groups undergo sufficient genetic change that they are no longer able to breed with members of the original population or of other subgroups. By definition, in fact, a species is a population whose members breed only among themselves to produce fertile offspring.

Occasionally, as on a small island, a species may change through time without producing additional species. In this case the new species simply replaces the old through a natural process of straight-line change. However, most new species are formed when isolated sub-groups undergo change sufficient to render them incapable of breeding with other sub-groups or with de-scendant members of the original population.

Our emphasis on variation is not meant to imply that genetic equilibrium does not exist. Under normal conditions, quite the opposite is true: new genes introduced by genetic novelty, whether a chromosomal aberration or point mutation, have little effect on the frequency of genes in a population unless some factor leads to the subsequent rapid generational increase of that genetic change. In general, rates of selection (except for lethal or semi-lethal characteristics) are sufficiently slow that they do not upset the genetic equilibrium; that is, the deviations they produce are not usually detectable. Thus it can be assumed for human breeding populations that genetic stability will be maintained over the generations. Even when two previously distinct breeding populations are fused for any reason into one, genetic equilibrium will come about in the next generation and be maintained thereafter. This concept is expressed in mathematical terms by the *Hardy-Weinberg Law.*

The Hardy-Weinberg Law was published simultaneously in 1908 by Hardy, a British mathematician, and Weinberg, a German physician. It demonstrates, quite simply, that under ideal conditions (including large population size and random mating) gene frequencies will not change from one generation to the next. The law is represented by an equation which takes into account the frequency of genes in a given population and predicts how these will be combined in separate individuals. Where p represents the relative frequency of a particular allele and q represents the relative frequency of a second allele, the formula reads as follows:

$$p^2 + 2pq + q^2 = 1 \text{ (totality)}.$$

The totality is calculated at 1.000, representing the total number of individuals in the whole population. The application of this formula to genetic data gives the genotypes of all the kinds of individuals possible in a population and the percentage frequencies of each.

Directions in Evolution

One problem in arranging fossil evidence chronologically is that, thus arranged, the evidence appears to demonstrate a predestined guidance of evolutionary change. Orthogenesis—the concept that evolution is guided in a preordained direction by natural selection or by other forces—rears its head even when the fossil record is accorded only cursory attention. Advocates of orthogenesis see in paleontological evidence a succession of transitional forms, linked by their progressive development toward the present. They fail to note those short-lived forms which, doomed to extinction, leave no descendants to represent their existence in later periods. It is only by ignoring the evidence of unsuccessful lines and concentrating solely upon surviving lineages that we see the error inherent in the theory of orthogenesis, for the fossil record is littered with the bones of evolutionary failures, forms which failed to readapt to rapid environmental change. In fact, prehistorians estimate that 98 percent of all species that have ever existed are now extinct. And there is no evidence to support a view of predestination. Indeed, the principles of natural selection preclude such a concept as applied to organic evolution.

It is equally misleading to view *Homo sapiens* as the culmination of evolutionary progress. To be sure, modern man represents the most successful—so far—of all species: he is the most recent product of hominid evolution, the most durable, and the most intelligent; he alone in the animal kingdom possesses the means to manipulate his own environment and, to a certain extent, his own destiny. But to consider man the *final* product of evolution is to deny that he is subject to natural law. Evolution does not stop with man.

Of course, it is with human beings that we are most directly concerned. We want to know ourselves, our origins, and our evolutionary history; but in order to do so, we must focus not on man alone but on the entire order from which man springs, viewing *Homo sapiens* against the larger background of primate development.

THE PRIMATE PATH TO MAN

While we must discount the notion of a mysterious predestination, we do note certain developmental trends. These emerge and are shaped by the trial-and-error nature of evolutionary progress. They reflect adaptations among a group of animals to a common environment and way of life. For the primates, such trends are prompted by modifications in response to arboreal life.

There are more than two hundred living species of primates, ranging from the insect-eating tree shrews to the complex erect-postured human being.[2] Primates are so varied, in fact, that it is sometimes difficult to believe that they belong within a single taxonomic order. Yet all members of the order are bound together by a common ancestry, and all are characterized by adaptations that point to a long evolutionary history lived at

---

[2] An increasing number of physical anthropologists and taxonomic specialists no longer believe that tree shrews are in the primate order.

tree-top level. Basically, primates are arboreal (tree-dwelling) creatures: they got their start in the trees, developed and flourished there, and most of them remain there today.

The first placental mammals appeared about 130 million years ago. This was the time when diverse species of giant reptiles stalked the earth, feeding by day and causing the few existing mammals, which were small, inconspicuous creatures, to depend for survival upon their nocturnal habits. Their shadowy existence, however, offered various evolutionary opportunities, the exploitation of which helped them to achieve an unprecedented degree of adaptability which would later serve them well in times of great and rapid change.

For example, the earth, which had been relatively stable for more than a hundred million years, began to shake with recurrent earthquakes and violent volcanic eruptions. As the land rose, retreating waters exposed vast continents that had once been islands. A cooler, drier climate favored the spread of dense forests, great open grasslands, and an abundant growth of grasses, trees, shrubs, and ivies. Swamplands dwindled, and with them the giant reptiles. The great dinosaurs, incapable of adapting to the changing conditions, produced fewer and fewer offspring with each generation. Their demise was not sudden: they disappeared gradually, though it is possible that their extinction was hastened by plant fungi or disease-bearing insects, or that their eggs, left in the open to be hatched by the heat of the sun, were eaten by night-feeding mammals. But by whatever forces, the giant reptilian forms were doomed. And there occurred then a dramatic increase in mammalian forms.

The warm-blooded mammals, unlike the reptiles, were able to maintain stable body temperatures; they thrived both in the heat of the day and in the cold of night. And they fell heir to a land abundant in food supplies. They soon multiplied and spread, competing for ecological zones formerly occupied by the many varieties of prehistoric reptiles. Many, venturing into the open grasslands, evolved into such familiar ground-dwellers as elephants, horses and other hoofed animals, and rodents; others evolved into aquatic mammals such as the sea cows and whales; and still others took to the trees. How they adapted to their new arboreal environment is of direct concern to man. Basic human structure is that of a forest animal; the human brain, limbs, sense organs, and reproductive system are derived from arboreal ancestors. More recent specializations represent modifications of an old pattern rather than the development of totally new structures.

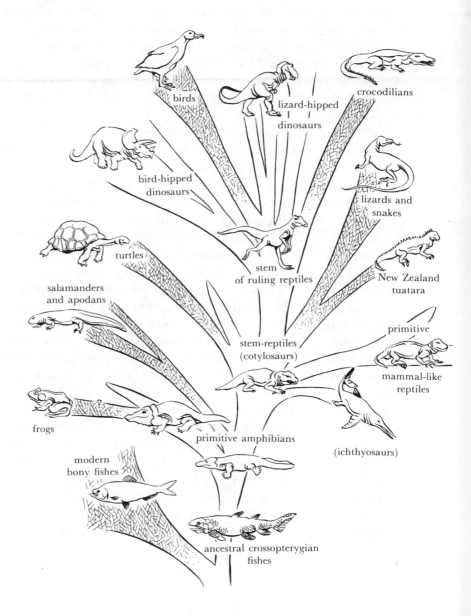

Among the earliest tree-dwelling mammals were the *insectivores,* insect-eaters which eventually gave rise to all the modern primates from monkey to ape to human being. All primates have in common numerous anatomical adaptations for life in the trees; one of these is an enlarged, modified brain, charac-

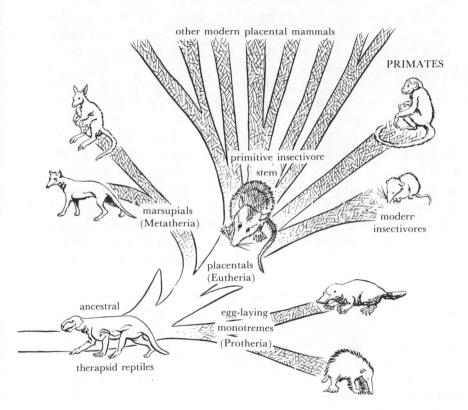

FIGURE 3. Family tree of the vertebrates and the position of the Primates. (Adapted from Alfred S.
Romer, *The Vertebrate Body,* Saunders
Co., 1962.)

terized by a pronounced expansion of the visual center and an accompanying reduction in the olfactory bulb. Ground-dwelling mammals, on the other hand, depend heavily upon their ability to sniff out food, while vision is of secondary importance. Hence the typical ground-dwelling mammal has a brain in which a large anatomical area is devoted to the sense of smell while a lesser region is reserved for sight. Most ground-dwelling mammals also tend to have long snouts with eyes set on either side making stereoscopic vision more difficult and unlikely, though not necessarily impossible.

Life in the trees, however, poses quite a different set of problems. Here the sense of smell is less critical, since smells do not waft about so freely at tree-top level. On the other hand, good vision is essential both to locating food and to getting about from branch to branch. Because most primates came into existence in the trees, their brains exhibit a reduction in the area devoted to the olfactory sense and a marked expansion, near the back of the brain, of the area reserved for vision. Eyes are set together on the frontal plane, allowing stereoscopic vision and depth perception. The higher primates also have color vision, enabling them to identify fruits and seeds high in food value and so extend their food resources.

In taking to the trees, the ancestral primates avoided the intense competition of terrestrial rodents, carnivores, and other rival species. At the same time, however, they faced the enormous evolutionary challenges of arboreal life, one of which was simply staying aloft—for while the ground is solid and dependable, brittle or swaying tree branches are not as reliable for resting, launching, or landing.

The solution to this problem lay in the primate retention of basic limb, hand, and foot structures that had been typical of the early amphibians. The limbs of most terrestrial animals differ markedly from the amphibian structure; in the horse, for example, parallel bones have fused together and a single functional digit remains. This is adequate in view of the fact that such ground-dwellers use their limbs solely for locomotion. The arboreal primates, however, need to use their limbs, hands, and feet for more varied purposes, and they are able to do so because they have retained and further developed the mobility and flexibility of early amphibian structures. The arboreal primates developed prehensile (grasping), five-digited hands and feet with thumbs and big toes that "oppose" the remaining digits. That is, the thumb can touch the other digits when the hand grasps a branch or other object. Humans are unable to use their toes in this manner because their feet have become specialized for the purposes of support and locomotion. Other primates, however, can usually grasp as well with their feet as with their hands.

Though firm evidence is lacking, experts believe that the earliest primates must have had claws, effective for climbing but disadvantageous for descent. Weight resting upon the primate foot and hand tended to force the first digit apart from the others, providing a foot or hand that curved smartly around a limb. The process of natural selection favored and perpetuated this form, and the evolutionary result was the development of opposable thumbs and big toes. Claws, except for those of the lowest primates, disappeared. The higher primates possess flat or slightly curved nails on the digits of both hands and feet.

Another feature of the adapted primate skeleton useful in an arboreal habitat is the retention and enlargement of the clavicle, or collarbone, which serves as a strut to hold each forelimb at the side of the body, and which provides unsurpassed mobility of the arms.

Once the hands are developed in an arboreal animal so that they can be used for grasping and exploring as well as for locomotion, the hindlimbs assume greater responsibility for support of the body. Various other adaptations follow in quick order. For example, although most primates are pronograde, they spend much of their time sitting in an upright position, a habit that favors the development of heavier, sturdier hindlimbs. The hands are free, then, for touching, holding, feeling, grooming, and scratching—all tasks that are both pleasurable and practical. Hence the differentiation of forelimbs and hindlimbs, the former being used for exploration while the latter assume the function of support. Primates, able to pick up objects for examination, feed chiefly with their hands; food can be carried to the nose or mouth, or held before the eyes for examination prior to consumption.

PRO′ NO GRADE walking on all four limbs as opposed to

OR′ THO GRADE walking on two limbs.

The advantages—and the adaptations that must have followed—are apparent. The primate sense of smell, never very important in the trees, became less so. The olfactory region of the brain decreased still further in size, especially among the higher primates. The hands could both carry and break up food, so there was no longer a need for large and powerful jaws; these gradually decreased in size as well. The long snout characteristic of the lower primate forms was also reduced among the higher primates, partly because of the reduced sense of smell and the increased need for visual acuity. A short snout meant that the eyes could lay closer together, and both sight and depth perception could thus be improved. The typical primate face, then, began to flatten out, becoming more "human-like" in appearance, with prominent front-facing eyes, and a small nose with the mouth directly beneath it. These modifications triggered a raft of others that improved the primate's chances for survival in the trees.

Is this in fact how it all happened; and is this the correct order of change? We can't know for certain; but from analyses of living species and from the examination of fossil forms, scientists have pieced together this rough history of primate development. Of course, not all the modern primates evolved in an identical manner, and no single primate possesses all the features that tend to arise from similar arboreal adaptation. Still, all primates shared to some extent the general primate pattern of evolution; and each demonstrates at least a trend toward the evolutionary modifications typical of the order as a whole.

FURTHER READINGS

Dunn, L. C. *Heredity and Evolution in Human Populations.* Cambridge: Harvard University Press, 1959.

Gardner, Eldon J. *Principles of Genetics.* New York: John Wiley & Sons, Inc., 1962.

Lerner, I. Michael. *Heredity, Evolution, and Society.* San Francisco: W. H. Freeman, 1968.

McKusick, Victor A. *Human Genetics.* Englewood Cliffs: Prentice-Hall, 1969.

Pilbeam, David. *The Ascent of Man: An Introduction to Human Evolution.* New York: Macmillan, 1972.

Savage, Jay M. *Evolution.* New York: Holt, Rinehart & Winston, 1963.

Simons, Elwyn L. *Primate Evolution: An Introduction to Man's Place in Nature.* New York: Macmillan, 1972.

Simpson, George Gaylord. *The Geography of Evolution.* New York: Bantam, 1971.

Srb, Adrian M., R. D. Owen, and R. S. Edgar. *General Genetics,* 2nd ed. San Francisco: W. H. Freeman, 1965.

Stebbins, G. Ledyard. *Processes of Organic Evolution.* Englewood Cliffs: Prentice-Hall, 1966.

Sutton, H. Eldon. *An Introduction to Human Genetics.* New York: Holt, Rinehart & Winston, 1965.

Volpe, E. Peter. *Understanding Evolution.* Dubuque: William C. Browne, 1972.

Watson, James D. *Molecular Biology of the Gene.* New York: W. A. Benjamin, 1965.

Watson, James D. *The Double Helix.* New York: Atheneum, 1968.

Watson, J. D. and F. H. C. Crick. "Molecular Structure of Nucleic Acids," *Nature* 171:737–738, 1953.

CHAPTER V

STUDIES IN PRIMATOLOGY

Perhaps no specialization in physical anthropology so captivates the public imagination as have recent studies in primatology. It is no wonder: the primates are, on the whole, alert and sociable animals; monkeys and apes are especially appealing, and they provide for most laymen amusing and often remarkable caricatures of human beings.

But entertainment aside, why should we study them? First, the primates provide us with a living context within which to analyze the meaning of fossil remains. If experts can relate structure to function, and function to behavior in living species, then they have the potential to hypothesize function in extinct primate forms. Secondly, the study of primate social behavior and social organization yields clues to the nature of the early hominids. By combining "living" evidence with paleontological evidence, we can then make more reliable assumptions about the past.

Like human beings, free-ranging monkeys and apes generally live in social groups, and they possess certain social traits highly similar to human behavior. Thus studies in primatology can also offer insights into the evolution of human culture. Problem-solving tests administered to monkeys and apes may help to isolate those factors responsible for the development of human capacity for culture. At the very least, scientists hope to utilize field observations in distinguishing between wholly learned human behavior and behavior that is shaped by genetic heritage.

Experimental primatology is applied directly in both medicine and psychology. The great apes, now endangered species in their natural habitats, are too rare and costly for all but the most crucial medical experiments, but monkeys can and often do serve as understudies to man in medical research. Research on rhesus monkeys, for example, led to the discovery of the Rh factor in red blood cells—a discovery that saved thousands of human lives. Today, medical investigation with primates centers upon organ transplants, with the hope that defective human kidneys, hearts, and livers can one day be replaced by healthy organs from apes and monkeys.

Behavioral studies of apes and monkeys are useful in testing hypotheses formulated in human psychology, where experimentation is difficult if not impossible. At the University of Wisconsin, for example, Professor Harry Harlow has used monkeys to demonstrate the importance of social contacts and interaction among growing primates. Harlow raised several groups of macaque monkeys in his laboratory, some of which were isolated from birth and denied all opportunity to see, touch, or play with other monkeys. Other macaques were permitted daily play periods with monkeys of their own age. The isolated monkeys grew into nervous, timid, highly disturbed individuals unable to copulate with or enter into friendly relationships with

FIGURE 1.   Surrogate mother situation with monkey conducted by Dr. H. F. Harlow, University of Wisconsin. (H. F. Harlow, University of Wisconsin Primate Laboratory)

other monkeys. In contrast, those that were permitted daily contact with others during infancy emerged as active, self-confident individuals able both to reproduce and to interact with others. These experiments point up the importance of peer groups in monkey development. Social contact is no less important among growing humans. (See Figure 1.)

In another experiment, Harlow tested the significance of motherly protection and reassurance among infant rhesus monkeys. He designed a playroom for the infants, complete with toys, gym equipment, and two artificial "mothers," one of which was a dummy constructed of bare wire, the other of wire wrapped in soft cloth. When research associates introduced factors of danger or stress into the playroom, the infant monkeys fled to the cloth mother for reassurance. In the absence of stress, the infants continued to cling to the cloth mother, even when the wire mother was mechanically rigged to provide a constant supply of bottled food. Occasionally driven by hunger to the wire dummy, the infants invariably returned to the cloth dummy after feeding. This series of experiments shows that, especially in times of stress, young primates tend to seek the warmth, protection and reassurance of their mothers, even if the "mother" is cloth.

Such experiments hold implication about human behavior based on the fact that man shares with other primates a common evolutionary history in which primate morphology *and* primate behavior patterns were conditioned, through habitat, long before evolution produced the first human populations.

THE LIVING PRIMATES

It is convenient to divide the order Primates into two suborders: Prosimii (lower primates) and Anthropoidea (higher primates). The first primates, which appeared about seventy million years ago, were the tree shrews, squirrel-sized creatures which seem not to have changed much since. Modern descendants of the group look remarkably like their fossil ancestors; they are so different in body structure and brain morphology that many modern scientists refuse to group them with the other primates, demoting them instead to insectivore status. The tree shrews have claws rather than nails, digits which are not truly opposable, and eyes set on either side of a long snout, which means that they lack stereoscopic vision. (See Figure 2.)

In any case, the earliest shrew-like mammals spread and multiplied, giving rise to the first lemurs.[1] Lemur brains are small and almost smooth, in contrast to the richly-convoluted brain surfaces typical in the higher primates. Nevertheless, lemur brains are large when compared with those of their insect-eating predecessors or with those of contemporary mammals. Many are nocturnal (active at night), avoiding competition with the diurnal (active by day) monkeys who inhabit the same regions. And some, like the dwarf lemur, are not able effectively to maintain stable body temperature, so that they fall into hibernation in cold weather, living off the fat reserves stored in their tails. Still, lemurs have endured for millions of years, and diverse forms of lemurs exist today. Modern representatives include the aye-ayes of Madagascar, the lorises of Asia, and the pottos and galagos, or bush-babies, of Africa.

Meanwhile, other evolutionary processes were occurring which, from our view, would prove to be more exciting. One lead to the tarsiers, monkeys, apes, and man. Rare and short-lived in zoos, modern tarsiers are so elusive that few scientists have been able to examine them properly. Native to Borneo, Sumatra, parts of Indonesia, and the Philippines, tarsiers are quite small, with heads and brains that are large in proportion to their bodies. Their eyes are also large, and set close together. Like the eyes of higher primates, the tarsier's eyes are set in a true bony socket,[2] but they lack color vision. Only one variety of tarsier now exists, though they were once as diverse as monkeys are today.

Experts have deduced from the fossil evidence, that the earliest prosimians were frugivorous (fruit eaters), and had relatively large brains in which the occipital and temporal lobes were expanded. These are the areas that are concerned, respectively, with the perception of visual stimuli and with the perception

---

[1] Lemurs are frequently subdivided into Lemuriformes and Lorisiformes. Because Lemuriformes are now found only on Madagascar and surrounding small islands, the term Lemur is often used to designate the Madagascar variety.

[2] Other prosimians have eyes that are enclosed by a ring of bone lacking a back wall.

FIGURE 2. Some examples of the lower primates. (a) Common tree shrew. (b) Mindanao tarsier with six-day-old infant. (c) Black and white ruffled lemur. (Ron Garrison, San Diego Zoo)

(a)

(b)

(c)

and memory of both visual and auditory stimuli. The same brain regions are similarly developed in modern prosimians, which suggests that some of the extinct prosimians lived in groups in which sight and hearing were important to social communication. Studies with living prosimians tend to support this hypothesis. If it is true, it is a surprising discovery, for experts held until recently that typical primate groupings and social organization could exist only among the Anthropoidea. Since prosimians do not perform well on standard intelligence tests, the evidence points to an early development of social organization—earlier, in fact, than the development of intelligence consistent with that displayed by the higher primates.

The primate suborder Anthropoidea includes the monkeys, apes, and man. Members of this group have eyes set on the frontal plane, producing stereoscopic vision in which each eye sees a given object from a slightly different angle, thereby increasing depth perception. Members of the suborder Anthropoidea also possess color vision; and their brains are larger and more highly developed than those of the prosimians.

Traditionally, the Anthropoidea have been divided into two infra-orders: the Platyrrhini, or New World monkeys, and the Catarrhini, including Old World monkeys, apes, and man. More recently, experts have preferred to divide the suborder Anthropoidea into three super-families: (1) Ceboidea, or New World monkeys; (2) Cercopithecoidea, or Old World monkeys; and (3) Hominoidea, including both apes and man.

By Oligocene times—some forty million years ago—several anthropoid groups had evolved. The monkeys had diverged into two distinct families and had ended their period of greatest evolutionary change. One group, ancestors of the modern Ceboidea, had spread across most of North and South America. A second large group, ancestral to the present-day Cercopithecoidea, had scattered across Africa, Asia, and southern Europe. The differences between these two vast and variable families are the results of their adaptation to different environments and are preserved by their long biological and geographic separation.

Modern Ceboidea, or New World monkeys, range in size from that of a kitten to that of a medium-size collie. The most familiar is the Cebus or "organ grinder" monkey, but there are more than one hundred other species. All but one of these species are diurnal: that is, they feed in the trees during the day and sleep there at night. New World monkeys failed to share fully in the development of the opposable thumb, but many species possess a useful aboreal adaptation lacking in Old World monkeys: they have prehensile tails which they use as balancing rudders or as an extra hand. With its sensitive ridged undersurface, this organ is both strong enough to hang by and also adapted for gripping. A few of the New World monkeys, notably

(a)

(b)

(c)

FIGURE 3. Some examples of New World monkeys. (a) Squirrel monkey at the Monkey Jungle, Florida. (Joseph Popp) (b) Golden marmoset, the smallest of New World monkeys. (Ron Garrison, San Diego Zoo) (c) Capuchin ("organ grinder") monkey. (Courtesy of the American Museum of Natural History)

the spider monkey, brachiate or move through the trees by swinging by their arms. This is a technique developed by some apes in the Old World. Experts have noted, in fact, numerous similarities between the New World spider monkey and the Old World gibbon. Such similarities demonstrate the principle of *parallel evolution,* the development of like structures or habits due to similar environmental circumstances.[3] Other examples of the principle, of course, among the higher primates would include stereoscopic vision and color vision.

(d)

(d) Red howler monkey. (San Diego Zoo) (e) Red uakari. (Ron Garrison, San Diego Zoo)

(e)

---

[3] Parallel evolution can occur between both related and unrelated species: for example, bats and birds are a case of partial parallel evolution of unrelated species.

While brachiation is known among New World monkeys, it is the exception rather than the rule. Most tree-dwelling monkeys run on all fours on top of the tree branches rather than swing from their arms below.

One final significant difference between the Ceboidea and their Old World cousins: the New World monkeys have a different dental distribution than do the Old World monkeys, apes, and man. Among the latter, the typical dental formula is 2:1:2:3, or

$$I\ 2/2\ +\ C\ 1/1\ +\ P\ 2/2\ +\ M\ 3/3\ \times\ 2\ =\ 32.$$

That is, on either side of each jaw, both mandible and maxilla, there are two inciser teeth, one canine tooth, two premolars, and three molars. Among the Ceboidea, there are three premolars rather than two. (See Figure 4.)

Further evolved than their New World cousins, but equally diversified, are the Cercopithecoidea, or Old World monkeys. Their hands, with broad nails and opposable thumbs, have the same shape as human hands, and the shape of their feet is also handlike. Some varieties of Old World monkeys have cheek pouches, useful for storing hastily acquired food that cannot immediately be devoured. Others, primarily leaf-eaters, such as the Colobus monkey, have sacculated stomachs, call "pre-stomachs" because they serve a similar temporary storage pur-

FIGURE 4. Dentition of New and Old World monkeys compared. (a) New World monkey *(C. albifrons)*. Note three premolars. (b) Old World monkey *(C. ascanius)*. Note two premolars. (Dr. N. C. Tappen and James Greer, Department of Anthropology, University of Wisconsin)

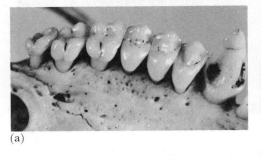
(a)

(b)

(a)

FIGURE 5. Some examples of Old World monkeys. (a) Hamadryas baboons. (San Diego Zoo) (b) Japanese macaque at Kyoto, Japan. (Irven DeVore) (c) Threat of an adult male savannah baboon, Nairobi Park, Kenya. (Irven DeVore)

(b)

(c)

pose. Numerous Old World monkeys are distinguished by their *ischial callosities,* those brightly colored patches of bare, toughened skin on the buttocks. This development accommodates constant resting on rough surfaces and in males of brightly colored species also serves as a sexual attractant.

Very little is known about the earliest monkeys, for relatively few fossil forms have been found which represent the time period in which the monkeys reached their evolutionary peak. Nevertheless, it is clear that they were generally highly successful animals that evolved to fill a wide variety of ecological niches in forest, woodland, and savanna.

The best known of the Cercopithecoidea are the modern baboons and macaques. Most researchers believe that both are basically woodland animals that have moved, in relatively recent times, into the vast treeless savannas of Africa. Hence, their social behavior cannot be judged typical and must be studied with constant reference to that fact. Baboons, for example, are known for their pronounced sexual dimorphism and the aggressiveness of the males. Earlier studies suggested that the aggressiveness of the male baboon, coupled with his huge canine teeth, was related to his function as defender of the baboon troop. Recent investigations however, reveal that closely related forest species show an equal development of sexual dimorphism, yet do not demonstrate the same aggressiveness toward intruders and predators. The implication is that extreme sexual dimorphism among the baboons has to do with sexual selection, or intermale competition within the baboon troop. Once they are developed, of course, canines and extreme aggressiveness prove useful for other purposes—in this case, defending the troop against ground predators.

SEXUAL DI MOR′ PHISM a difference in bodily characteristics and behavior of the two sexes in a species.

The monkeys, of course, are not as closely related to man as the apes are, and this must be kept in mind when using them as models for the behavior of the earliest hominids. Still, they are useful in, for example, studies of the mechanical changes in jaws and teeth that occurred in the hominid lineage.

But it is with the hominoids that researchers are most concerned. Ape-like forms began to appear some thirty million years ago, and within a short time several species of true apes inhabited the vast tropical forests that ranged from West Africa to the

East Indies, an extensive region that was at that time uninterrupted by water barriers.

These apes were not "super primates" or overgrown monkeys, nor were they derived from monkeys; they were members of a group of primates anatomically distinct although descended from common primate ancestors. They lacked external tails and cheek pouches, and, according to numerous experts, they shared a long evolutionary history of brachiation. Except for the very few American exceptions noted earlier, tree-dwelling monkeys run on all fours atop tree branches, where as the early apes apparently swung by their arms below the limbs of trees.

BRA CHI A′ TION the hand-over-hand form of swinging locomotion practiced by some apes and by a few New World monkeys.

Brachiation was made possible by the development of long, agile fingers. As a pattern of locomotion, it reinforces the habit of upright posture: for example, in brachiating animals and in man, the clavicle acts as a strut which permits free arm movement in almost any direction; and the pelvis is modified to bear the brunt of support in erect stance. Whether or not all the early apes brachiated is a controversial issue among physical anthropologists; but many experts argue convincingly that all the apes show signs of a long history of brachiation in their short, compact trunks and long, free-swinging arms. On the ground they move on all fours in a uniquely ape-like manner. Although they are capable of walking upright like humans, they do so with obvious distaste and discomfort. Their preferred gait—except for the gibbon—is quadrupedal: they get about by leaning forward to rest their weight on the bent knuckles of their hands.

The hominoids are divided into three families: Hylobatidae (gibbons and siamangs); Pongidae (gorillas, chimpanzees, and orang-utans); and Hominidae (man). Investigations in biochemistry and comparative anatomy demonstrate the interrelatedness of these forms and their distinctiveness from other primate forms. All have brains that are markedly larger and more intricately convoluted than those of the monkeys. All demonstrate a lengthy period of infant dependency, indicating that a greater percentage of their total behavior is learned rather than instinctive, and is therefore more adaptable.

Numerous attempts have been made to chart the course of evolutionary development for the apes; but there occurs, shortly after the appearance of the first ape forms, one of those frustrating gaps in the fossil record, a great chunk of time for which we have few truly significant fossils. Although prehistorians and physical anthropologists are increasingly filling in these gaps, this work is still not complete and, in some cases, the evidence may be forever lost to us. Meanwhile, all we know for certain is that, of the numerous prehistoric ape species, only four descendant groups survive: the gibbons and orang-utans from East Asia, and the chimpanzees and gorillas from Africa. They are man's nearest primate relatives, sharing with him numerous similarities in anatomical structure, cellular structure, and blood chemistry. Of them, the small brachiating gibbon bears the least resemblance to human beings. The gorilla, because of his specialized man-like foot, appears to be the most closely related to man of the living apes. (See Figure 6.)

(a)

(b)

FIGURE 6. Some examples of hominoids. (Ron Garrison, San Diego Zoo) (a) White-haired gibbon. (b) Chimpanzee (Congo). (c) Orangutan, adult pair. (d) Lowland gorilla, adult male.

(c)

(d)

The same annoying gap in the fossil record that obscures ancient ape history also obscures the history of the earliest human development. There are never sufficient fossils for study, and the fossil evidence for the earliest phase of human existence is particularly scant. Bones left on the ground are scattered or eaten by free-roaming animals, and even when they are covered with earth or stone, they decay rapidly. In order to be a likely candidate for fossilization, one must manage either to die in a cave (where the bones can become impregnated with mineral salts) or to fall into a lake bed (where sediment can cover and preserve the form).[4] Such conditions aren't met very often, and only a tiny fraction of living populations die under conditions or in regions favorable for fossilization. Of these, an even smaller fraction are unearthed for examination.

Human beings evolved in regions unfavorable for fossilization. The earliest humans lived in small bands, and their scattered remains, if preserved at all, have for the most part been discovered by accident. Invariably, fossil evidence is meager or fragmentary. One goal of primatology, then, is to add evidence which will compensate for the scarcity of early human fossils.

Down from the Trees

At one time, all primates—including the ancestors of the modern monkeys, apes, and man—were arboreal creatures. At some point, however, certain primates abandoned the trees, perhaps in search of new or more abundant food supplies. Whatever the motivation, this departure gave rise to numerous biological and social adaptations that characterize the modern higher primates.

For life in the trees, agility and lightness of body are advantageous. Most modern monkeys, for example, are small and remarkably nimble. They easily evade snakes and carnivores, and as long as they avoid the very tops of the trees in which they dwell, they are also safe from predatory birds.

Life on the ground, however, involves new dangers, particularly from ground-dwelling predators, and for the early primates

---

[4] Other modes of preservation and fossilization are peat bogs, amber, and tar; but early hominids have not been found under these conditions.

who abandoned arboreal life, natural selection favored adaptations that permitted survival in the face of such dangers. The
baboons, who spend most of their waking time on the ground,
developed long, pointed canine teeth for defense, and, of course,
a longer snout to accommodate these teeth. In addition, they
developed strong jaws, powerful shoulders, sturdy torsos, and
aggressive temperaments.

More important to survival, however, was the baboon's social
evolution. Because they faced fierce, ground-dwelling predators,
the earliest baboons learned to cooperate in order to defend
themselves and came to live always in closely knit bands. Thus
they evolved a cohesive social organization in which almost every
aspect of their daily lives is conditioned by their membership
in the group.

Most scientists believe that group solidarity, for the common
defense and for the added protection of infants and pregnant
females, is the result of the primate descent from the trees, not
only for the baboons, other monkeys, and apes, but for humans
as well. Many authorities believe that, from this early social
organization are derived other primate social phenomena, such
as babysitting, struggle for leadership and dominance, and inheritance of status.

METHODS OF PRIMATE INVESTIGATION

The importance of social life to human beings is extrapolated
from primate studies, and there are three primary means by
which these studies may be pursued: the animals involved may
be studied (1) within their natural habitat, (2) in artificially
established colonies such as those seen in zoos, national parks,
and animal refuges, or (3) in the laboratory. Each approach
has inherent advantages and disadvantages, but each contributes
to the accumulation of knowledge regarding man's relatives and,
by inference, concerning early man's life patterns.

Field observation has the advantage of preserving as fully as
possible normal patterns of primate behavior. It may be argued,
of course, that the mere presence of a human investigator is
a disruptive influence, inducing abnormal behavior. A trained
observer, however, takes great pains to minimize the effects of

his presence, and in most cases, the investigator plots into his field schedule a lengthy period at the outset during which he attempts to establish a neutral relationship with the group under study. He seeks from the animals neither approval (through hope of reward) nor disapproval (through fear of punishment). Most observers find that, following this period, the primate group will revert to normal behavior, tolerating or ignoring the human investigator. At this time, the normal behavior of the animals may be observed and recorded. Later, the investigator may wish to experiment, injecting deliberately some disruptive factor in order to judge reactions to new or unfamiliar situations.

Field studies, however, are expensive and demanding, and the natural habitat of a given primate group may be inaccessible to all but the hardiest of investigators. Further, in order to obtain the most reliable results, field studies must be of long duration, taking into account seasonal patterns of behavior. This is necessary regardless of whether climatic, geographical, or financial limitations threaten to preclude prolonged investigation.

Early attempts to glean information from the observation of artificially established primate colonies invariably failed, largely because investigators knew too little about the animals they observed. In 1925, a baboon colony was established at the Regent's Park Zoo in London, beginning with a group of one hundred individuals, most of whom were male. Within two years, only fifty-six animals had survived; the rest had died in sexual battles. Hoping to match the sexes better and thus to reduce combat, the zoo officials added thirty females and five immature males. Within two months, fifteen females were dead. By 1930, only thirty-nine males and nine females were left, the females being "owned" by the eight dominant males of the group. Out of fifteen baboons born during the duration of the colony, only one survived. The others were accidentally squeezed or crushed to death during sexual battles.

Modern colony studies are more successful, and notable among these are the ongoing investigations with semi-wild Japanese monkeys. Japanese scientists observe these subjects in their natural habitat, taking care that experimental methods are subtle and carefully introduced, and that the monkeys do not develop strong attachments to or dependence upon the investigators.

Laboratory studies, for those animals that are suitable, have the distinct advantage of permitting mental and psychological testing. While such investigation tends to shed little light on group behavior in the wild, it yields excellent data regarding intelligence, memory, and social behavior. Scientists have devised numerous tests to gauge in nonhuman primates the influence of past experience, the concept of future, means of intercommunication, and tool use and manufacture. These represent only a few of the many expanding fields open to inquiry in the primate laboratory.

For an example of a typical laboratory test, we can refer to the classic "Chimp-O-Mat" experiment conducted in the 1920's by W. Kohler in order to gauge past experience and concept of future. Kohler used a vending machine filled with raisins; the chimpanzee under observation was forced to work for tokens, which he could use later in "buying" raisins from the machine. The chimp complied with relative ease. When the machine was purposely put out of order, the chimp continued to work for tokens, saving them in apparent anticipation of a buying spree once the machine resumed its normal operation. Kohler concluded, however, that neither memory nor concept of future was a factor in the chimp's behavior. Instead, he thought, the chimp's reactions were the result of conditioned response. His conclusions were based on the fact that the chimp was interested not in a future goal, but in an immediate desire for food.

Kohler's methods and conclusions have been challenged by modern investigators, and the fact that his views have been attacked illustrates another limitation on laboratory studies of nonhuman primates—the human factor. Whatever testing is done can be only as reliable as the human analysis of test results.

Today's laboratory studies on primate intelligence, personality traits, and social behavior are designed to eliminate as fully as possible the factor of human error; and the scope of such tests is increasingly wide. Scientists at primate centers around the world focus on such problems as learning processes; thought and memory; use and manufacture of tools and implements; personality development and disturbance; maternal instinct; addiction to drugs or alcohol; and the possible origins of human art. Certainly comparisons with human beings must not be carried too far, for humans differ from their primate relatives in distinct and important ways. Nevertheless, the behavior of baboons, chimps, orangs, and gorillas offers clues to the origins of certain human behavioral patterns.

Such clues may be used in reconstructing the history of human development, but this has only recently been recognized. Investigations were carried out on animals under controlled laboratory conditions or in artificially established colonies without reference to their behavior in the wild and numerous studies were conducted with animals only remotely related to man. Over the past two decades, however, there has been increasing emphasis on correlating laboratory and field studies, and there has been a corresponding increase in the number of careful investigations of primates in their natural habitats. Two journals and an international society have been founded to provide a forum for the free exchange of ideas and investigative conclusions among scholars interested in primatology.

MODERN FIELD STUDIES

Early field investigations established the fact that primates tend to live in socially organized groups and perpetuated the notion that a "typical" primate group consisted of a single dominant male, several sexually mature females, their infant offspring, and a brace of subordinate males. According to most early primatologists, behavioral patterns within each group were dictated by dominance and sexuality. The dominant male exerted absolute control over other group members, enjoyed exclusive sexual rights with the females, and retained his dominance through incessant combat with subordinate males who challenged his leadership.

Recent field studies show, however, that primate behavior cannot be characterized so simply. Each species occupies its own territory, facing the needs and dangers inherent in that environment. Hence social organization varies greatly from group to group. Baboon troops, for example, are relatively large, consisting of from forty to one hundred individuals led by not one but several dominant males. Baboons have developed the most intense social organization of all the nonhuman primates, and survival of the troop itself depends upon the preservation of this closely knit society. Dominant males are fiercely protective, particularly of the females and the young, but they do not form the front line of defense against potential predators. Whether a baboon troop is on the move or at rest, expendable subordinate males take up positions at the front and rear of the group, while dominant males remain at the center of the troop near the females and infants. It is only when danger threatens that the dominant males move forward, leading subordinates into action while the females and infants retreat to safety. A rigid social hierarchy within the troop assures order and discipline and provides for the protection of the weakest members.

For gibbons, however, the basic social unit is the nuclear family: an adult male, a sexually mature female, and their offspring. Sexual dominance, aggressiveness, and physical combat are almost unknown.

Free-ranging gorillas live in bands of from two to thirty individuals, and size determines which are the dominant males. The leaders are large, silver-backed males; lesser males dominate in a linear hierarchy. Social organization is not as rigid as in baboon society: since the few carnivores that inhabit the region occupied by the gorillas seldom attack, there is therefore no need for the elaborate defensive posture and displays of aggression so common among baboons in the wild.

In short, recent field studies have shown that it is risky to generalize about primate behavior. For example, sexuality, so long considered the primary factor in primate social organization, is periodic; hence it serves as only one of several factors that shape the behavioral patterns of each group. Dominance varies between species, and leadership patterns are much more complex than previously suspected.

More has been learned about primate behavior and social organization over the past ten years than ever before, and exciting advances will no doubt be made in the future, for primatology is a relatively new field in which dramatic developments may yet be expected.

Until recently, for example, the gorilla was little known and much misunderstood. In 1959, however, John Emlen and George Schaller of the University of Wisconsin set out to map the distribution of the mountain gorilla. Schaller stayed on to observe the daily life of this largest of primates, and he found that wild gorillas are mild-mannered vegetarians whose ferocious reputations are unwarranted. In the face of danger, gorillas prefer to bluff, standing erect and posturing wildly or beating their chests and charging for short distances. When forced into physical combat, their usual battle strategy is to bite and retreat. When they are not threatened, however, the wild gorillas live a quiet, placid existence, feeding and playing among themselves.

The gorilla's great body bulk demands excessive quantities of food, and adults spend from six to eight hours a day in feeding, beginning immediately after awakening. The gorilla simply stations himself in the midst of lush vegetation and eats everything within arm's reach. After two or three hours of steady feeding, the gorilla builds a crude ground nest and rests. Feeding is resumed after noon and continues (with frequent interruptions for play and grooming among females and infants) until late afternoon when the group retires to nests on the ground or in trees. The tree-nests are seldom higher than ten feet from the ground, for while young gorillas are agile and adventurous climbers, adults climb with extreme caution. They are simply too large for the trees: adults spend more than eighty percent of their time on the ground.

Schaller noted a wide range of temperament among members of the gorilla groups, but they all tended to be shy and reserved, and few appeared to be inherently aggressive. Although dominant males have complete control over the actions of other group members, leaders tend to be benign and approachable.

Schaller occasionally spotted lone males who might continue to live a solitary existence or may rejoin one group or another, seemingly at will. There is no animosity between gorilla groups, and neighboring troops have repeated, tolerant contacts with one another.

New knowledge about free-ranging chimpanzees has also come from recent field investigations, notably through the efforts of a young British zoologist, Jane van Lawick-Goodall. Mrs. van Lawick-Goodall has established a field station in a remote section of Tanzania in East Africa. She waited patiently for fourteen months before she was able to approach her subjects, and in the years since, she has provided some of the most startling evidence yet to come from primate studies in the field.

Mrs. van Lawick-Goodall was the first to document what some scientists had suspected for a long while: that wild primates can and do fashion crude implements from materials at hand. Until recently, anthropologists had defined man as the "tool-making primate." The definition is no longer valid. Quietly watching her chimpanzee subjects, Mrs. van Lawick-Goodall noticed that a wild chimp would occasionally be attracted to a teeming termite hill. He would search about for a twig or a bit of straw, break it to the proper length, lick it once or twice, and plunge it deep into the termite hill. After waiting a moment—giving the insects time to bite into the straw—the chimp would withdraw his simple probe and nibble off the clinging termites.

This is tool manufacture, however crude or primitive, for it demonstrates the chimp's ability to see a problem, decide upon a solution, and carry out a procedure that requires the manufacture of a fashioned implement. Laboratory tests have confirmed that both chimps and gorillas can assemble crude tools with or without human direction.

Van Lawick-Goodall was also first to film chimpanzees killing and eating a monkey. This is rare among the primates and remarkable for chimpanzees, who were previously assumed to be vegetarians. Clearly, the chimpanzee must now be classed as omnivorous, for monkeys and bush-pigs provide occasional feasts for free-ranging chimps in East Africa.

Unlike the baboons, who exhibit a linear social organization, the basic social unit for the wild chimpanzee consists of a temporary association of individuals of varying duration. The only stable group observed is that of the mother and infant, who are joined periodically by other males and females of differing ages. Mature chimps, both male and female, are seen alone.

Presumably because of their fluid social grouping, patterns of dominance are not distinct among chimps. Aggressive-submissive relationships are rare, and there is no clear leader, for any chimpanzee who initiates group movement or regulates its route or speed assumes, for the duration only, leadership status. Rank carries no particular privilege and there is no male dominance in mating. Males and females have equal sexual access to each other, although in individual interaction, mature males dominate over females and juveniles, while mature females dominate over infants. On the whole, there remains a conspicuous lack of stable dominance.

Such facts tell us that while most primates are born into a social world, not all primate species demonstrate similar patterns of behavior. Obviously, each species has evolved behavioral patterns and social organizations appropriate to its needs, and all primates, including human beings, must be studied with constant reference to their social context. This is not to say, however, that studies in primatology cannot yield insights into the evolution of human culture. Through field observations, scientists hope to distinguish between behavior that is learned and that which is shaped by genetic heritage; and in the laboratory, they hope to isolate intelligence factors responsible for the development of human capacity for culture.

FURTHER READINGS

DeVore, Irven (ed.). *Primate Behavior.* New York: Holt, Rinehart & Winston, 1965.

Eimerl, Sarel, Irven DeVore, and the editors of *Life Magazine. The Primates.* New York: Time, Inc., 1965.

Hahn, Emily. *On the Side of the Apes.* New York: Thomas Y. Crowell, 1971.

Jay, Phyllis C. (ed.). *Primates: Studies in Adaptation and Variability.* New York: Holt, Rinehart & Winston, 1968.

Morris, Desmond. *The Naked Ape.* New York: McGraw-Hill, 1968.

Morris, Desmond (ed.). *Primate Ethology.* Chicago: Aldine, 1967.

Napier, J. R. and P. H. Napier. *A Handbook of Living Primates.* New York: Academic Press, 1967.

Schaller, George B. *The Year of the Gorilla.* Chicago: University of Chicago Press, 1964.

Southwick, Charles H. (ed.). *Primate Social Behavior.* Princeton: D. Van Nostrand Co., Inc., 1963.

Van Lawick-Goodall, Jane. *In the Shadow of Man.* Boston: Houghton-Mifflin, 1971.

Van Lawick-Goodall, Jane. *My Friends The Wild Chimpanzees.* Washington, D.C.: National Geographic Society, 1967.

CHAPTER VI

THE FOSSIL PRIMATES

Our interest in the early fossil history of the primates as a group is guided initially by our curiosity about human origins. It is no longer a question of whether man has evolved from some prehuman primate, but rather a question of *when* and *from which* ancestral primate form he evolved. Clues must be taken from the meager and fragmentary prehistoric evidence that has been preserved. The rarity of fossil primates has always frustrated attempts to pinpoint the evolutionary appearance of human and related forms, although the years since 1950 have been relatively productive, not only of new discoveries but of reasoned interpretive reports. And although anthropologists bemoan the scarcity of sound fossil evidence, they have been able to reconstruct a fairly good picture of the many types of primates that flourished long before the first human beings appeared on earth.

According to the fossil record, primates first appeared about seventy million years ago; the date is approximate, again, because of the inadequacy of the fossil evidence available. A few bone fragments and teeth are all that paleontologists have to establish the earliest boundary between certain mammalian forms and the earliest primates. However, it is known that toward the end of the Mesozoic—and especially during the early epochs of the Cenozoic—the climate was warm and moist, and extensive forests covered large areas of both the Old and New Worlds. This was a rich habitat for the development of small tree-dwelling primates.

The following discussion of the more significant fossil primates is divided, for convenience, into the chronological sequence of Tertiary periods.

FIGURE 1. Generalized family tree of the order of Primates with modern prosimians originating among the lower branches and anthropoids among the upper branches. Time at the bottom center is the Cretaceous Epoch, ending about 70 million years ago, and progresses gradually upward and outward. Extinct lineages are represented loosely by closed branches.

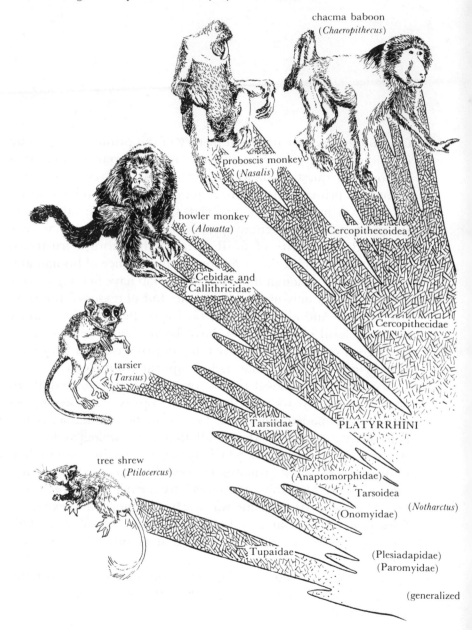

chacma baboon
(*Chaeropithecus*)

proboscis monkey
(*Nasalis*)

howler monkey
(*Alouatta*)

Cercopithecoidea

Cebidae and
Callithricidae

Cercopithecidae

tarsier
(*Tarsius*)

Tarsiidae

PLATYRRHINI

tree shrew
(*Ptilocercus*)

(Anaptomorphidae)

Tarsoidea

(Onomyidae)

(*Notharctus*)

Tupaidae

(Plesiadapidae)
(Paromyidae)

(generalized

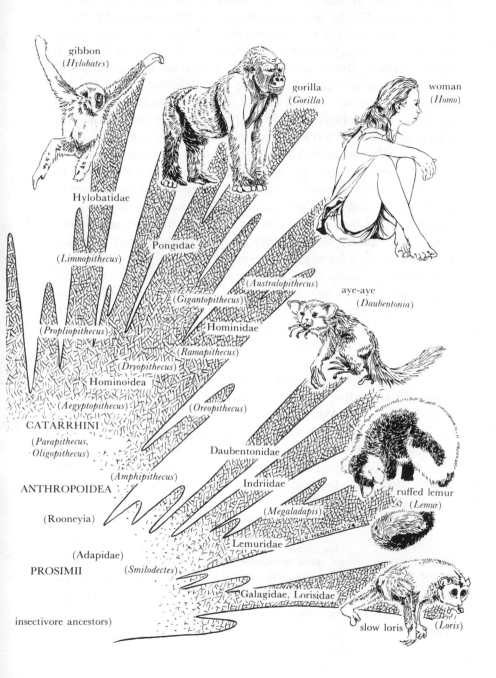

gibbon
(*Hylobates*)

gorilla
(*Gorilla*)

woman
(*Homo*)

Hylobatidae

Pongidae

(*Limnopithecus*)

(*Australopithecus*)

(*Gigantopithecus*)

aye-aye
(*Daubentonia*)

(*Propliopithecus*)

Hominidae

(*Ramapithecus*)

(*Dryopithecus*)

Hominoidea

(*Aegyptopithecus*)

(*Oreopithecus*)

CATARRHINI

(*Parapithecus,
Oligopithecus*)

Daubentonidae

ANTHROPOIDEA

Indriidae

ruffed lemur
(*Lemur*)

(*Amphipithecus*)

(Rooneyia)

(*Megaladapis*)

(Adapidae)

PROSIMII

(*Smilodectes*)

Lemuridae

Galagidae, Lorisidae

insectivore ancestors)

slow loris

(*Loris*)

PALEOCENE

The earliest primates known have been classified, as we
have discussed in the preceding chapter, in the suborder Prosimii,
which includes such forms as the tarsier and lemur. It is impossible, however, to examine the earliest fossil evidence for such
forms without contemplating their ancestral relationships to
other mammalian groups. During the Paleocene and Eocene
periods in Europe and in North America there existed two
families of extremely primitive primates—Plesiadapidae and
Paromomyidae—which exhibited characteristics similar to those
of the tree-shrews, which were classified at one time (and continue to be so classed by some zoologists) as insectivores. On
the other hand, these early forms also possessed traits reminiscent
of the lemur and other prosimians. Thus the early homologous
relationship of these ancient forms suggests that the insectivores
would best qualify as ancestors to the primates, and they are
regarded as such by many experts.

In the early part of the Tertiary epoch, tarsoids were widely
distributed over the world. Including both Paleocene and Eocene
fossils, some twenty-five different genera of tarsoids have been
established. They came from North America, Europe, and China,
and have been grouped into two families, Anaptomorphida and
Omomyidae.

Paleocene lemurs are represented by the widespread family,
Adapidae, including two subfamilies, the Adapinae from the Old
World and the New World Notharctinae. These Paleocene prosimians varied in size from that of a squirrel to that of a well-fed
house cat. They were quadrupeds with claws, and they looked
very much like rodents, typically having small braincases, long
snouts, and large, forward-slanting incisor teeth.

EOCENE

Primate beginnings were sporadic in the Paleocene, but with
the dawn of Eocene times came a tremendous increase in the
development of primate forms. Large and diverse numbers of
them have been identified from North America, Europe, and
Asia.

Lemurs were represented by *Notharctus* and *Smilodectes* in North America as well as by some late Eocene forms in France and Switzerland. It is believed that the family Notharctinae may have provided the ancestral stock from which the New World monkeys have derived.

Tarsier-like forms continued to develop rapidly during Eocene times. In fact, the Eocene genus *Pseudoloris* had already exhibited the characteristic specializations of the modern tarsier in skull and hind limb. It is unfortunate that nothing is known of the paleontological history of the Tarsoidea after the close of the Eocene: no more than two fragmentary exceptions, from lower Oligocene deposits of North America and China, are known.

Unlike that of the tarsiers, the fossil record for the lemurs continues throughout the Tertiary and is distinguished by the remarkable appearance of a giant form during Pleistocene times in Madagascar. *Megaladapis* was probably one of the largest prosimians ever to exist; it is said to have exceeded the modern gorilla in bulk.

Eocene primates were the first to demonstrate the specific arboreal adaptations so typical of later primates: They had larger brains than their Paleocene ancestors; their snouts were shorter, and their eyes were directed forward rather than sideways; claws disappeared and were replaced with nails; and the hands and feet became grasping organs with the thumb and great toe set apart from the other digits. All these and other anatomical changes made it easier for these early primates to climb by grasping. But there was, in addition, a major locomotor adaptation: the Eocene primates were not quadrupeds but vertical clingers and leapers, and, on the rare occasions when they ventured to ground level, they became bipedal, progressing by hopping and walking with their trunks held semi-erect.

Obviously, the Eocene was a period of great evolutionary activity among the prosimians, and the progressive nature of this activity was well demonstrated by some of the late Eocene forms. *Amphipithecus,* from the late Eocene of Burma, provides a good example. This form, represented by a small jaw fragment, has been classified at various times as an independently evolved lemur, a possible cercopithecoid, and, by some, as a very small, primitive pongid. Wherever he belongs, *Amphipithecus* and fossils like him demonstrate the great diversification and radiation of the primate forms some forty to fifty million years ago.

OLIGOCENE

Oligocene deposits have yielded a fascinating sample of fossil primates. The prosimians, which reached a developmental peak during the Eocene, are represented in fewer numbers, whereas the cercopithecoids and pongids now make their debut.

The earliest evidence comes from the lower Oligocene beds of western Texas. A small skull, classified as *Rooneyia viejaensis,* exhibits a curious combination of characteristics, some of which are typically prosimian while others are described as demonstrating anthropoid affinities. It is possible, in other words, that *Rooneyia* may approximate parallel morphological or even linear stages in the ancestry of Old World primates. Unfortunately, *Rooneyia* is, so far, the only known survivor of his kind. Paleontologists, quite naturally, dislike having to deal with single samples; to do so is to proceed without knowledge of variation and to permit the entry into the fossil record of aberrant forms. On the other hand, discoveries must be examined and interpreted, as rationally as possible, when they emerge. Even puzzling single representatives like *Rooneyia* cannot be ignored.

The Fayum Desert in Egypt has produced three significant fossil forms which date from middle- to late-Oligocene. These are *Parapithecus, Propliopithecus,* and *Aegyptopithecus. Parapithecus* is represented by a lower jaw with a full complement of teeth. The tiny creature represented by these remains exhibits a mosaic of traits that recall the prosimians (especially the tarsier) as well as Old World monkeys and primitive apes. It is possible that *Parapithecus,* as well as *Oligopithecus,* a recent find from the same geographic area, may represent a welcome clue to the existence of a transitional stage between the lower and higher primates. More evidence and more sound interpretation are needed.

On the other hand, the *Propliopithecus* jaw has been evaluated by many experts as having belonged to an ancient gibbon-like form. This would indicate that as early as thirty million years ago the differentiation of the Pongidae had begun, producing apes that are clearly recognizable even by current standards.

Aegyptopithecus possessed dentition that is typically pongid but had a skull which exhibits many cercopithecoid features and, in some cases, prosimian ones. *Aegyptopithecus* had a tail as well as the hands and feet of a typical arboreal quadruped, all demonstrating an interesting combination of ape and monkey characteristics. The form is the earliest known representative of the Dryopithecinae, coming from the Fayum Oligocene deposits of the Egyptian desert, and dating from some twenty-eight to thirty million years ago.

The subfamily Dryopithecinae includes the largest known sample of Tertiary apes. The first member of the group, *Dryopithecus fontani,* was recovered from the middle Miocene deposits of France in 1856, and over the years a large number of dryopithecines have been recovered in many areas of the Old World. The earliest of these was found by members of expeditions led by Professor Elwyn Simons of Yale University. Dentition is typically pongid, but the skull with its long snout looks more like that of a monkey than that of an ape. This form is known as *Aegyptopithecus,* discussed above.

It is interesting to note that the pongids make a rather abrupt appearance in the last half of the Oligocene period and that they show wide morphological variation. This aspect of the fossil Pongidae becomes even more dramatic during the last two periods of the Tertiary.

Miocene and Pliocene

These two epochs have been combined because they are continuous relative to the development of the Pongidae. They represent a time of dramatic primate diversification and radiation.

The gibbonoid tendency initiated by the Oligocene fossil *Propliopithecus* continued throughout the last two epochs of the Tertiary. *Limnopithecus* from East Africa, and *Pliopithecus* from Europe, while exhibiting traits suggestive of both monkeys and gibbons, demonstrate the progressive development of the gibbon. In fact, these fossils represent the most complete paleontological record, for any of the modern apes, from recent to most ancient times.

As for the remaining pongids, more than twenty genera of

extinct forms have been classified or at least recognized by
various paleontologists. However, recent taxonomic revisions by
Simons and Pilbeam have translated this early confusion into
a simplified system which combines the late Tertiary fossil apes
into three distinct genera: *Dryopithecus, Gigantopithecus,* and *Ramapithecus,* the first containing at least three species.

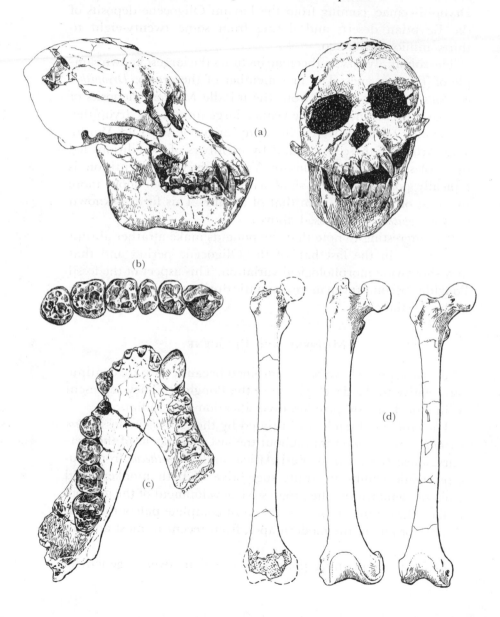

The fossil remains of *Dryopithecus* have been collected from both Miocene and Pliocene deposits since the middle of the nineteenth century. Their bony inventory, however, includes mostly durable teeth and jaw fragments, making the total reconstruction of individuals speculative at best. The dryopithecines appear to have had a wide geographic distribution in Europe

FIGURE 2. *Dryopithecus (= Proconsul)*. (a) Skull of *Dryopithecus africanus* from the Lower Miocene of Africa. (b) Upper right cheekteeth of *D. africanus*. Note the large canine and irregular premolars. (c) Lower jaw of *D. major*, possible ancestor to the modern gorilla. Compare this with the chimpanzee jaw in Figure 3, Chapter VII. (d) Right femur of *D. Africanus* (left), modern chimpanzee (center), and fossil *Homo sapiens* (right), reduced to equal lengths. (e) Reconstruction of *D. africanus* standing upright.

(e)

(*Dryopithecus*), Asia (*Sivapithecus*), and Africa (*Dryopithecus, Xeno-pithecus,* and *Proconsul*). Also, their body size seems to have been highly variable, ranging from that of a modern gibbon to that of a modern gorilla.

It is difficult to characterize this large, diverse group of fossil apes, but they did have certain distinctive traits that separate them from the other late Tertiary primate genera. Probably the most important of these traits has to do with the arrangement of cusps on the molar teeth, known as the *Dryopithecus* pattern, or Y-5 pattern, which consists of five cusps rather than the usual four so that the fissures between the cusps resemble the letter Y. This pattern exists in modified form among modern pongids and in humans, thus establishing the ancestral relationship between modern primates and the early Dryopithecinae.

The only available evidence for the skull and postcranial skeleton of *Dryopithecus* comes from East Africa. This material was excavated through the efforts of the late L. S. B. Leakey from Rusinga Island in Lake Victoria as well as from the nearby shores of the lake, and it was originally assigned to the genus *Proconsul*. The discovery of this important material has yielded a more comprehensive picture of the complete animal, and the results are most interesting. *Dryopithecus* was an ape-like form that exhibited a number of advanced cercopithecoid characteristics together with features that suggest hominoid status, particularly in the face, jaws, and dentition. Thus in *Dryopithecus* we have an ape whose traits demonstrate ancestral relationships to the earlier cercopithecoids and also anticipate the later hominoids. The postcranial skeleton also exhibits a number of significant features. Unlike those of modern pongids, these ancient apes had forelimbs that were shorter than their hindlimbs, and the bones of the extremities are extremely difficult to differentiate from those of modern monkeys. It is clear that morphological changes during the evolution of the higher primates proceeded at different rates in functionally distinct parts of the anatomy.

Gigantopithecus differs little from *Dryopithecus* except in the size of its jaws and teeth. Skeletal remains of this animal, representing a form somewhat larger than a modern gorilla, have been found in both China and northern India, where *Gigantopithecus* existed

during late Pliocene and early Pleistocene times. Once again,
however, authorities are frustrated by the incompleteness of the
skeletal sample that represents this form; the only remains of
Gigantopithecus that are available so far are some jaws and an
assortment of teeth. *Gigantopithecus* is obviously one of the largest
primates in the fossil record and seems to have met extinction
sometime during the middle Pleistocene.

Perhaps the most intriguing of the late Tertiary primates is
represented by the fragmentary remains that have been classified
as *Ramapithecus*. This genus has a wide geographic range, having

FIGURE 3. *Ramapithecus*. (a) Fragments of upper and lower jaws with reconstruction of surrounding bone structure and teeth. (b) Upper right cheekteeth
of *R. punjabicus*. Here the premolars are almost the same size. (c) Reconstruction of the palate of *R. punjabicus* based on fragments and teeth. Compare
this with Figure 2, Chapter VII. Note the similarities to the skull of modern
Homo sapiens. (d) Mandible of *Ramapithecus* from India with three molars and
a second premolar. Note the broad flattened crowns and increasingly thick
enamel toward the rear, both characteristics of human teeth. (Adapted in
part from F. Clark Howell and the editors of Time-Life Books, *Early Man*,
New York: Time-Life, 1965, and David Pilbeam, *The Ascent of Man*, New
York: Macmillan, 1972.)

(a)

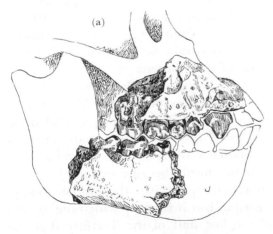

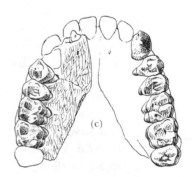

(c)

(d)

(b)

been found in India (*Ramapithecus, Bramapithecus*), East Africa (*Kenyapithecus*), and possibly in China. A reconstruction of the upper jaw is remarkably hominid in appearance, indicating a foreshortened face with small incisors and short canine teeth. It lacks a maxillary diastema, and the curve of the dental arcade is human in form. Many authorities believe that *Ramapithecus*, with its many hominid features, represents a transitional form between ape and man. Intense interest has accordingly been focused on this form, and new discoveries are eagerly awaited.

MAXILLARY DI AS′ TE MA the gap between canine and lateral incisor in the maxilla (upper jaw) which permits the projection of the canine teeth in the mandible (lower jaw) that is typical for all primates except man.

Oreopithecus, a fossil group from Italy, must also be included in the Miocene and early Pliocene time zone. The remains of this form come from a coal mine in the Tuscany Hills of central Italy. Since their discovery almost a century ago, abundant samples have been collected and the accumulated evidence has been studied by Johannes Hurzeler, a Swiss paleontologist. *Oreopithecus* is described as having been a large ape, about the size of a modern adult chimpanzee. *Oreopithecus* had a short, relatively flat face, in contrast to the long snout-like face of *Dryopithecus*. Studies of its pelvis and extremity bones indicate the possibility that *Oreopithecus* walked erect. It would seem, in fact, that this form had most of the characteristics that would qualify him as a direct ancestor to the hominid family; but recent studies of the dentition strike *Oreopithecus* from the list of possible ancestors to modern humans, and it is now believed that this genus became extinct by the end of the Pliocene.

In the history of the Tertiary primates, authorities expect great variability and differentiation. It was during the Miocene and Pliocene that the primates reached their developmental peak, with diverse types and sizes of apes inhabiting many areas of the Old World. Then, following the Pliocene, their numbers began to decrease, and many forms became extinct. Today a mere scattering of representatives survive: the gibbon, orang-utan, chimpanzee, and gorilla. But it is to the wide-ranging and variable populations of the last half of the Tertiary that the present day pongids owe their existence.

Although the preceding pages have concentrated upon the primate fossil record as observed in the Old World, it should be noted that primate evolution in the Tertiary was continuing in the New World as well. Here, however, it culminated in the production and further development of the *Ceboidea,* or New World monkeys. Fossil pongids have never been found in the Americas, and authorities eliminate the New World from consideration in their search for fossil evidence for human evolution.

FURTHER READINGS

Altmann, Stuart and Jeanne Altmann. *Baboon Ecology.* Chicago: University of Chicago Press, 1970.

DeVore, Irven, (ed.). *Primate Behavior.* New York: Holt, Rinehart & Winston, 1965.

Leakey, M. D. (ed.) *Olduvai Gorge.* Vol. 3. Cambridge: Cambridge University Press, 1971.

Pilbeam, David. *The Ascent of Man.* New York: Macmillan, 1972.

Simons, Elwyn L. *Primate Evolution.* New York: Macmillan, 1972.

Tuttle, Russell, (ed.). *The Functional and Evolutionary Biology of Primates.* Chicago: Aldine-Atherton, 1972.

CHAPTER VII

THE FOSSIL HOMINIDS

However scant and fragmentary they may be, fossil bones provide us with direct evidence for the course of hominid evolution. Thus, the story of human evolutionary history rests initially on the paleontological evidence that has accumulated in laboratories, museums, and storerooms over the past two hundred years.

The collection of these specimens has been, for the most part, accidental and haphazard, so that in many cases the evidence is poorly documented. Nevertheless, those who seek to discover the most distant human origins have managed to construct, with bits of teeth and fossil bone, a number of hypotheses regarding human evolutionary history. It is appropriate that each new generation of scholars sift through the preceding mass of information, adding to it their new evidence and devising their own interpretations for future consideration.

Students of human evolution often complain that hominid taxonomy is disorderly and confusing, and much of the current taxonomic confusion stems from the over-zealous attempts of earlier prehistorians to classify each and every piece of fossil evidence and to place it within some phylogenetic context. Since authorities have seldom reached unanimous agreement, many specimens have been encumbered through the years with multiple taxons. Early attempts to classify fossil remains were handicapped, of course, by the lack of adequate material for comparison. Today, however, responsible authorities tend to withhold the assignment of official nomenclature until a fossil can be examined thoroughly and compared rigorously with known fossil evidence. Thus, recent fossil discoveries may be referred to by geographical location or by the name of their discoverers; and, until adequate supporting evidence has accumulated, this is a sound procedure.

There have evolved special rules to govern the naming of paleontological evidence. These rules, established by the International Code of Zoological Nomenclature, exist to assure coherent terminology, to avoid duplication, and to give functional names to newly discovered fossil specimens. Ideally, a scientific name should serve as a statement of relationship, but because new evidence may emerge to necessitate the revision of earlier interpretations, scientific names are always subject to change, regardless of the care with which they have been selected. New discoveries constantly test the framework of earlier interpretations, and for this reason any taxonomic system devised to explain evolutionary hominid development must remain both tentative and flexible. Modern authorities, all too aware of the paucity of their fossil evidence, recognize the many gaps that exist in their knowledge of man's distant past.

IDENTIFYING FOSSIL HOMINIDS

When a fossil is found and identified (and when interpretations are considered sufficiently sound to warrant tentative taxonomic classification), the life form which it represents is generally assigned two names, one generic and one specific (e.g., *Homo erectus,* a fossil population assigned to the genus *Homo* and to the species *erectus*). In very close phylogenetic relationships, a subspecies designation may be added. Anthropologists assume, for example, that all *erectus* populations were sufficiently similar to permit interbreeding, which is the test to determine whether a population can be included within a given species. Yet they also recognize a number of local varieties of *erectus,* each with physical differences sufficiently significant to warrant a subspecies differentiation. Hence authorities refer to *Homo erectus erectus, Homo erectus pekinensis, Homo erectus modjokertensis* (also known as *Homo erectus robustus*), *Homo erectus lantianensis, Homo erectus mauritanicus,* and *Homo erectus leakeyi.* But more of *erectus* later.

The system utilized by most modern authorities is represented, in part, below:

Genus	Species	Subspecies
Homo	*sapiens*	*sapiens*
Homo	*sapiens*	*neanderthalensis*
Homo	*erectus*	*erectus*
Homo	*erectus*	*pekinensis*
Australopithecus	*robustus*	
Australopithecus	*africanus*	

This system represents a new emphasis on simplicity and forms an excellent basis for future expansion. It does not include the numerous "problem cases" pending—those which will either be fitted into one of the above taxons or added as an entirely new taxonomic category—whichever new supporting evidence warrants.

The following pages review the more significant fossil evidence for hominid evolution. We shall see that many of these fossils fit easily within the existing taxonomic framework, while others, at least for the time being, seem to fit nowhere. Human evolutionary history remains subject to rigorous re-evaluation and constant revision. All that can be summarized here are the important known fossil populations, the varied interpretations of these fossils, and some educated speculations regarding the trend of ongoing human evolution.

One problem in seeking remains of the earliest human forms stems from the fact that early primates display curious combinations of anatomical traits—characteristics of both apes and humans together with features that seem typical of neither. And when paleontologists begin to uncover fossils that seem half-man, half-ape, it is time to stop and decide how to separate the men from the apes. Man is, after all, grouped with the apes in taxonomic classification because he shares with them numerous anatomical similarities.

But clearly human beings differ from the apes, too, in many important ways. It is easy enough to spot those differences in living forms, but in tracking down man's earliest fossil relatives, even experts run the risk of unearthing fossils that are difficult to classify. When this occurs, it is necessary to fall back on skeletal traits which distinguish humans from apes—differences which are easily obscured when all we have to work with are a few heaps of dusty bones and a handful of crumbling teeth. Our problems multiply when we realize that there was no magic moment in prehistory when man crossed the line from pongid to hominid status. Nevertheless, we must find some way of distinguishing the curious forms found in ancient deposits.

How is it possible to spot a human being in the fossil record? Experts once argued that the only sure way to distinguish ancient men from ancient apes was to find stone tools buried with them in clear and certain association. Early anthropologists defined man, in fact, as a tool-making primate, a form possessing the intelligence and manipulative ability necessary to manufacture tools and weapons. But we mentioned in the beginning of this book that the search for fossil man centers not only on excavated evidence but also on the observation of living forms, particularly of wild monkeys and apes whose behavior helps us to reconstruct the lives of prehistoric men. Just such observations as these have forced a revision of the traditional definition of man. Prehistorians know now that apes are capable of assembling crude tools with or without human direction. And so anthropologists have been forced to devise a new definition of man as a primate both intellectually and physically capable of *systematic* tool manufacture through *consistent* methods of production. He makes *patterned* tools and implements, and he is capable of teaching succeeding generations his techniques of manufacture. The earliest man-made tools, of course, are of stone, with flakes chipped off one or both sides to form a jagged cutting edge—they are crude tools, but patterned ones nonetheless, and they have not yet been duplicated by a nonhuman primate. Some ancient human populations are known solely from the distinctive patterned tools they left behind.

We can tell a fossil man from a fossil ape readily enough, then, as long as the former was considerate enough to get himself buried with his tool kit. Few prehistoric men were so inclined, and the majority of fossils are found without direct associations with ancient tools. Thus anthropologists and prehistorians must

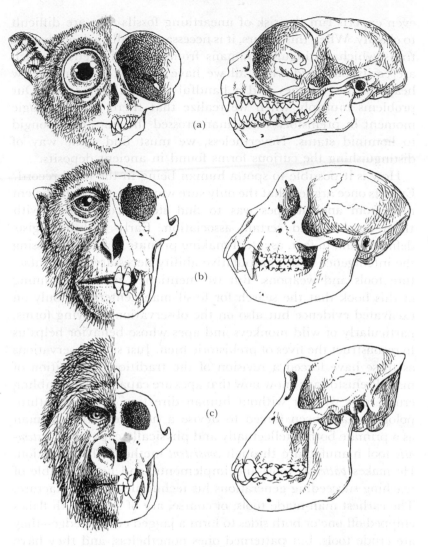

FIGURE 1.　Half-front and side views of skulls of (a) tarsier, a prosimian from the forests on Indonesia. The skull and teeth are relatively primitive, but the eyes are enormously developed for binocular vision at night. (b) Rhesus monkey, female. (c) Lowland gorilla (male in front view, female in profile). The male has prominent canine teeth and a sagittal crest. (d) *Australopithecus boisei*, male. Like the gorilla the skull has prominent brow ridges and a sagittal crest, but the canine teeth are very small and the base of the skull is directed downward rather than backward as in the gorilla. (e) *Homo sapiens* (modern man). The braincase has become enormously inflated and the forehead has become a dominant feature of the facial region.

focus upon anatomical or morphological traits that reliably distinguish man from ape in the fossil record.

Nineteenth-century investigators solved the problem by measuring the cranial capacity of each recovered fossil skull. Cranial capacity, of course, refers to the volume of the inside of the cranium, and it gives a good estimate of brain size. Comparisons of past and present primates could thus be made by utilizing the following average values as a rough rule of thumb:

Average Brain Size in Cubic Centimeters

Modern man	1500
Neanderthal (European)	1600
Australopithecine	500
Gorilla	600
Chimpanzee	400
Orang-utan	400
Gibbon	100

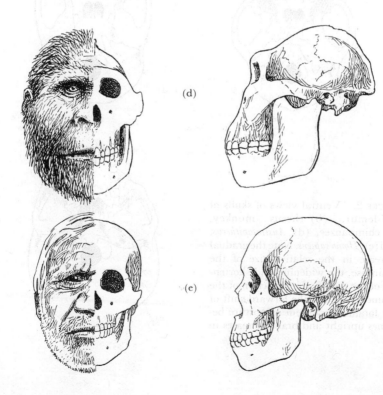

(d)

(e)

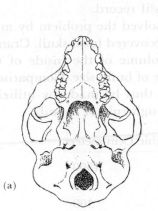

(a)

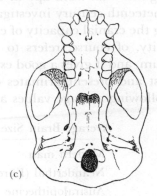

(c)

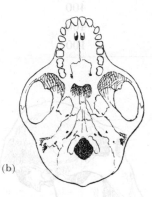

(b)

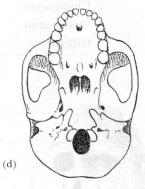

(d)

FIGURE 2.   Ventral views of skulls of
(a) lemur,   (b) rhesus   monkey,
(c) chimpanzee, (d) *Australopithecus*,
and (e) *Homo sapiens.* Note the gradual
increase in the relative size of the
braincase, the widening and shorten-
ing of the palate, the reduction of the
canine teeth, and the forward shift of
the foramen magnum as posture becomes upright and brain increases in
size.

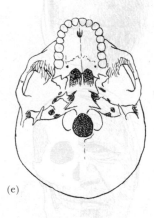

(e)

Early anthropologists simply dubbed their discoveries human if the brain size were reasonably large; if small, they dismissed them as apes.

As it turns out, however, a large brain size relative to total body weight is a trait typical not only of man but also of apes. While it is true that humans have a larger cranial capacity than do the apes, there is no absolute numerical value that separates man from his primate relatives on the basis of brain size alone. The average cranial capacities noted above are statistical means only taken from *modern* rather than ancient specimens. Individuals, whether hominid or pongid, can vary enough to place them at the mean of a higher or lower category. Nineteenth-century investigators had no way of knowing the average brain size for the earliest hominids, and in attempting to measure ancient remains by modern yardsticks, they succeeded only in confusing the issue.

More reliable than absolute brain size in distinguishing humans from apes in fossilized remains are the relative limb proportions. Because man has a habit of walking erect, his legs tend to be longer than his arms: exactly the opposite is true of the apes, who developed long arms for efficiency in the trees.

Skull features other than cranial capacity are important, too. In humans, the forehead is generally high and the brow ridges small; in apes, there is no forehead and the brow ridges are large and bony. Hominid skulls exhibit both chin and nasal bridges, features which are generally absent in ape skulls; and while man's canine teeth are small, pongid canines are large and projecting, with adjacent gaps in the jaw to accommodate these toothy weapons. (See Figures 1, 2, and 3.)

Again, because man walks erect, his *foramen magnum*—the opening in the skull where the spinal column joins the brain—is positioned near the center of the skull base. In the ape, whose head tends to hang forward, the *foramen magnum* is located nearer the back of the skull, though not, of course, so far back as is typical for animals with an even more horizontal, or pronograde, posture. Man's dental arcade is parabolic, while that of the ape is more U-shaped (see Figure 3). All these features help to distinguish human from ape remains. And, in addition, modern anthropologists look for patterns or mosaics of anatomical features;

it is not the presence or absence of a single trait that distinguishes man from ape, but a total configuration of distinctively human morphological characteristics.

The main factor which accounts for these differences, of course, is man's unique way of life. He walks erect, his head balanced on top of his spinal column. He is omnivorous. He makes and uses tools rather than depending upon such evolved body struc-

FIGURE 3.   Lower jaws of (a) chimpanzee, (b) *Australopithecus robustus,* and (c) *Homo sapiens.* Note the simian shelf in the chimpanzee and the reduced canines in the two species of human beings.

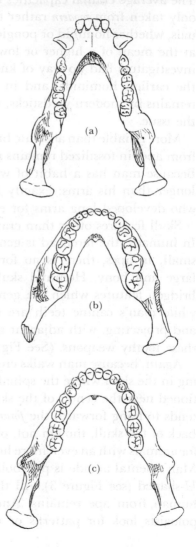

(a)

(b)

(c)

tures as projecting canine teeth or fierce jaws. In hunting, eating, and defending himself, man uses cultural rather than anatomical equipment.

The similarities between man and ape have been known for more than a century and have supported the theory that the two groups shared at some time in the past a mutual primate ancestor. What was not known, however, was the way in which man diverged from his primate stock and developed into his present unique state.

How does an ape-like ancestor evolve, through a long period of time, to emerge in human form? Until the missing fossil links between man and ape could be located, there could be no

FIGURE 4. Shoulder, rib, lumbar and pelvic regions in (a) macaque, (b) gorilla, and (c) *Homo sapiens.* Note the progressive changes in the angle of the shoulder blades and the number of lumbar vertebrae. The lumbar region in the gorilla is stiff and inflexible, conferring great strength but making it very difficult for the gorilla to stand upright. The macaque is a quadruped. (After Irven DeVore and the editors of Time-Life Books, *The Primates,* New York: Time-Life, 1965.)

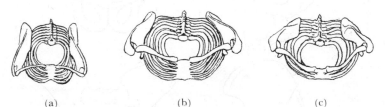

(a) (b) (c)

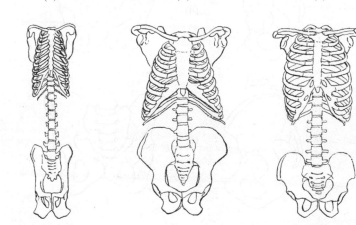

FIGURE 5. Side and front views of the pelvis of (a) lemur, (b) macaque, (c) gorilla, (d) *Australopithecus*, and (e) *Homo sapiens*. Note progressive modifications toward erect posture.

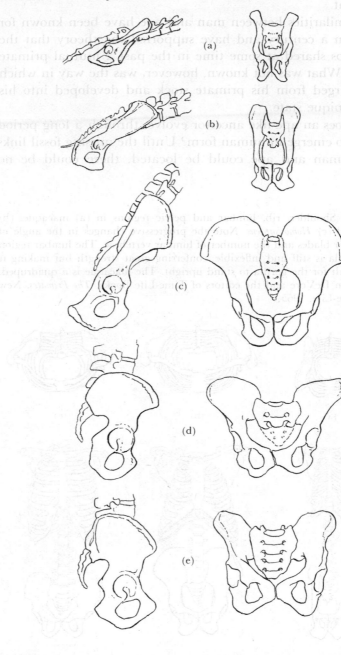

convincing justification for Darwin's theory of organic evolution
—at least not for those who continued to insist upon exempting
man from the laws of evolution. But in 1925, a few elusive links
began to appear. Intriguing new discoveries in South Africa
hinted at the prehistoric existence of fossil populations whose
hominid status remains in dispute today.

FIGURE 6.   Feet and hands of (a) lemur, (b) macaque, (c) gorilla, (d) *Homo
sapiens,* and (e) foot of *Australopithecus.* In man the big toe ceases to function
as a thumb and becomes part of the support apparatus necessary for walking
and running upright. Note that *Australopithecus* had an essentially human foot.
(Adapted in part from Adolph H. Schultz, *The Life of Primates,* New York:
Universe Books, 1969 and W. E. LeGros Clark, 1959.)

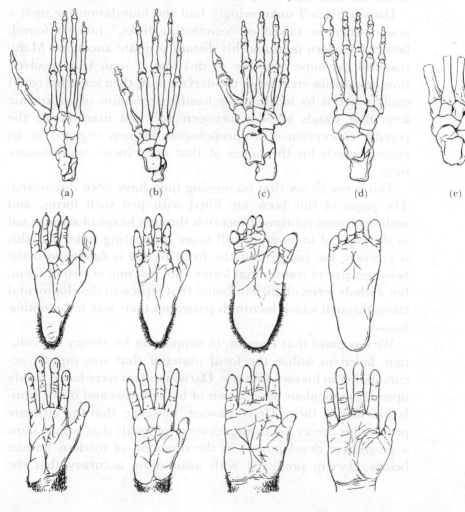

The Australopithecines

Charles Darwin informed a skeptical world that man descended from a primate form that lived many thousands of years ago, and that this remote primate was ancestor not only to all modern human varieties but to all living monkeys and apes as well. Early misinterpretations of Darwin's theory triggered and sustained the erroneous idea that somewhere there existed a single "missing link." Since the initial publication of Darwin's works, a steady stream of exuberant scientists have come forth with their fossil discoveries, each proclaiming his own as the best possible candidate for that title.

Darwin himself unknowingly laid the foundation for such a notion when he talked of "connecting links," not yet found, between modern man and his distant primate ancestors. Many reasoned (as some continue to do) that if man truly evolved from an ape-like creature of the darkest past, then scientists could easily prove it by locating the fossilized remains of an archaic form that stands midway between ape and man—hence the popular conception of anthropologists as men engaged in an endless search for the bones of that one elusive transitionary form.

This is not to say that no missing links have been discovered. The pages of this book are filled with just such forms, and anthropologists continue to scratch through heaps of ancient soil in the hope of uncovering still more connecting links. But this is precisely the point: that the fossil record is *littered* with the bony remains of transitional forms—not just one or two of them, but a whole series of ancient bones that represent developmental stages through which hominids passed on their way to becoming human.

We have said that Darwin, in supporting his theory of evolution, failed to utilize the fossil material that was rapidly accumulating in his own lifetime. Darwin's ideas were based firmly upon his meticulous observation of living forms and of the similarities among them. He was aware, however, that the ultimate proof of his theory lay in the recovery of fossils that would show a progressive development in the direction of modern human beings. Darwin predicted with astonishing accuracy that the skeletal evidence for man's most ancient precursor—the one clearly intermediate between the apes and man—would one day appear somewhere in Africa.

In prehistoric times, most of the world's land masses were subject to violent upheavals. The earth buckled with the formation of vast mountain ranges and trembled with the fiery eruption of active volcanos. Numerous times, catastrophic glacial advances swept across the globe, smashing forests in their frigid advance. South Africa, however, escaped these cataclysms. Serene and undisturbed, this land might hold the fossilized remains of man's most distant representatives. It was here therefore that many scientists were drawn in their search for the link that would complete an evolutionary chain leading to man. A few spent their entire lives engaged in that frustrating task—and many remain there today, their efforts contributing to an ever-growing inventory of revealing skeletal evidence.

It was not until 1924—forty-two years after Darwin's death —that scientists actually picked up the trail there. Workmen quarrying lime from deposits near Taung, South Africa, blasted loose from ancient breccia (cave debris) a small skull that looked strangely—though not quite—human. Puzzled, they mailed it to Raymond A. Dart, Professor of Anatomy at Johannesburg's Witwatersrand University. Dart knew at once that this was the fossil that had been sought for so long: that of a man in the making, a creature not yet fully human but one that provided proof of the evolutionary leap from anthropoid to hominid—from ape to preman.

The Taung skull was marvelously complete for so ancient a fossil. Many parts were available for study. The skeletal face was almost intact, and the lower jaw was present. At least half of the brain cast—an impression in the brain itself upon prehistoric rock—was clearly visible. And there were teeth.

These were deciduous, or "baby" teeth: the Taung skull represents a child about six years old at the time of his death, which occurred in early Pleistocene times. The youth of the fossil spelled trouble for Dart. Taxonomic classification is normally based upon *adult* traits, and immature bones merely hint at adult morphology. Further, identifying either an existing animal or a newly discovered fossil on the basis of a single specimen is at best a risky business. Because all living individuals vary, reliable classification is made through analysis of a *group* of specimens—the more the better.

Nevertheless, Dart was satisfied with the conclusions he was able to draw from the single juvenile skull. "The specimen," he wrote, "is of importance because it exhibits an extinct race of apes intermediate between living anthropoids and man." In describing the "Taung Baby," Dart made special note of numerous anatomical features that seemed to him to demonstrate a closer approach to man than to any of the living or known fossil apes. Since the fossil was decidedly prehuman rather than human, he named it *Australopithecus africanus,* the "South African ape."

Dart rushed enthusiastically into print, publishing his preliminary conclusions barely six weeks after receiving the skull for analysis. The reaction to his report was immediate and devastating. Both British and American scientists complained that Dart was irresponsible in publishing so radical an opinion without first consulting an older, better established scientific authority.

FIGURE 7. Skull and endo-cranial cast of *Australopithecus africanus* from Taung, South Africa. (Courtesy of the American Museum of Natural History)

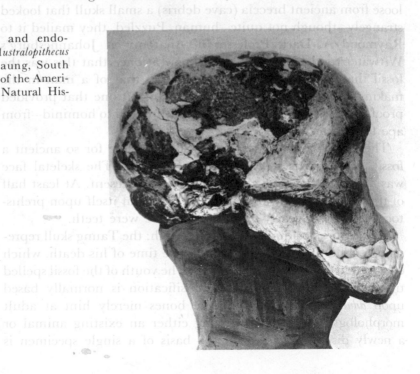

They ridiculed Dart's attempts to classify an immature specimen and labeled as gross exaggerations his statements regarding the human-like qualities of the skull. "Dart's Baby," the disgruntled experts insisted, was no more than a primitive form of chimpanzee. Even Dart's closest colleagues refused to accept his interpretations. Many wrote disparaging letters, while others published disdainful papers criticizing Dart's rash conclusions based on a hasty examination of the specimen. Dart was enveloped in a cloud of protest, contempt, and ridicule.

The man who came to Dart's rescue was a Scottish medical doctor who had distinguished himself as an extraordinarily competent paleontologist. At an age when most men look forward to a comfortable retirement, Robert Broom—then sixty-eight years old—accepted the demanding post as Curator of Vertebrate Paleontology and Physical Anthropology at the Transvaal Museum at Pretoria, South Africa. After his examination of the Taung skull, Broom was convinced that the worldwide criticism of Dart's work was unwarranted. Dart was right, Broom insisted, and the proof that would vindicate him lay in the eventual recovery of additional fossil forms. What was needed to settle the true taxonomic fate of *Australopithecus* was the discovery of mature specimens of the same type. Broom set out to accomplish just that.

His method was deceptively simple. Broom realized that quarry workers often used dynamite to remove limestone locked in the caves and crevices common to this section of South Africa. He notified the mining managers of every quarry in the region—a two-hundred-square-mile block of the Transvaal—and instructed each to keep a vigilant eye out for fragments of fossil bone that might be uncovered through blasting. This done, Broom had only to wait and hope.

Between 1925 and 1950, Dart and Broom reported a number of intriguing fossil forms from the region, most of which were quite literally blasted from caves. As the skeletal inventory grew, with additional sites recognized, most authorities concluded that the collected sample was significant, and that it represented more than a single fossil population. The reconstructed forms from such sites as Taung, Sterkfontein, and Makapansgat appeared to be smaller, more slender, and more graceful than those found

at Kromdraai and Swartkrans. The two populations seemed to
have lived at different times during the early Pleistocene, the
slender, gracile form appearing earlier. Eventually, it was decided
that the differences between these two fossil populations were
sufficiently great to justify the assignment of two specific names:
Australopithecus africanus and *Australopithecus robustus*.

AFRICANUS.   Dart's early description of *africanus*, based solely
upon the infant skull from Taung, mentioned numerous ape-like
features (including the small size, 500 c.c., of the brain), but
also emphasized the fact that there were a number of traits in
both skull and dentition that were definitely hominid in character. Dart suggested initially that this fossil species should be
placed intermediate between the pongids and the hominids,
giving rise to the popular notion of *africanus* as a "missing link."
Later, however, Dart revised his opinion; he and Broom were
convinced, on the basis of further evidence, that *africanus* was
a true hominid. Their conclusions were met with skepticism at
first, but as more material emerged through the efforts of the
tireless Professor Broom, the list of experts accepting hominid
status for *africanus* began to grow.

Today our knowledge of *africanus* has been expanded, due in
part to explorations undertaken in 1967 in the Omo Valley of
Ethiopia. Here Professor F. Clark Howell has reported both
africanus and *robustus* finds. Most authorities have come to recognize *africanus* as a small gracile creature who habitually stood
and walked erect though he probably was not capable of the
unique striding gait typical for modern man. He weighed no
more than 60 to 70 pounds, and his height was barely more
than four feet. Brain size was small, averaging about 500 c.c.,
which is comparable to that of the modern gorilla. Although
resembling in numerous respects an erect-walking ape, *africanus*
exhibited traits that are unmistakably hominid. His braincase
is set rather high above the face, and the frontal lobes of the
brain surmount the eye sockets. Thus the bony contour of the
frontal region is arched and rounded. The brow ridges are only
moderately developed, and the occipital region of the skull is
rounded. Dentition is extremely human-like. Incisor teeth are
small and implanted vertically in upper and lower jaws. Canine

FIGURE 8. *Australopithecus africanus.* (a) Skull of female from Sterkfontein with a reconstruction of a jaw based on a fragment found at Makapanskat. (b) Front view of (a) with reconstructed teeth. (c) Female mandible from Makapanskat. (d) Portion of upper right toothrow of a skull from Sterkfontein. Note the reduction of the canine tooth. (e) Pelvis from Sterkfontein.

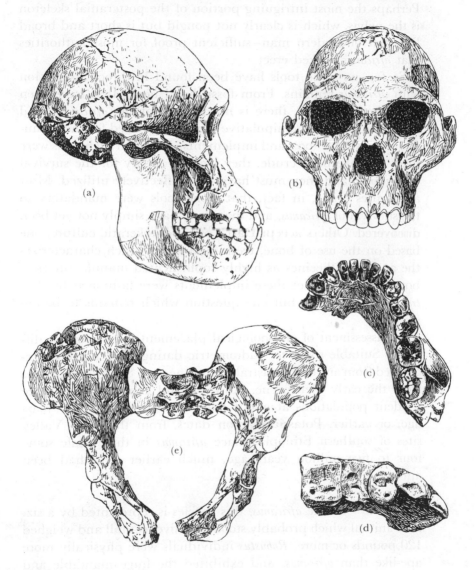

teeth are also small, and spatulate, barely projecting beyond the occlusal (chewing) surfaces of the dental arcade. Although pre-molars and molars are large and relatively broad, this condition is typical for almost all middle- to late-Pleistocene populations. Perhaps the most intriguing portion of the postcranial skeleton is the pelvis, which is clearly not pongid but is short and broad like that of modern man—sufficient proof for most authorities that *africanus* walked erect.

So far, no stone tools have been found in direct association with *africanus* remains. From fossil hand bones that have been unearthed, however, there is no doubt that the *africanus* hand was capable of the manipulative motions required for the manu-facture of simple tools and implements. Although such tools were likely to have been crude, they were necessary for the survival of *africanus,* and they must have been effectively utilized. Most authorities argue, in fact, that stone tools were mandatory to the survival of *africanus,* and that these have simply not yet been discovered. Others accept Dart's osteodontokeratic culture, one based on the use of bone, teeth, and horn, which characterizes the australopithecines as highly sophisticated manufacturers of bone tools—if in fact these implements were fashioned by *Aus-tralopithecus.* This is but one question which remains to be an-swered.

An assessment of chronological placement for *africanus* is dif-ficult. Suitable rocks for radiometric dating have not been re-covered from any of the australopithecine sites. Sterkfontein dates from the early Pleistocene, however, and expert guesses place resident populations at about two and one half million years ago, or earlier. Potassium-argon dates, from the Omo Valley sites of southern Ethiopia, place *africanus* in that locale some four to five million years ago, much earlier than had been anticipated.

ROBUSTUS.   Unlike *africanus,* this species is represented by a siz-able animal which probably stood over five feet tall and weighed 120 pounds or more. *Robustus* individuals were physically more ape-like than *africanus,* and exhibited the huge mandible and robust cranial superstructure so typical of the present day gorilla. They also featured greater facial prognathism, larger brow ridges,

FIGURE 9. *Australopithecus robustus.* (a) and (b) Swartkrans skull. (c) Swartkrans mandible. (d) Top of femur of *A. robustus* (left) and *Homo sapiens* (right). (e) Pelvis (right half) from Swartkrans. (Adapted in part from Pilbeam, 1972.)

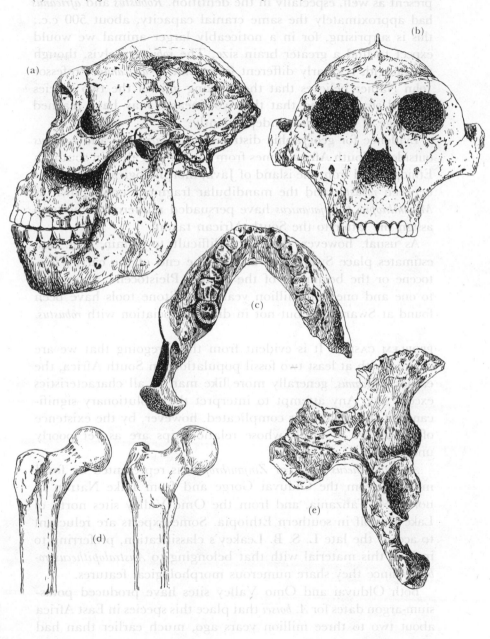

and marked muscle attachment areas that are more rugged, suggesting much greater robustness. But hominid features are present as well, especially in the dentition. *Robustus* and *africanus* had approximately the same cranial capacity, about 500 c.c.; this is surprising, for in a noticeably larger animal we would expect to find a greater brain size. The *robustus* pelvis, though not pongid, is clearly different from that of *africanus.* Professor John Napier believes that the walking gait of the two species differed sharply, and that the two lineages may have reached the stage of bipedalism independently.

Evidence for geographic distribution of *africanus* and *robustus* outside of South Africa comes from the Omo Valley in southern Ethiopia and from the island of Java; morphological similarities between *robustus* and the mandibular fragment now known as *Meganthropus paleojavanicus* have persuaded numerous experts to assign the latter to the South African taxon.

As usual, however, dates are difficult to obtain. The best estimates place Swartkrans around the end of the early Pleistocene or the beginning of the middle Pleistocene, about one to one and one half million years ago. Stone tools have been found at Swartkrans but not in direct association with *robustus.*

PROBLEM CASES. It is evident from the foregoing that we are dealing with at least two fossil populations in South Africa, the earlier, *africanus,* generally more like man in all characteristics except size. Any attempt to interpret the evolutionary significance of the material is complicated, however, by the existence of a number of fossils whose relationships are as yet poorly understood.

Australopithecus boisei, or *Zinjanthropus,* is represented by fossil material from the Olduvai Gorge and from Lake Natron in northwest Tanzania, and from the Omo Valley sites north of Lake Rudolf in southern Ethiopia. Some experts are reluctant to accept the late L. S. B. Leakey's classification, preferring to include this material with that belonging to *Australopithecus robustus* since they share numerous morphological features.

Both Olduvai and Omo Valley sites have produced potassium-argon dates for *A. boisei* that place this species in East Africa about two to three million years ago, much earlier than had been expected from the speculations made for the South African species.

Homo habilis, another stepchild of L. S. B. Leakey, was found in the lowest bed of the Olduvai Gorge site in Tanzania, East Africa. The fragmentary remains represent the skeletal portions of several individuals with a potassium-argon date of almost two million years. The morphology of these fossil remains contrasts markedly with both *A. boisei* and *A. robustus,* but is similar in many respects to *A. africanus,* especially in dental traits. However, a reconstruction of skull fragments indicated a cranial capacity of between 640–650 c.c., well above the average known range for *africanus.* This significant difference seems to be the primary problem in deciding whether to accept *Homo habilis* as a valid

FIGURE 10.   *Australopithecus boisei.* (a) Skull discovered by Dr. Mary Leakey at Olduvai Gorge. (b) Side view, with missing portions of the braincase and the lower jaw restored. (c) Palate of *A. boisei* (above) compared with that of a modern Australian Aboriginee. The massive cheekteeth are adapted to an herbivorous diet of nuts, roots, seeds, and other small hard food items. (d) A lower jaw from the Omo River basin in Ethiopia.

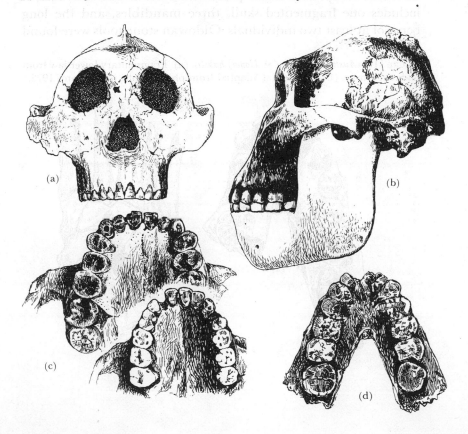

taxon or to reclassify it as a slightly advanced *africanus.* One additional point: stone tools, known as Oldowan, were found with *Homo habilis;* but whether these were made by him or by some more advanced population is another area of contention.

Telanthropus capensis was discovered by Robert Broom at Swartkrans in the same geological zone containing the remains of *A. robustus.* The fossil material includes one mandible, other facial and jaw fragments, and a small piece of radius (forearm bone); it is sufficient material from which to conclude that *T. capensis* shares similar features with both *A. africanus* and *A. robustus* but with greater resemblance to the former. Also, this form has been characterized by some authors as being closely allied to *Homo erectus.* A total re-evaluation of *Telanthropus capensis* is in process, but there seems even now to be a general consensus that *T. capensis* should be assigned to either *A. capensis* or *A. africanus.*

Another intriguing discovery was made by Richard E. Leakey in 1972; the material has not yet been classified nor has it been described completely in the professional literature. However, it includes one fragmented skull, three mandibles, and the long bones of at least two individuals. Oldowan stone tools were found

FIGURE 11.   *Australopithecus (= Homo) habilis.* (a) Fragmentary lower jaw from Olduvai Gorge. (b) Left foot. (Adapted from photographs in Pilbeam, 1972.)

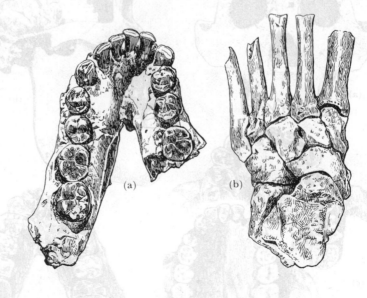

in association with this material. The site is located east of Lake Rudolf in western Kenya, East Africa, and the site date has been given as 2.6 million years ago.

A description of the reconstructed skull comes as something of a surprise: it does not appear to fit with any of the other early Pleistocene fossil populations of South or East Africa; and it differs radically from the skulls of the australopithecines as well as from the middle Pleistocene *Homo erectus* populations. Indeed, the material looks amazingly recent considering its obvious age. Briefly, the skull lacks the heavy, protruding brow ridges of *Homo erectus,* yet it has an estimated cranial capacity of approximately 800 c.c.

Richard Leakey interprets his discovery as representing a large-brained bipedal form of the genus *Homo,* existing contemporaneously with the australopithecines some two and one half million years ago. It has been suggested that the more recent *Homo habilis* may have been part of this lineage, but detailed phylogenetic relationships must await further examination of the material.

Summing up our knowledge of the australopithecines, most authorities believe that we have at least two lineages of fossil hominids, *robustus* and *africanus,* dating from late Pliocene and early Pleistocene times. Some anthropologists, though, believe that Loring Brace's unilinear theory is a better representation. Brace holds that *robustus* and *africanus* are sexually dimorphic forms of the same australopithecine species, *robustus* being the male and *africanus* the female of that species. Whichever view one holds, *robustus* was roughly twice the weight and size of *africanus* (sometimes called *gracilus* or gracile form), which weighed somewhere between fifty and ninety pounds and was about four feet tall. While this is a greater difference than exists between the sexes in any modern human population, it is not unknown among primates. Male orangutans and many baboons are twice the size of the females and, as with *robustus,* have much larger canine incisors. On the other hand, investigators have found *robustus* fossils that are about three-fourths of a million years more recent than the latest *africanus* fossils. In addition, deposits containing numbers of australopithecine fossils have most often been segregated—all *robustus* or all *africanus.* Finally, and without going into detail, the differences in dentition are qualitative as well as quantitative: that is, *robustus* teeth and jaw configuration are both bigger than and structurally different from those of *africanus*.

John Robinson maintains that these differences in dentition are great enough to suggest that *africanus* was primarily an earlier, carnivorous (meat-eating) species while *robustus* was an herbivorous (vegetarian) species, overlapping in time. This view is not wholly accepted by most experts. While many opinions in anthropology have been changed radically by the discovery of new evidence and new methods, current opinion must always be based on the contemporaneously available evidence. One

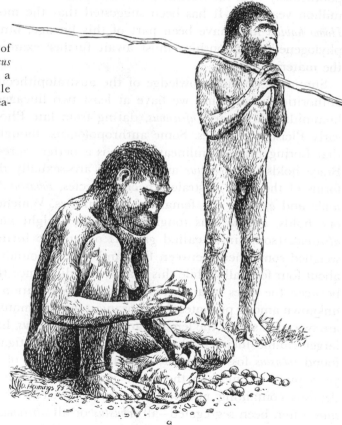

FIGURE 12. Reconstruction of an adult female *Australopithecus africanus* cracking nuts with a stone hammer and a male standing vigilantly with a weapon.

cannot state, then, that either of the opposing views represented
by Brace and Robinson is incorrect, but only that the evidence
now available is not sufficient to convince most physical anthropologists and prehistorians. Even seemingly contradictory evidence can mean that what has been discovered is not typical
of the species it represents. While this is possible in the case
of australopithecines, the fairly high number of sites and individuals uncovered decrease the probability that we are dealing with
atypical cases.

Trying to represent the major view, *africanus* shows greater
evolutionary change than *robustus* and is the best candidate for
ancestor to the *Homo erectus* forms which emerged in the mid-

FIGURE 13. Reconstruction of an adult
male *Australopithecus robustus*.

Pleistocene. *Homo erectus* radiated throughout most of Africa and probably also to Europe and Asia. Approximately coinciding with the appearance of *Homo erectus* was the disappearance of *robustus,* and although some anthropologists believe that *robustus* was hunted and killed by *erectus,* which is possible, such an explanation is just not needed. Simple displacement of one species by a more recent, better adapted species more effectively exploiting limited resources (such as food) is a more common pattern among animals and easily accounts for the disappearance of *robustus.*

A third lineage in the early Pleistocene of East Africa may be represented by Richard Leakey's find in 1972. It has been speculated that this third lineage represents a direct line to *Homo sapiens,* by-passing *Homo erectus* completely; and there are just enough unexplained fossils in the middle Pleistocene of Africa and Europe to make this an exciting hypothesis. Certainly the diversification and radiation of the hominids during early Pleistocene times was much more complicated than authorities had previously supposed.

Homo Erectus

The fossil evidence indicates that, by approximately a half million years ago, true hominids had spread over most of the Old World. Their skeletal remains have been recovered from Java (*Pithecanthropus erectus*), China (*Sinanthropus pekinensis*), and Africa (*Atlanthropus mauritanicus,* Chellean Man-Hominid 9).

About forty years before the appearance of the first *Australopithecus* skull, a young Dutchman, Eugene Dubois, dreamed of finding in Africa primitive fossils that would help to illuminate the widest and most mysterious gaps in human prehistory.

Dubois was born in 1858, his earliest years coinciding with the initial period of fossil discovery in Europe. In those days, the infant science of anthropology was taking its first uncertain steps; furor and controversy greeted the announcement of each new fossil find. Dubois was determined to be a part of this great excitement. He prepared at first for a career in medicine, but his interests shifted increasingly to anatomy and natural history. By the time he was nineteen, Dubois had become obsessed with the idea of finding a truly primitive and ape-like fossil that would validate Darwin's radical new theory of evolution as it applied to man. Later, as a lecturer in anatomy at the University of Amsterdam, he was constantly distracted from his work by visions of the sensational discoveries that awaited him in Africa if only he could get there. It was on the African continent that man's closest animal relatives—the chimpanzees and gorillas—survived in great numbers, and in the African forests that the ancestors of these advanced primates must have arisen. Surely, Dubois reasoned, human beings originated there also, in which case meticulous excavation would result in the dramatic recovery of fossils previously unimagined. It was inconceivable to Dubois that someone else should have the satisfaction of finding them.

But for Dubois, who was young, inexperienced, and had neither reputation nor specialized training, an African expedition was impossible. At first reluctantly, and then with renewed enthusiasm, he turned to the sites he considered next best. The Asiatic islands of Java and Sumatra, like South Africa, had escaped the prehistoric glacial advance, and were also the home of advanced primates. An abundance of extinct animal bones had been found on Java, suggesting that game had been plentiful even during times of bitter cold. There was therefore a chance that early humans had inhabited these islands as well and that their fossilized bones remained. Dubois had only to find them.

He readily tossed aside his teaching career, resigned his post at the University, and wrangled an appointment as Surgeon in the Royal Dutch Army. This position would take him to Sumatra, where he would at last have a crack at locating the bones of the earliest humans.

Once settled, Dubois performed his hospital duties with vigor, dispatching them as quickly as possible so that he might devote every spare moment to his quest. He spent every hour that he was away from the operating room roaming the countryside, digging in fossil-rich streambeds, and scouring the island's many caves.

Frustrating weeks of endless grubbing yielded nothing but a handful of teeth from an extinct variety of orang-utan. Then word came from a neighboring island that human bones—ancient ones—had been found. Dubois bombarded the Army with urgent appeals: it was essential, he insisted, that the Dutch government have an accurate record of the extinct vertebrate fauna native to its island territories—and his training in anatomy and natural history would enable him to submit a superior report. When his request for transfer was granted, Dubois rushed to Wadjak, on the southern coast of Java.

He wasted little time there. He purchased the skull that had been found earlier and almost immediately unearthed another. Both seemed disappointingly recent, but he kept digging. Working near Trinil, a small village on the banks of Java's Solo River, he recovered a fragment of jawbone—prehuman, he thought— with a single molar tooth still in place. The deposits in which he was digging contained abundant fossils. At about 350 feet deep, their stratigraphy dated back to Tertiary times. Dubois was certain that at any moment he would find the bones of a crucial missing link.

To his despair, the rainy season intervened, making further excavation impossible. Dubois paced impatiently, resuming his search on the first clear day. Soon he unearthed an ape-like molar, and then a handful more. A month later he stumbled upon the prize for which he had risked his career: a single heavily fossilized fragmentary skull. Mostly braincase, the skull was unlike any that had been seen before: it was too large and heavy to represent the skull of an ape, and yet it was too small to be that of a human. The forehead was low and receding; huge bony brow ridges projected in a bar across the front, lending a brutish appearance. It seemed to Dubois a perfect transition form, one that bridged the gap between ape and human. Excitedly, he plotted large-scale excavations.

Maddeningly, the rains resumed, halting operations once more. Again Dubois waited, resenting each wasted hour. Then, digging at the same level as before, but about forty-five feet away from where he had found the skull, he recovered a complete femur, or thigh-bone. Amazingly, it appeared to be fully human in form, hardly distinguishable from that of a modern human being. After agonizing appraisal, Dubois decided that it belonged with the previously excavated skull.

Dubois had gone looking for the earliest man. Now, it seemed, he had found something even better: a creature half-human, half-ape. Announcing his discovery of a "human-like transition form from Java," he named the fossil *Pithecanthropus erectus,* the name chosen by an earlier scientist to designate the hypothetical creature linking man and ape, if and when such a form could be found.

The scientific community received Dubois' report with open skepticism. Dubois, after all, was an amateur paleontologist making a preposterous claim for a mismatched heap of fossils found on an out-of-the-way island. And if science was hostile, the Church was aghast. *Pithecanthropus,* complained an irate and unified clergy, made an unsatisfactory Adam; the notion of a missing link was unacceptable on religious grounds.

Dubois, unable to make any further discoveries along the Solo River, hastened to Europe to defend his report. Exhibiting the controversial bones at scientific meetings at Paris, London, Berlin, Edinburgh, and Dublin, he fielded angry questions from assembled experts. Humiliated, outraged, stinging from the verbal assault, Dubois removed his precious fossils from public view. Burying them in a strongbox beneath his dining-room floor, he vowed he would have no more to do with science or scientists: he was done with the lot of them. Later, when experts became more responsive to the suggestion that *Pithecanthropus* did in fact represent a transition form, the irascible Dubois was reluctant to display his treasured fossils. He rejected urgent appeals from the presidents of both the American Museum of Natural History and the prestigious Dutch Academy of Sciences. Finally he relented, permitting Aleš Hrdlička, Curator of Physical Anthropology at America's Smithsonian Institution, to examine the long-hidden bones.

By that time, important new fossils had begun to emerge from China which would provide evidence to vindicate both the peevish Dubois and his ape-like protégé. An ancient Chinese tradition holds that "dragon bones" (which are in fact the fossilized remains of many different sorts of animals) can be ground up and made into potions powerful enough to cure almost any ailment from heartburn to lovesickness. Since 1903, when the German scientist Max Schlosser purchased a Pleistocene molar tooth in a Peking chemist's shop, paleontologists had made it a habit to browse in Chinese apothecaries.

The Chinese government permitted little excavation by out-siders, but Western scientists, intrigued by the "dragon bones" that kept turning up in Chinese drugstores, suspected that, if they could excavate the hills surrounding Peking, they might very well encounter valuable skeletal evidence concerning early man. The suspicion became a certainty when a Swedish geol-ogist, J. G. Andersson, acting as Mining Advisor to the Chinese government, came across the first tantalizing clue to Chinese prehistory—a clue that would lead to the discovery of one of the richest and most productive archaeological sites ever known.

Conducting an extensive geologic survey of the limestone cliffs near Choukoutien—about thirty miles south of Peking—Anders-son noticed among other rocks broken bits of quartz, a material not native to the region. Surely these had been brought in by human beings, but who would transport such quantities of raw quartz? And for what purposes?

For Andersson, there seemed but one compelling answer: blocks of quartz had been carried to Choukoutien in the remote past by primitive stone-age men who fashioned weapons and tools from stone, leaving behind these discarded flakes. Andersson ordered immediate excavations in the hope of locating the bones of these ancient tool-makers.

He was soon joined by Davidson Black, a Canadian anatomist working at Peking Union Medical College. Black was convinced that mankind had originated in Asia, and now, agreeing with Andersson, he would sift all of Choukoutien if necessary, to find the fossils that would prove man arose in Asia. But his investi-gation, he decided, must be thorough. He made plaster casts of all the Asian fossils so far uncovered and carried them to the Rockefeller Foundation, where he pleaded for funds sufficient to conduct an exhaustive study. Not only did he receive a grant from the Foundation, but he convinced China's reluctant officials that he should proceed—with the understanding, of course, that the Chinese government would retain possession of any valuable specimens recovered.

Black broke ground in April, 1927. Within six months his field director had unearthed a molar tooth that was both huge and primitive, but undeniably human in form—so human, in fact, that Black did not hesitate to use it to create a special new hominid genus. He called this new form of man—represented only by a single molar—*Sinanthropus pekinensis.*

Two years passed before the first *Sinanthropus* skull was found by the eminent Chinese paleontologist W. C. Pei. But this was followed by a veritable flood of fragmentary fossils. The skull of *Sinanthropus* is so strikingly similar to that of *Pithecanthropus* that it settled the taxonomic fate of the Javanese specimen. No doubt remained that Dubois' "erect ape-man" was in fact, the earliest known true human. But the unpredictable Dutch eccentric suddenly reversed his original interpretation. *Pithecanthropus,* he now insisted, was neither an ape-man nor a fully fledged human but an extinct variety of giant gibbon: the newly discovered *Sinanthropus* was no more than a degenerated Neanderthal that had inexplicably strayed to China. There was no relationship between the two fossils. Clearly, *Pithecanthropus* would have to take his rightful place in prehistory without the support of his erratic discoverer.

Most of the taxonomic labels for these early middle Pleistocene hominids have been discarded, and all have been transferred to the same genus and species, *Homo erectus.* Thus we have not only simplified the taxonomic situation but have also revealed the evolutionary relationship of each of these populations to the others. Although the evidence we have for them places them many thousands of miles apart, all date from the same period and have in common numerous morphological similarities.

Reconstructions based on the skeletal remains show a short (averaging a little over five feet tall), powerful individual with a well-developed upright posture. His pongid ancestry is easily discernible in the general formation of the skull, which was small, with an average cranial capacity of about 1000 c.c., and had a low crown and no forehead. The postcranial skeleton, on the other hand, appears to be quite modern, implying that in human evolution the postcranial skeleton approached modern standards earlier than did the skull.

African populations established the production and use of large bifacial core tools (hand axes), while the Asiatic hominids relied on cruder unifacial core tools (choppers). Each type represented a technical and functional improvement over the earlier Olduwan pebble-tool even though the latter was still being used in many areas. Evidence of man's knowledge of the use of fire at this time exists in the large hearths and charred bone from Choukoutien.

Clues to the possible origin of *Homo erectus* are to be found in both Africa and Asia. Both *Homo erectus* and his forerunner, *Australopithecus,* appear in Africa, and it has been strongly suggested that *Homo erectus* originated there. But if *Meganthropus paleojavanicus* from Java is generally accepted as a far-flung representative of *A. robustus,* and is therefore a precursor of *Homo erectus*

FIGURE 14. *Homo erectus.* (a) Reconstruction of adolescent and adult males. (b) Restoration of skull and jaw based on a cranium from Olduvai Gorge. (c) Cranium of *"Sinanthropus"* from Choukoutien Cave, China. (d) Femurs of *H. erectus* (left) and *H. sapiens* (right). (Growth on left femur is from a bone disease.) (e) Portion of mandible of an early *H. erectus* or late *A. habilis* from Java with two unworn teeth of typical *H. erectus.* (Adapted in part from photographs in Pilbeam, 1972.)

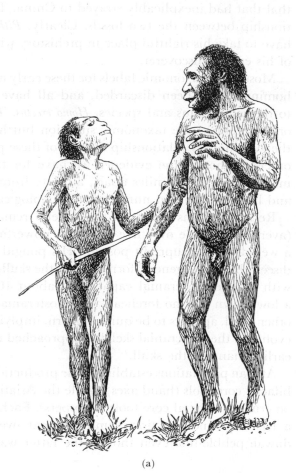

(a)

as well, then the same situation exists in Java. It is difficult, however, to conceive that *Homo erectus* originated in such a small, restricted area.

The evolutionary direction of *Homo erectus* is another problem. The general trend of morphological change between *Homo erectus* and modern man is characterized by increasing brain size (from about 1000 c.c. to about 1450 c.c.), the reduction in size of jaws and teeth, and an increase in body size as well as a number of adjustments in locomotor behavior. Some authorities

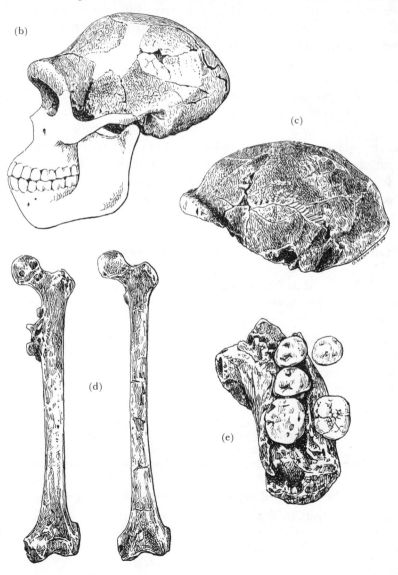

(b)

(c)

(d)

(e)

have calculated rates at which these changes are likely to have occurred, and, according to these rates recognize *Homo erectus* as modern man's direct ancestor. Others consider that the differences between *Homo erectus* and modern man are too great for these necessary changes to have occurred in the time that existed for such a transition. Thus they are convinced that *erectus* became an extinct species and that the evolutionary development of *Homo sapiens sapiens* was a slow, gradual process that must have started long before *erectus* appeared. These and other speculations are interesting and provocative, but the many gaps in the fossil record of the Pleistocene continue to frustrate our research into the true nature of hominid evolution.

PROBLEM CASES. The Heidelberg mandible, found in 1907 by Otto Schoetensack at Mauer near Heidelberg, Germany, is dated at over 400,000 years old. However the mandible demonstrates more physical similarities to the more recent Neanderthal populations of Europe than it does to the Asiatic and African hominids that date from the same time period. Some claim that the Heidelberg mandible represents a direct ancestral link to the Neanderthals; others see the mandible as representative of *Homo erectus* in Europe.

In 1965, an occipital bone and a few teeth were recovered from a quarry near Vertesszollos, Hungary. The site contains evidence of living-floors, hearths, and Oldowan-type tools, and has also been dated at around 400,000 years ago. The teeth are similar in many ways to those of *Homo erectus,* but the occipital bone looks slightly more advanced. The Vertesszollos material obviously comes from a fairly large skull with an estimated cranial capacity of 1400 c.c. The final disposition of the Vertesszollos material cannot be completed until more details of this population are known.

Homo sapiens neanderthalensis

The first detailed description of the Neanderthals was made by M. Boule in the early 1900's and was based on a complete skeleton taken from a rock shelter near the village of La Chapelle-aux-Saints in France. Boule pictured these people as short (a little over five feet tall) and extremely robust. Their skulls, although very low and long, were huge: cranial capacities exceeded 1600 c.c. in a number of cases, a figure well over the average for modern man. The face was dominated by strongly-developed brow ridges; the eye orbits were large and round; and the face was generally long and prognathic (having a projecting forehead); and the lower jaws were rugged and chinless.

We now know that Boule's description represented only one variety of Neanderthal, that lived in western Europe between 70,000 and 50,000 years ago. Also, many of Boule's conclusions about posture and skeletal articulation were not accurate. Actually, the Neanderthals were a highly variable population that left its mark in most of the geographic areas of the Old World and covered a time span of from 40,000 to 200,000 years ago. From the rock shelters and caves of western Europe, to the zinc mine at Broken Hill in Rhodesia, and to the caves on Mount Carmel in Israel come the variable representatives of this subspecies.

The western European variety, as described by Boule, have been categorized as "typical" or "classic," and have been located at only one other site outside Europe, the Shanidar Cave in Iraq. Their lithic industry, called *Mousterian,* is well known and is based on tools made from stone flakes that have been removed from a core. Thus the assemblage is dominated by such flake tools as scrapers and points, and these are quite distinct from the core tools or hand-ax domination of the early Pleistocene industries.

In Africa, a variety of Neanderthal is found that is reminiscent of the "classic" Neanderthal of Europe but which exhibits some very distinct differences. The fossil evidence comes from Broken Hill, Rhodesia, and the Saldanha site on the Atlantic Coast of southwestern Africa. Although robust and fairly short, these African Neanderthals had much smaller skulls (about 1200 c.c.) and brow ridges that would rival those of the modern gorillas. Their faces were narrower and much longer than those of the European Neanderthal.

Evidence of another Neanderthal variety comes from the shores of the eastern Mediterranean. These specimens differ from the classic type in that their general morphology is much closer

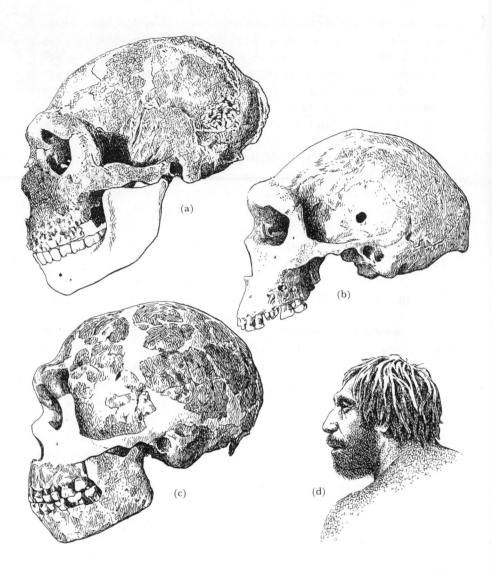

FIGURE 15.   *Homo sapiens neanderthalensis.* (a) Skull from Monte Cicero, France, together with the skull from la Chapelle represents the classic Neanderthal type. (b) "Rhodesian man" from Zambia thought by some to be an African version of Neanderthal and by others to be an intermediate between *H. erectus* and *H. s. sapiens.* The hole may have been the result of a primitive but successful attempt at surgery. (c) Tabun skull from Mt. Carmel, Israel, an advanced Neanderthal. (d) Reconstruction of classic Neanderthal profile based on the Monte Cicero skull. (Adapted from photographs in Howell, Time-Life, 1965.)

to modern *sapiens* populations; they have therefore been labeled as "progressive" Neanderthals. For this variety, the cranium is not as large as that which is typical of the European population (about 1400 c.c.); the brow ridges are smaller, the facial profile is more orthognathus (flat-faced), and the vault is higher. The fossil evidence for these more advanced Neanderthals has been concentrated in the Near East but clues to their existence have also come from North Africa (at Haua Fteah in Lybia) and Europe (at Ehringsdorf in Germany and Krapina in Yugoslavia). Also, the Mousterian-type tools are found with these progressive Neanderthals, but their makers had adopted the Levallois technique which created a kind of mass-produced flake; these industries are known as Levalloiso-Mousterian.

Speculation is still rampant concerning the role played by the Neanderthals in the evolutionary development of modern humans. Either the Neanderthals were an aberrant form that became extinct during the late Pleistocene, leaving no genetic heritage among modern living populations, or their transition from a Neanderthal to a *sapiens* stage of evolution is supported by the more anatomically progressive varieties. A certain answer depends upon more thorough knowledge of the variability of these early populations as well as of their genetic potential for progressive phyletic change.

PROBLEM CASES. Physical anthropologists know Neanderthal better than any other fossil population, but problem cases abound in spite of this familiarity. For example, the fossil remains of at least eleven individuals were excavated from the banks of the Solo River at Ngandong, on the island of Java. Only skull caps, teeth, and the shafts of two long bones were recovered, from which age of "Solo Man" has been estimated at 150,000 years. A thorough analysis of this material has never been completed, and many experts consider the Solo population as representing an Asiatic Neanderthal. However, Franz Weidenreich, who died before he could finish his study of this material, was adamant in rejecting this interpretation. The skulls are small, exhibiting an average cranial capacity of about 1100 c.c. Their brow ridges are prominent, and the muscle attachment areas of the occipital bone are rugged. When reconstructed, Solo man looks more like an advanced *Homo erectus* than a Neanderthal, which has caused some to suggest that the Solo hominids were the last of the Asiatic *Homo erectus* lineage and may reflect the destiny of other *erectus* populations, namely those from China and northwest Africa.

Another puzzle is "Swanscombe Man." The Swanscombe site in Kent, England, has produced parts of a skull that are as-

FIGURE 16. Family group of advanced Neanderthals from the Middle East. The man is making a flint hand-ax.

sociated with Acheulean hand-axes and date from about 250,000 years ago. Only the back portions of the skull are present, the occipit and both parietals, but these reveal an interesting mixture of both Neanderthal and modern features. Without the face and important postcranial material, however, it is extremely difficult to associate the Swanscombe remains with either Neanderthal or *sapiens* populations of Europe.

FIGURE 17. Reconstruction of a Magdalenian ice-age hunter and a woman *(Homo sapiens sapiens)* from Europe about 10,000 years ago.

A single distorted skull, lacking a lower jaw, is all we have from the Steinheim site in Germany, but it too is enough to mystify and intrigue authorities. Because the Steinheim skull dates from the same time as the Swanscombe material and exhibits a number of morphological similarities, many experts insist that these two finds are remnants of the same middle Pleistocene population. Both have moderate brain volumes (1200–1300 c.c.), long, low skulls, and fully rounded occipital bones. The Steinheim face is large, supporting well developed brow ridges. Both have been classified, at various times, as both *neanderthalensis* and *sapiens.*

A complete mandible, some teeth, and a vertebra represent the fossil remains from the Coupe Gorge cave near Montmaurin, France. The date is designated as 250,000 years ago. Only the mandible has been described and has been considered to be of a general neanderthaloid type but with features reminiscent of the Heidelberg mandible. Thus a Heidelberg-Montmaurin-Neanderthal lineage has been suggested.

An even more intriguing discovery comes from the Fontechevade site in France. Two cranial fragments, associated with a Tayacian lithic industry[1] and dated about 100,000 years ago, seem surprisingly modern except for the thickness of the bone. Most authorities have classified these remains as *Homo sapiens sapiens,* recognizing that they date from earlier times than any other known European *sapiens* specimen.

The most recent discovery of fossil man in the middle Pleistocene comes from the Caune de l'Argo Cave near the village of Tautavel in southeastern France. The human skeletal remains include two mandibles and the anterior portion of an adult skull. The mandibles are massive and chinless, very much like the Heidelberg and Montmaurin mandibles. The facial portion of the adult skull is probably that of a young male with pronounced brow ridges, receding forehead, low and rectangular eye orbits, and pronounced facial prognathism. The cranial capacity is estimated to be small. In general, the Tautavel remains appear to be more primitive than the Neanderthal but distinctly more advanced than *Homo erectus.* Also, the cultural associations are similar to those noted at Vertesszollos, with Tayacian and Acheulean tools found in these deposits.

[1] See Chapter X.

The early dates and morphological similarities of the Montmaurin, Tautavel, Swanscombe, and Steinheim finds make them
difficult to place in human developmental history, but the problem is vastly intriguing. The missing portions of any of these
fossil representatives would certainly add to our knowledge and
aid our attempts to understand the true nature of hominid
evolution.

Homo sapiens sapiens

The fossil record indicates that modern human forms began to
appear about 40,000 years ago. These populations introduced
a new morphology, a new emphasis in tool types, and, in Europe,
a remarkable artistic development. Their appearance was note-
worthy because it occurred in most areas of the Old World
at approximately the same time. The following brief list of sites
demonstrates the wide geographical distribution of these earliest
sapiens populations:

Cro Magnon—France
Chancelade—France
Obercassel—Germany
Predmost—Yugoslavia
Grimaldi—Italy
Afalou—Algeria, North Africa
Oldowan—Tanzania, East Africa
Boskop—South Africa
Hotu—Iran (Mesolithic?)
Choukoutien—China
Wadjak—Java
Keilor—Australia

Like our modern populations, these early groups were extremely variable, and some experts have seen this variability
as evidence of early racial differentiation. In most cases, however,
the representatives of these skeletal races number less than two
or three individuals, a sampling that leaves much to be desired.

FIGURE 18. *Homo sapiens sapiens.* (a) Two views of the Skhull V skull, an adult male from Mt. Carmel, Israel. (b) and (c) Skulls from Combe-Capelle, France, and Grimaldi, Italy, showing two extremes in variability. (Adapted in part from photographs in Frederick S. Hulse, *The Human Species,* Random House, 1971.)

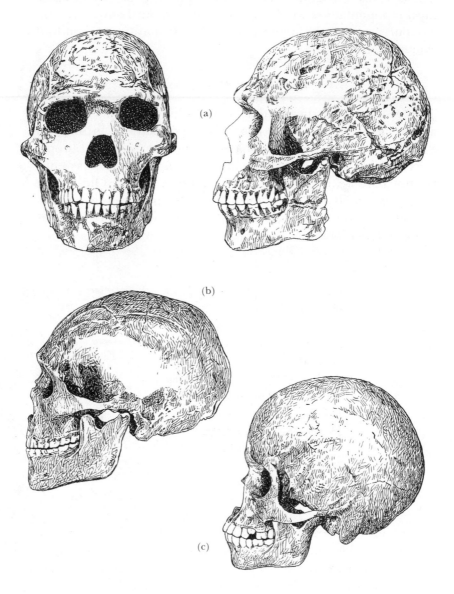

The origin of *Homo sapiens sapiens* is, obviously, an extremely complex story; there is simply too little evidence available to carry our ideas further than intriguing speculation.

FOSSIL INTERPRETATION

It is the ultimate responsibility of any scientist to use what evidence he has to add to the theoretical development of his discipline. In studies of human evolution, the essential problem is to place the variety of fossil forms into some meaningful developmental or phylogenetic system that attempts to reconstruct human biological history from the ancient past to the present.

Obviously, there are many logical ways of interpreting the fossil evidence, and there were times when numerous schools of thought dominated the discipline. Today, the general theoretical situation can best be documented by diagramming a number of individual interpretations. Figure 19 illustrates the hypotheses of W. E. LeGros Clark, Loring Brace, P. Tobias, and L. S. B. Leakey.

Sir W. E. LeGros Clark, the noted British paleontologist, considers both the robust species of *Australopithecus* and the Neanderthals to represent extinct species, playing no role in the phylogenetic development of modern man. C. Loring Brace of the University of Michigan interprets the fossil evidence as representing a simple monogenetic system, with all forms included as developmental stages to *Homo sapiens sapiens.* Phillip J. Tobias of the University of Witwatersrand, South Africa, begins his human family tree with *Australopithecus boisei* and *Homo habilis;* he views the other two species of *Australopithecus, africanus* and *robustus,* as extinct. L. S. B. Leakey listed the highest number of extinct branches including both species of *Australopithecus* and the Neanderthals. Also, he did not count *Homo erectus* among the ancestors of modern man. Leakey was one of the few who saw a straight line of evolutionary development from *Homo habilis* to *Homo sapiens sapiens.*

All of these arrangements are tentative at best, since analysis of new evidence as well as reanalysis of old evidence forces a constant shifting of hypotheses within the general structure

FIGURE 19.   A comparison of interpretations of the fossil evidence for human evolution by various experts.

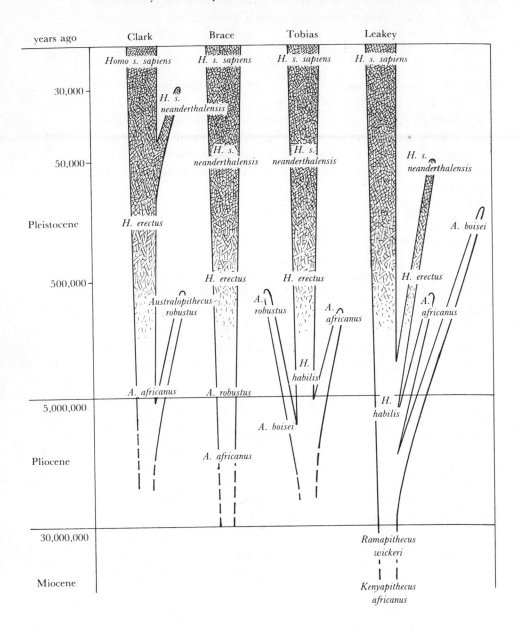

of hominid evolution. Nor do the schemes reproduced here represent all current views; they are chosen for diagramming because they indicate how varied are ways in which the evidence might be interpreted. The over-all picture of human evolutionary history during the past five million years is one of morphological change and geographic radiation, with populations resembling modern humans occurring only in more recent times. As far as a more detailed knowledge of human evolutionary development is concerned, future fossil discoveries and more refined methodologies will help to solve many of our current problems. For example, Richard Leakey's latest discovery has not yet been described completely and thus it is not included in any of the present phylogenetic schemes. Yet there is no doubt of its importance to the history of the hominids. As might any new fossil discovery, this one could initiate a new approach to the interpretation of man's earliest origins.

FURTHER READINGS

Brace, C. Loring. *The Stages of Human Evolution.* Englewood Cliffs: Prentice-Hall, 1967.

Broom, Robert. *Finding the Missing Link.* London: C. A. Watts, 1950.

Clark, W. E. Le Gros. *The Fossil Evidence for Human Evolution.* Chicago: University of Chicago Press, 1955.

Coon, Carleton S. *The Origin of Races.* New York: Alfred A. Knopf, 1962.

Dart, Raymond A. *Adventures with the Missing Link.* New York: Harper & Bros., 1959.

Dobzhansky, Theodosius. *Mankind Evolving.* New Haven: Yale University Press, 1962.

Hooton, Ernest A. *Up From the Ape* (rev. ed.). New York: Macmillan, 1947.

Howells, William W. *Mankind in the Making.* Garden City: Doubleday, 1950.

Leakey, Louis S. B. *Adam's Ancestors.* New York: Harper & Bros., 1960.

McKern, Thomas W. and Sharon S. *Human Origins.* Englewood Cliffs: Prentice-Hall, 1966.

McKern, Sharon S. and Thomas W. *Tracking Fossil Man.* Praeger, 1970.

Oakley, Kenneth Page. *Man the Tool-Maker* (3rd ed.). Chicago: University of Chicago Press, 1964.

Simpson, George Gaylord. *Life of the Past.* New Haven: Yale University Press, 1961.

Von Koenigswald, G. H. R. *Meeting Prehistoric Man.* New York: Harper & Bros., 1957.

Weidenreich, Franz. *Apes, Giants, and Man.* Chicago: University of Chicago Press, 1946.

CHAPTER VIII

HUMAN VARIATION

Modern human beings are classed collectively within a single polytypic species because they vary in an infinite number of ways. It was this bewildering human variability that caused early scholars to attempt to bring order and understanding to the apparent chaos of physical diversity. Unfortunately, more effort was expended in classifying the diverse types of modern man than in attempting to understand the causes of his variability. Certainly classifications are necessary, but only to improve our understanding of the distribution of human varieties throughout the world.

Ideally, such groupings lead to solutions of specific problems. We compare human populations in order to trace historical relationships and to illuminate the mechanics of human evolution. Since generations are linked physically through gene transmission, we attempt to ascertain the genetic component of human variation. This is made difficult since very few traits are inherited in simple form and gene action leads to different consequences under different circumstances, making it clear that we must learn more about the effects of diverse environments on man.

Classifying Human Beings

Kelso[1] has summarized the three different kinds of classification that are currently used as typological, populational, and clinal. Typological classification, the more traditional approach, divides human beings according to biological traits that occur regularly within certain geographical locations. Most commonly

---

[1]Kelso, A. J. *Physical Anthropology*. Philadelphia: J. B. Lippincott, 1970, pp. 301–317.

utilized in this system of classification are such visually percepti-
ble features as skin color, average stature, hair form, and limb
proportions. Less obvious characteristics such as blood groups,
serum proteins, taster, and secretor, are also used when such
data are available.

Typological classifications are useful in summarizing the complex distribution of human biological variations. They also divide
mankind into units which vary, of course, depending upon the
number of characteristics utilized in the division. These units

FIGURE 1. A montage demonstrating the variability of biological traits that
may be used in typological classifications. (Copper Eskimo, American Museum
of Natural History; others, Harrison Foreman World Photos)

Moslem, India.	Berber, Morocco.	Patriarch, Israel.

Quiche, Guatemala.	Galla, Ethiopia.	Peoples Republic of China.

are useful in suggesting hypotheses concerning possible relationships between trait clusters and the environment in which they are expressed. They also act as convenient aids to teachers in leading students through the maze of information regarding human variation.

Populational classifications divide mankind into breeding populations, which are the basic units of evolutionary change. Classifications based on inherited traits are founded on the fact that evolution represents change in the genetic structure from

Afghanistan.

Zulu, South Africa.

Copper Eskimo.

Peoples Republic of China.

Russia.

Uganda.

one generation to the next; therefore the logical unit of evolutionary analysis is the reproductive unit, a group of individuals that mate and produce subsequent generations.

Although easily defined, populational classifications are hard to come by. Since descriptions of breeding populations are presented almost exclusively in terms of gene frequencies, and since these frequencies may be influenced by a number of variables impossible to include in the final estimate, the system itself would seem to be both inefficient and impractical. It is used, however, and the best results are derived when typological and populational approaches are combined.

FIGURE 2.   Clinal map showing average stature in human beings. (After Joseph B. Birdsell, *Human Evolution: An Introduction to the New Physical Anthropology*, New York: Random House, 1972.)

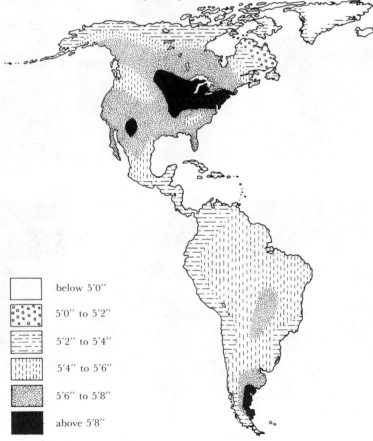

below 5′0″

5′0″ to 5′2″

5′2″ to 5′4″

5′4″ to 5′6″

5′6″ to 5′8″

above 5′8″

In the past several years, clinal classifications of human variability have begun to come into some use, most notably in the work of Joseph B. Birdsell, who is still improving on their usefulness and on the kinds of information that can be presented. Clinal maps are based on the fact that the occurrence (frequency) of virtually all traits (size, color, etc.) and entire species varies in a relatively continuous manner over a given area. A trait example is offered by a small salamander of the genus *Ensatina* which is reddish-brown on the coast of California; but spotted yellow-orange individuals are increasingly common towards the Sierras, where all individuals are of the spotted variety.

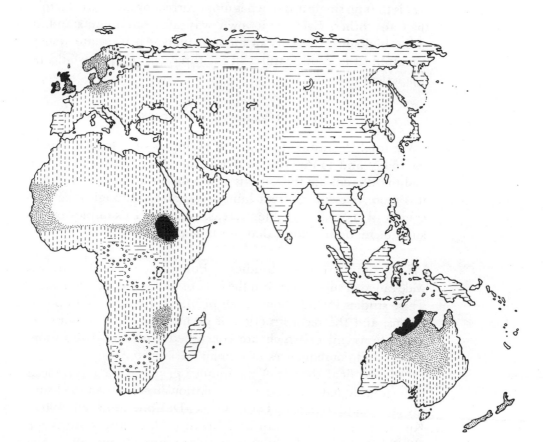

The problems encountered in applying this kind of observation to humans are the enormous number of significant traits which one is usually trying to work with, and the difficulty in obtaining these data across wide spans of territory without gaps in sampling. In addition, of course, human distribution is often as much the result of cultural factors as of environmental conditions. To illustrate, the purchase of Alaska and subsequent discovery of gold resulted in a discontinuous distribution of caucasians. Someone studying the distribution of caucasians would have to allow for the cultural factor, but such factors are not always as clear and obvious as this one.

Probably one truth eclipses all others in our methodological attempts to bring order to the realities of human variation, and that is that no single approach is more correct or more satisfactory than any other. Each in its own way aids our understanding of the biological diversity of modern man. An ultimate system combining the good features of all three approaches would be a practical goal.

Human Variation Studies

We might continue to consider examples of classifications in use today and to describe in detail the characteristics that are said to differentiate the various groupings of human beings. But it is more relevant to treat human variation through a consideration of its major problem areas, with brief examples of the kinds of modern studies that are typical of each.

DEMOGRAPHIC STUDIES.   Studies in human demography cover a wide range of subjects within the field of biological anthropology. These studies include nonhuman primates, living human populations, and the reconstruction of prehistoric and ethnohistoric populations, all of which are concerned with the description, causes, and consequences of human variability.

Detailed field studies of nonhuman primates have produced demographic data relative to the relationship between food supply and population size. For example, DeVore and Hall (1965), Kummer (1968), Gartlan and Brain (1968), and Southwick (1969) have all found that aggression is more pronounced among

groups who live in environments that are rich in food. Since
a high level of aggression in any primate species causes a significant increase in mortality, the links among food supply, aggression, and population size seem obvious, a conclusion that runs
counter to an earlier assumption that primate population size
is controlled by food resources alone.

Information that is more revealing about human nature comes
from Baker and Sanders (1972) in their report on the apparent
similarities among the basic demographic features of chimpanzees, gorillas, and human hunting and gathering groups. They
noted that the females of all these groups have reproductive
spans of about 20 to 25 years; that all average about three years
between single births; and that all three groups seem to have
similar mortality curves. Humans, of course, live longer than
gorillas and chimpanzees, but only because of a longer period
before reproductive maturity. If longevity is calculated from the
age of sexual maturity, then all three groups live approximately
the same number of years. This contrasts sharply with mortality
curves found in human peasant and industrial societies.

Data from descriptive demographic studies of living human
populations are usually applied to various problems of population density and resource utilization, with special emphasis on
hunting and gathering groups. Thus Dunn (1968) surveyed the
general health, diseases, nutrition, and causes of mortality among
South African bushmen, Australian aborigines, Eskimos, African
pygmies, and the Semang.

The size and distribution of the aboriginal populations has
always been a puzzle to scientists; results of early studies were
dubious. However more sophisticated statistical methods have
initiated studies such as those which attempt to reconstruct the
demographic structure of a population through a detailed analysis of the skeletal remains. These studies are often called *paleode-
mography*. Investigations by McKern and Stewart (1957), Giles
(1970), Phenice (1969), and Armelagos (1969) are examples of
this type of approach relative to the determination of age, sex,
and disease in ancient human populations.

In many ways the following study areas are also demographic
or utilize demographic data. These are treated, however, as

separate categories of investigation because the problems they attempt to solve have strong disciplinary emphases usually originating outside the general area of human demography.

GENETIC STUDIES. Most genetic studies in biological anthropology are concerned primarily with establishing the frequency of the distribution of genes in human populations, and with the ways in which such data contribute to population genetics theory. These studies have always included traits such as skin color, blood groups, multiple births, and dermatoglyphics; but more recent information comes from investigations of such inherited systems as red-cell enzymes, serum polymorphisms, and abnormal hemoglobins.

Selection may be the major source of human population difference in gene frequencies. This area is being investigated by scholars such as Crow (1958), Johnston et al. (1969), and Neel (1968), who have attempted to test selection processes on the basis of fertility and mortality patterns.

Since human variation is in part caused by changes in allelic frequencies, it is vital that we know more about gene activity in populations.

NUTRITION STUDIES. Nutrition studies have been conducted for a variety of world populations, demonstrating the complex influences of both environment and culture. For example, Buck et al (1969) reported that, among Andean Indians, those who chew the coca leaf show an inferior nutritional status, a higher prevalence of symptoms resulting from poor hygiene, and diminished work performance. They suggest that such conditions arise from the fact that chewing coca leaves blunts the sensation of hunger.

Many nutritional studies have dealt with the distribution of lactase deficiency (McCracken 1971). Milk contains *lactose* which is assimilated by the enzyme *lactase*. A defective lactose absorption among some infants causes malnutrition and may be due to a deficiency of the enzyme. Some individuals lose their lactase activity with age and thus experience gastrointestinal discomfort when they drink milk; that is, they become intolerant to lactose. The problem lies in explaining how this adult condition is related to the infant lactase deficiency, and why it occurs more frequently in some human populations than in others. The condition is found more frequently among American Indians and Negroes than among Europeans, and there is some evidence that the deficiency is a recessive trait. Thus it has been suggested that man may be polymorphic for the loss or retention of lactase activity in adulthood; that prior to the domestication of animals, the deficiency was widespread but when milk was introduced into the adult diet, new selective pressures were created to operate against the deficiency.

DENTITION STUDIES.   Dental data, both descriptive and functional, have been accumulating for many years. The distributions of numbers, age changes, comparative asymmetry, and disease have been reported for both living and ancient populations. A good example has been reported recently by Bailit and Workman (1970). Their investigations have demonstrated that dental asymmetry in human populations increases as environmental conditions deteriorate; that is, the condition can be shown to be much more a function of environment than of heredity.

Studies of individual features of the teeth include quantitative analyses of the incidence of standard features such as shovel-shaped incisors, Caribelli's cusp, and peg-shaped maxillary lateral incisors. Mayhall and Dahlberg (1970) report that the incidence of the *torus mandibularis*—a bony ridge running along the inside of the mandible below the teeth—appears to decrease among Eskimos as the native diet is abandoned. As data on lineage are continually collected, our understanding is increased concerning the mode of inheritance of specific traits such as these. The result is a greater general understanding of the appearance of diverse traits among the living races of mankind.

GROWTH AND DEVELOPMENT STUDIES.   Most current studies in human growth and development deal with the analysis of one or more contributing factors in the observed variation of growth processes. Some of the studies which cover populations in most of the continents of the world include birth-weight variation related to parental age, parity, and sex; growth and development through preadolescence and adolescence; and the timing of the onset of puberty and menarche (the onset of menstruation).

An interest in secular trends for various periods of time is represented in reports from a number of countries. A good example of this type of study is Froehlich's report (1970) on the plasticity of physique after migration. His investigation of Japanese-Americans in Hawaii covers two generations following migration from Japan and shows a significant increase in average stature. Also, secular trends among Negro and white children in Cuba in height and weight are reported as being much more marked for the white boys than for the Negro boys (Laska-Mierzejewska 1970). There are additional studies that treat the growth of specific portions of the body: the variability of the cephalic index (the ratio between length and breadth of head) with age; or the average degree of spinal curvature in different populations. These represent only a few of the documented interests in the area of growth and development, and they are vital in our quest for a better understanding of human variation.

ANTHROPOMETRIC STUDIES.   Probably the most traditional area in the investigation of human variation is the comparative measurement of man. A study by Valaoras (1970) is typical. He reports on a large sample of army conscripts in Greece, born between 1927 and 1945, and notes that the mean stature demonstrated substantial geographic variation as well as an interesting secular trend; stature increased during periods of normal social and economic development but decreased during times of social and economic deterioration.

Anthropometric data have long been of interest to both military and industrial agencies: for example, the United States Army uses such data to establish clothing standards for both male and female personnel. A more recent example is found in Harrison and Marshall's report (1970) in which they used photogrammetric data on the length of limbs and limb segments for young British women to establish normal standards in clothing and industrial design.

MORPHOLOGICAL STUDIES.   Somatotype studies are not as common as they were in the early days of physical anthropology, but one example of an area of investigation which is still considered to be valid is found in Falkiewicz's work (1969) in mountain areas of Egypt, where he studied the variation of constitution indices with blood groups, and the relationship between body type and performance.

The relationship of the incidence of particular morphological characteristics to the mode of inheritance has been investigated for such features as cleft chin, types of mucosa relief of the palate, pilosity, hair structure, and blood antigens; but, for most, the pattern of inheritance remains obscure.

PHYSIOLOGY AND ADAPTATION STUDIES.   This problem area in- cludes studies in exercise physiology and environmental adapta- tion. The former is represented by such articles as "Possible Effect of a Vegan Diet upon Lung Function and the Cardiorespiratory Response to Submaximal Exercise in Healthy Women," by Cotes et al 1970. Knibbs (1971) has found, in a study of the physio- logical effects of exercise on young nonathletic females, that as the intensity of training increases, so does its effectiveness in improving oxygen uptake and reducing heart rate.

Of more crucial interest to most physical anthropologists are studies in environmental adaptation. Although there is still a need to standardize terminology and procedures, much has been accomplished in the study of populations living at high altitudes. Scholars have studied the growth and development of children in such areas and have reported late sexual dimorphism, slow and prolonged growth, late and poorly defined adolescent growth spurt, and greater development of chest size (Frisancho and Baker 1970). Interpretations relating these recorded events to physiological adaptation to high-altitude living have been care- fully worded. It has been pointed out that not all alterations (for example, cardiorespiratory characteristics) are necessarily adaptive; some may be pathological. Also, it is still impossible to determine the genetic components in these developmental responses.

Many physiological studies have investigated human adapta- tion to heat and cold stress, comparing various world populations. Little, Thomas, Mazess, and Baker (1971) found that the adult highland Indians of Peru maintained higher hand and foot skin temperatures than the younger Indians, while all Indian subject groups could maintain higher skin temperatures than could whites. They suggest the possible operation of developmental acclimatization as well as genetic adaptation in the response of skin temperature to cold.

From the foregoing brief survey of problem areas within the general field of human variation, it is clear that a great deal of investigation remains to be done. Variability is the very essence of evolution; through a better understanding of the causes of human variation we can achieve a better grasp of the mechanics of human evolution. This is the new physical anthropology.

REFERENCES CITED

Armelagos, G. J. "Disease in Ancient Nubia." *Science,* 163:255–259, 1969.

Bailit, H. L., P. L. Workman, J. D. Niswander, and C. J. MacLean. "Dental Asymmetry as an Indicator of Genetic and Environmental Conditions in Human Populations." *Human Biology,* 42:626–638, 1970.

Baker, P. T. and W. T. Sanders. "Demographic Studies in Anthropology." *Annual Review of Anthropology,* Vol. 1 (B. J. Siegel, ed.), Annual Reviews Inc., Palo Alto, Calif., 1972.

Buck, A. D. et al. "Association of Coca Leaf Chewing with Malnutrition." *Nutrition Review,* 27:187–88, 1969.

Cotes, J. E. et al. "Possible Effect of a Vegan Diet Upon Lung Function and the Cardiorespiratory Response to Submaximal Exercise in Healthy Women." *Journal of Physiology.* London. 209:30–32P, 1970.

Crow, J. F. "Some Possibilities for Measuring Selection Intensities in Man." *Human Biology.* 30:1–13, 1958.

DeVore, I., and K. R. L. Hall. "Baboon Ecology." I. Devore (ed.). *Primate Behavior.* New York: Holt, Rinehart & Winston, 1965.

Dunn, F. L. "Epidemiological Factors: Health and Disease in Hunters-Gatherers." *Man the Hunter.* R. D. Lee and I. Devore (ed.). Chicago: Aldine, 1968.

Falkiewicz, B. "Constitutional and Functional Typology in the Acclimatization and Adaptation of Man." *Przegl. Anthropologia.* 35:261–280, 1969.

Frisancho, A. R. and P. T. Baker. "Altitude and Growth: a Study of the Patterns of Physical Growth of a High Altitude Peruvian

Quechua Population." *American Journal of Physical Anthropology.* 32:279–292, 1970.

Froehlich, J. W. "Migration and the Plasticity of Physique in the Japanese-Americans of Hawaii." *American Journal of Physical Anthropology.* 32:429–442, 1970.

Gartlan, J. S. and C. K. Brain. "Ecology and Social Variability in *Cercopithecus aethiops* and *C. mitis.*" P. C. Jay (ed.). *Primates.* New York: Holt, Rinehart & Winston, 1968.

Giles, E. "Discriminant Function Sexing of the Human Skeleton." *Personal Identification in Mass Disasters,* T. D. Stewart (ed.). Washington, D.C.: Smithsonian Institution, 1970.

Harrison, J. M. and W. A. Marshall. "Normal Standards for the Relationships Between the Lengths of Limbs and of Limb Segments in Young British Women: A Photogrammetric Study." *Human Biology.* 42:90–104, 1970.

Johnston, F. E. and K. M. Kensinger. "Fertility and Mortality Differentials and Their Implications for Microevolutionary Change among the Cashinahua." *Human Biology.* 43:356–364, 1971.

Kelso, A. J. *Physical Anthropology: an Introduction.* New York: J. B. Lippincott, 1970.

Knibbs, A. V. "Some Physiological Effects of Intensity and Frequency of Exercise on Young Non-athletic Females." *Journal of Physiology.* London 216:25–26P, 1971.

Kummer, H. *Social Organization of Hamadryas Baboons.* Chicago: University of Chicago Press, 1968.

Laska-Mierzejewska, T. "Morphological and Developmental Difference between Negro and White Cuban Youths." *Human Biology.* 42:581–597, 1970.

Little, M. A. et al. "Population Differences and Developmental Changes in Extremity Temperature Responses to Cold among Andean Indians." *Human Biology.* 43:70–91, 1971.

Mayhall, J. T., Dahlberg, A. A., and D. G. Owen. "Torus Mandibularis in an Alaskan Eskimo Population." *American Journal of Physical Anthropology.* 33:57–60, 1970.

McCracken, R. D. "Lactase Deficiency: An Example of Dietary Evolution." *Current Anthropology.* 12:479–517, 1971.

McKern, T. W. and T. D. Stewart. *Skeletal Age Changes in Young American Males.* Quartermaster Res. Develop. Center, U.S. Army, Environmental Protection Research Division, Technical Report. EP-45, 1957.

Neel, J. V. "The Study of Natural Selection in Primitive and Civilized Human Populations." *Human Biology.* 30:43–72, 1958.

Phenice, T. W. "A Newly Developed Visual Method of Sexing the *os pubis.*" *American Journal of Physical Anthropology.* 30:297–301, 1969.

Southwick, C. 1969. "Aggressive Behavior of Rhesus Monkeys in Natural and Captive Groups." *Aggressive Behavior,* S. Garattini and E. G. Sigg (eds.). Excerpta Medica.

Valaoras, V. G. "Biometric Studies of Army Conscripts in Greece: Mean Stature and ABO Blood Group Distribution." *Human Biology.* 42:184–201, 1970.

PART 3

STUDIES IN
ARCHAEOLOGY

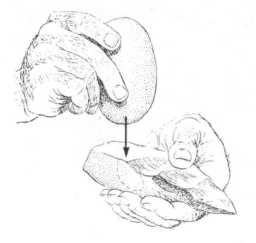

CHAPTER IX

METHODS IN ARCHAEOLOGY

While physical anthropologists take much of their evidence for past human life from fossilized skeletal material, archaeologists draw primarily upon the artifacts and other cultural remains left behind by vanished peoples. For a few important cultures, such as those of ancient Egypt and pre-Columbian Peru, archaeologists have gathered copious remains, reconstructing them into rich patterns of human achievement. We know more, in fact, about the Middle Kingdom of ancient Egypt than we do about medieval England, simply because scientists have collected more abundant archaeological materials from Egypt.

For the most part, however, archaeologists, like physical anthropologists and other prehistorians, make their deductions from meager collections of fragmentary ruins and artifacts. Even under the best circumstances, the archaeologist can hope to reconstruct only a fraction of the total record of human behavior. He makes his discoveries like a Sherlock Holmes: with the few clues he can wrest from the grudging earth, he does the best he can to deduce a rough history of past human behavior.

For most of man's existence on earth, we have no written records. Prehistory, of course, comprises that long, preliterate period of human existence; and when written histories do exist these records are, more often than not, inadequate for our purposes. For centuries after its development, writing was used primarily for temple records and commercial transactions. Even when writing was well established, little was written about the daily lives of people, and not much of that survived. What historians have learned about daily life in ancient Rome, for example, was gleaned not so much from the writings of the time but from the records of archaeological excavations at sites such as Herculaneum and Pompeii. Archaeology is the most reliable anthropological means for discovering the facts about past human cultures.

An archaeologist deals with four primary problems:

1. TYPOLOGY, the classification of excavated remains;
2. SPATIAL DISTRIBUTION of these materials;
3. DATING, the temporal distribution of archaeological materials; and
4. INFERENCE, or forming conclusions about certain aspects of culture and society from excavated remains.

TYPOLOGICAL CLASSIFICATION

Typology is the study of the forms and functions of archaeological objects and their relationships with other objects. Like other scientists, archaeologists can make use of the data they collect only after it has been made manageable through classification. The alternatives are chaos and the misinterpretation of evidence.

Classifications are made by human beings and thus are tailored to suit specific problems; their utility can be judged only in terms of these problems. Most archaeologists classify artifacts on the basis of function. In a prehistoric site, for example, the archaeologist will divide stone tools and implements into groups of axes, adzes, spear-points, etc., in order to make inferences concerning the economics and ecology of the population under investigation. If, however, the archaeologist faces a different problem—the historical development of stone tool types, for instance, or the historical relationships between two human cultures—he will classify his material in quite a different manner. In any case, the chosen system of classification is utilitarian; it is designed to facilitate further study.

SPATIAL DISTRIBUTION OF ARTIFACTS

Spatial distributions of artifacts yields further information regarding the culture of the people who made them. By grouping artifacts geographically, the archaeologist may be able to gain some understanding of a group's origins and prehistoric migrations. Often, he can pinpoint ancient trade routes or infer other kinds of contacts among specific prehistoric cultures. For example, a distinctive type of incised pottery found in Valdivia, Ecuador, and dating from about 3200 B.C., is amazingly similar to pottery made at about the same time in Japan,[1] which some archaeologists take as supportive evidence of prehistoric transoceanic contacts between cultures of the Old and New Worlds. Although archaeologists have not yet found conclusive evidence of long or continued Old World contacts in the prehistoric Americas, most admit—chiefly on the basis of the Valdivia pottery—that favorable winds and ocean currents might have carried an occasional Japanese fishing boat to the coast of Ecuador in pre-Columbian times.

When culture contact has occurred in prehistoric times, the spatial distribution of a given type of artifact can be used to date or cross-date archaeological sites. If objects of European manufacture are found, for example, in a certain stratum of an American site, archaeologists know at least that this stratum is not pre-Columbian.

ARCHAEOLOGICAL INFERENCE

Archaeological inference is the most subjective of the archaeologist's methods, but it is necessary if he is to describe the culture under study and not just the artifacts he has excavated. We have discussed in an earlier chapter the use of ethnographic analogy. If an archaeologist classifies a given object as a decorative earspool, he does so because he is aware that certain contemporary peoples use similar objects as earspools.

Inferences can also be made through experimentation. If an archaeologist does not know whether a given stone hand-ax might have been used to skin an antelope, he may be able to find out by trying to skin an antelope with it. Louis S. B. Leakey, Don Crabtree, Francois Bordes, and other imaginative archaeologists have experimented in this way. Crabtree, a specialist in stonemaking, can skin and butcher a bear using obsidian tools in less than two hours; it would require more than three hours with steel blades.

---

[1] Meggers, Betty J., *Prehistoric America.* Chicago: Aldine, 1972, pp. 35–36.

By specifying the sources of certain raw materials, the archaeologist can infer much about patterns of prehistoric trade. By
studying ancient animal remains, he can make sound inferences
about a group's ecological adaptation, patterns of subsistence,
and methods of butchering. He can, taking care to stay within
the limits of his evidence, make certain deductions about social
structure, kinship patterns, and even religious beliefs. Insights
into residential patterns can come from studying the floor plans
of ancient dwellings. If houses tend to be small, the archaeologist
assumes that in the society under investigation the nuclear family
was the basic residential unit; if dwellings tend to be large and
complex, he hazards the guess that extended families shared
the same accommodations. By comparing several dwellings

FIGURE 1. Polychrome murals from Bonampak offer rare insights into daily
life among the ancient Maya. (Courtesy Organization of American States,
United Fruit Company)

within a single prehistoric city or village, the archaeologist can determine whether a strong class distinction existed there in ancient times. This was the case in Central America, where elaborate Mayan temples are set apart from clustered huts. Even details of house construction can have social implications: at Machu Picchu, an ancient Inca city in Peru, several groups of dwellings appear to have been constructed with special care, suggesting that they were intended for nobility. Here too, altars and accompanying artifacts indicate that certain buildings served as ceremonial centers while others were used as residences, barracks, and jails.

In much the same way, art objects and burial patterns yield clues to the religious beliefs of ancient peoples. An ancient Mayan city at Bonampak in Central America has on its temple walls huge polychrome murals which serve as a prime source of information about Mayan costumes, customs, and ways of life. In one building, three rooms of wall paintings show the Mayas in scenes of classic importance: conferring with their priests, conducting raiding parties, taking captives and passing judgment on enemies, offering sacrifices to their gods, and celebrating sacred festivals. Egyptian tombs, rich in burial offerings, hint at the nature of the Egyptian view of the afterlife, while microscopic grains of ancient pollen found in Neanderthal burials suggest that the Neanderthals were the first to make grave offerings of flowers. Similarly, archaeologists infer that paintings found on the walls of caves in prehistoric Spain were of magical significance; the paintings depict hunted animals, and it is believed that they were made not for decoration but to bring luck to hunters who depended upon such animals for food.

DATING TECHNIQUES

A bone, fossil, or artifact whose age cannot be determined is of little scientific value. It becomes a mere museum curiosity, interesting enough on the shelf but sadly stripped of the clues that could place it in its proper context. Today every effort is made to deduce as accurately as possible the age of each archaeological discovery. Scientists often accomplish this in much the same way that geologists date rocks. We have seen that, on land or in water, geologic deposits are laid down in horizontal layers, one after the other. Each layer is older than the layers above it, and younger than those below, which leads one quite reasonably to expect that in undisturbed stratigraphy any fossil or artifact excavated from a given level must be older than objects found in levels above and younger than objects found in levels below. And if the task of dating skeletal remains and archaeological artifacts were indeed dispatched so simply, prehistorians could spend their summers lolling around their neighborhood swimming pools instead of hunching bleary-eyed over cluttered laboratory tables.

Frustrations abound when archaeological sites are disturbed through construction or careless digging, or when geologic deposits are disturbed through erosion, volcanic action, sliding, faulting, or other natural earth movement. Under conditions such as these, and to the dismay of those who dig for relics of the distant past, objects begin to wander into inappropriate layers. Intrusions (or intrusive burials), which occur when objects make their way into levels in which they do not belong, must be noted and dealt with, usually (but not always) through the application of trace-element tests.

Traditionally, archaeologists have recognized two distinct types of chronology: *relative* chronology and *absolute* chronology. An absolute date, of course, is one that may be expressed in years or other specific measures of time. Absolute dating techniques specify the number of years, or the amount of time, that has elapsed since the occurrence of a certain past event such as the making of a hand-ax or the death of an organism. Relative dates, on the other hand, specify no time lapse; they indicate only that an object in question is older or younger than another object. Numerous relative dating methods have been devised, the most common of which are listed below:

TYPOLOGICAL DATING.   This early technique, used in dating fossil material, considers the form or structure of the specimen with reference to the evolutionary trend toward greater complexity. The simpler forms are the most ancient, while complexity denotes more recent age. This is a comparative device, largely subjective.

Typological classification of artifacts may also help to date archaeological sites, which is often used with ceramic sequences. In regions where pottery has been in use for a long period of time, distinctive methods of manufacture are apparent as are decorative techniques and styles typical for different periods. Pottery can also be useful in cross-dating sites. If, for example, an absolute date is established for a particular site through dendrochronology, pottery found in that site may be dated approximately—and pottery at other sites can then be cross-dated according to style and method of manufacture. Cross-dating can also be accomplished with trade objects, as we have seen. Numerous Minoan sites have been dated through the presence of certain Egyptian trade objects.

FLUORINE ANALYSIS. This method provides relative dates for bone materials, indicating whether a given bone is of the same age, older, or more recent than another bone. Fluorine analysis, a trace-element test, depends upon the known fact that the chemical composition of buried bone changes through time. Bone takes from its burial medium (the soil) minute quantities of fluorine. Stated simply, the older the bone, the more fluorine it contains. The Galley Hill skeleton, discovered in England in 1888, was once credited with great age on the basis of the deposit in which it was found. In 1948, however, scientists demonstrated through fluorine analysis that Galley Hill represents an intrusive burial. The remains date from a relatively recent time in prehistory.

Although the archaeologist may have to settle for relative dates, he strives for absolute dates. Among the dating techniques which yield absolute dates are the following:

DENDROCHRONOLOGY. Tree-ring dating provides excellent seasonal records. A tree adds a new growth ring each year, and by counting the annual layers one discovers the age of the tree at the time it was cut down. Thus some trees—notably the redwoods in northern California—are known to be thousands of years old. Tree-rings vary in width and spacing according to the effects of moisture, temperature, and light, all of which vary seasonally. By comparing the tree-ring sequences of many trees in a given region, a master chart can be constructed to show the typical tree-ring sequence for that region. This chart may be extended back in time as progressively older trees are found whose tree-ring sequences overlap those of younger trees. While many people have been involved in dendrochronology, the system now in most common use was conceived by A. E. Douglass about 1913 at the University of Arizona. By about 1930 Douglass had developed dendrochronology into a highly useful methodology.

This method has been used primarily in the American southwest, where established tree-ring sequences extend back to the time of Christ. Beams found in excavated ruins are cut into cross-sections and compared with known tree-ring sequences. Archaeologists can thus establish the year in which the beam was cut and, by implication, the probable year of the construction of the building under investigation. By continually finding more beams, trees, or sizeable pieces of wood, and matching their innermost (earliest) ring sequences with the outermost

FIGURE 2.   Diagram illustrating how dendrochronological dating is accomplished. (Bryant Bannister, Laboratory of Tree-Ring Research, The University of Arizona, Tucson)

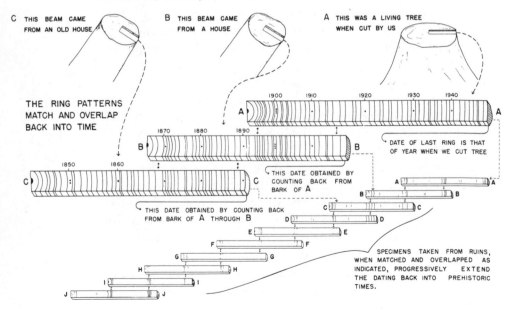

sequences (latest) of an earlier sample, the record can be dated backward as long as any lumber survives.

As it is currently constructed, the method depends on three conditions for its accuracy. First, it requires a fair amount of annual variation in rainfall; otherwise, all tree rings are the same size and no comparisons can be made. Secondly, the tree must not have tapped any permanent source of water, since when this occurs ring distinctions nearly disappear in warm climates. Trees near streams, ponds, springs, or underground water tables are generally useless. Finally, the climate should be warm and dry for best preservation. The usefulness of this method in the American southwest is thus explained.

While trees or beams preserved in mud, ice, or water should be usable, two problems have arisen in most such cases. First, for a variety of reasons, wood preserved in any of these media can seldom be tied to the locale in which it is found. Generally, they have come from other sources (through glacial movement, human transport, and so on). Secondly, not enough samples have been available to construct a continuous record.

VARVE ANALYSIS.   Like dendrochronology, varve analysis reflects seasonal variations. Varves are annual layers of sediment deposited by ice sheets in glacial lakes. During warm (summer) periods, melting glacial ice runs to the lake bottom, carrying coarse sediment with it. In colder (winter) periods, the lake freezes over, and melting ceases; fine sediment slowly sinks to the bottom of the lake, covering the layer of coarse sediment deposited earlier. Varves vary from less than a half-inch to more than fifteen inches in thickness, depending upon the warmth and duration of summer periods. Counting varves gives a date in years for the period of the melting and retreat of glaciers, and counting is done on the assumption that each varve equals one year, which is not always the case. Nevertheless, the technique has provided considerable accuracy for dating late Pleistocene and later sites in northern Europe. In Sweden and Finland, sequences have been established that extend back farther than 10,000 years B.C. Artifacts, of course, are unlikely to be found in glacial lakes, but estimates can be made of the possible range of human settlements for any given time period. Hence the method can be used to date bones or archaeological artifacts provided one knows the geography of the ice sheets at the time in question. Since these depositions of alternate kinds of sediment depend upon the annual freezing and melting of very large amounts of water, this method has been useful primarily in northern Europe. Developed in Sweden by Baron Gerare DeGeer in the 1870's, it is one of the oldest geochronologic dating methods.

ARCHAEOMAGNETISM OR PALEOMAGNETISM.   This recently developed technique depends upon the peculiarities of the earth's magnetic forces to yield dates from fired clay (if all facts are available) with an accuracy of within fifty years. When clay is fired, the magnetite and hemetite grains align with the magnetic field of the earth. If the approximate locale of firing is known, as well as the position and angle in which the object was fired, a date can be assigned by knowing at what time the magnetic field of the earth was in a matching plane. The restriction of this method is that the movement of the earth's magnetic center is neither wholly uniform nor entirely predictable; nor were records kept until recent times. Thus, while this is theoretically an exact method, it is in actual practice used primarily to confirm dates arrived at by other methods.

RADIOCARBON DATING (C-14).   The best known and most widely applied of all archaeological dating techniques is radiocarbon dating. This method is based upon the discovery that all living organisms, both plant and animal, contain a radioactive carbon known as carbon-14. Plants absorb this element from the atmosphere, while animals ingest it by eating plants or by eating other animals which have eaten plants.

The amount of carbon-14 present in a living plant or animal is known. Although some disintegration of radioactive carbon may occur during the life of an organism, it is balanced by the intake of C-14; thus in a living organism the amount of radioactive carbon remains relatively constant. After the organism dies, however, no additional carbon-14 is taken in, and disintegration of carbon-14 proceeds at a steady rate. Since the rate of disintegration is known, it is possible to date the time of death of various organic materials by the amount of radioactive carbon remaining. Charcoal is the most desirable material for C-14 analysis; shell, bone, seeds, wood, and so forth, may be subjected to the test but are less reliable.

Radiocarbon dating is not foolproof, and dates obtained by the C-14 analysis include a standard deviation, or margin for error; thus a site may be dated as $1,000 \pm 50$ years. Sometimes a sample is contaminated, for example when there occurs an accidental decrease or increase of C-14 following the time of death. Early atomic research tests conducted in the state of Nevada so significantly raised radiation levels that samples being processed as far away as Chicago were rendered useless. The same problem arises with other radioactive dating methods, including the usually reliable potassium-argon as well as those using the transformation of thorium to lead, uranium to lead, and rubidium to strontium. Ideally, archaeological samples are protected from the very instant they are discovered; they are sealed immediately in lead containers and rushed to process in specially constructed laboratories. Such protective measures are seldom practical, however, and the hard-working archaeologist, habitually pressed for both time and money, does the best he can by quickly wrapping his samples in aluminum foil and placing them in sealed glass jars. Whatever the limitations, radioactive dating techniques are the best tools we have so far for determining the age of geological and archaeological specimens—at least within a range of 60,000 years.

POTASSIUM-ARGON DATING (K-40). This method, mentioned above, is based on the fact that a radioactive form of potassium decays at a given rate to form and release argon, enabling scientists to date the ages of numerous rocks by measuring the potassium-argon ratios. The primary advantage of the potassium-argon technique is that it can be used to date sites older than those which fall into the 60,000-year carbon-14 range. More recent archaeological sites must be dated by methods other than K-40, as this technique is used chiefly for sites dating to 500,000 or more years ago. *Zinjanthropus,* the famous fossil found by L. S. B. Leakey at Olduvai Gorge, was dated at 1,750,000 years through application of the potassium-argon test. In effect, this method dates the time that has elapsed since the molecular structure of a mineral was last disturbed by any kind of intense heat. Volcanic refuse is the most complete and common case of minerals reformed from igneous material. An example is volcanic ash (tuff) deposited over the remains of a campsite: dating the volcanic ash also dates the campsite fairly closely. The limitation on the method is that the rate of argon loss varies from mineral to mineral. The accuracy of the date depends upon accurate knowledge of the loss rate in the mineral being dated.

While the theories which involve using trace elements to determine age are relatively simple, results of applications have failed to yield consistent figures. Difficulties arise from contamination, from unresolved questions regarding the original state of the earth and its chemical constituents, and from the purely mechanical uncertainties in the use of infinitely small samples of material. The chief limitations arise from the fact that dates derived from small samples or areas cannot be related meaningfully to their surroundings.

The C-14 test has been criticized on the basis of the many inconsistent and obviously incorrect dates derived. Discrepancies may stem from contamination, but archaeologists must also consider the possibility that the original hypothesis underlying the method is invalid; it has been suggested that the rate of C-14 production has not in fact been constant over the last tens of thousands of years. So far, the potassium-argon method has yielded results that are much more consistent.

Whatever the limitations of the trace-element tests, radioactive dating techniques will continue to be used and improved upon. With advances being made continually in atomic research, we can expect that, in the future, dating techniques will be applied with increasing consistency and reliability, and that reasonable explanations will be found for most of the current discrepancies.

Some other techniques should be mentioned here. Pollen analysis, while not used primarily as a dating technique, provides valuable records of ecological conditions to which man had to adjust at different times in the past. And examination of associated fauna may provide clues to chronology, particularly when extinct forms are found. It is the goal of the archaeologist to reconstruct as fully as possible the total life of early man—and such details as available flora and fauna add depth to the study.

In recent years, several new methods have been added. *Thermoluminescence* (TL), first developed by Kennedy and Knopff just over ten years ago, depends upon the fact that pottery traps a relatively fixed number of electons each year. Heating the piece releases these electrons which, in an excited state, emit a low level of luminescence as they enter the atmosphere. By measuring the intensity of this glow and then calculating the number of electrons released, one can estimate the time since the last firing (that is, when the piece was originally made). Quite recently, *obsidian hydration dating* has begun to look like a viable method in light of the work of Joseph Michels at Pennsylvania State University. Obsidian is volcanic glass which usually contains less than 0.3 percent water by weight and tends to adsorb water from the surrounding air or soil, forming a film of molecular thickness. A process of diffusion then begins: when viewed through a microscope water drawn from the surface film appears to advance into the obsidian as a sharply demarcated front. The depth of this layer is used to determine the time that the surface has been exposed. Obsidian found in conjunction with habitation sites has generally been fractured in some way to make it useful as a tool or weapon. This exposes one or more

FIGURE 3. Obsidian hydration dating. Mother piece of obsidian and slice cut from it for study of its hydration level under a microscope. (William M. Rosenthal)

surfaces, thus making it possible to determine the date of manufacture. This method depends for its accuracy upon fair amount of knowledge about past weather, since ambient temperature affects the hydration rate.

SITE SELECTION

Before a site can be excavated and analyzed, of course, it must be located, and this is not always easy since most archaeological materials are buried. Burial is often deliberate, as in the case of human burials and grave offerings. Other times burial results from dramatic natural causes, as at Pompeii, where the entire city was covered with lava and ashes from a volcanic explosion; or burial can result when a scene of human activity is covered by a tidal wave, by a river as it changes course, or by flood deposits of alluvium or silt. More frequently burial is the natural result of human change. Archaeologists often find that one culture after another has settled on a single site, erecting crude campsites or elaborate cities upon the ruins and refuse of earlier peoples. Modern Mexico City is built upon the site of ancient Tenochtitlán, the treasure-laden Aztec capital that was at its peak five times the size of sixteenth-century London. (See Figure 4, Chapter XI.)

Nature itself can camouflage the most massive structures. This has been the case for many of the immense Mayan temples of Central America. Beginning around 900 A.D., the Mayan Empire began to disintegrate in an abandonment process which took less than a century. While the reasons are still very much in dispute, the most acceptable guess is that the environment in which Mayan culture reached maturity—the tropical lowlands of Mesoamerica—ultimately proved too hostile for continued habitation (Meggers, 1972). Whatever the reasons, city after city was abandoned. Large-scale public projects were left partially completed, and the quality of pottery and art declined. A few survivors lingered—at least for a time—trying in vain to prolong a vanished way of life; then they moved on as well. Year by year the lianas crept closer until the great stone cities, shrouded in dense vegetation, were lost from sight. In numerous instances, the encroaching jungle camouflaged entire prehistoric cities.

More than eighty percent of all archaeological sites come to light by accident. Ruins or artifacts may be found by farmers plowing their fields or by laborers in the course of construction. Numerous important ruins were discovered in Mexico City by municipal workers building a vast subway system; and some of the richest archaeological treasures in the Valley of Mexico were unearthed by peasants constructing simple irrigation ditches for their farms. Mining often gives the archaeologist a chance to see what lies beneath the earth's surface, as does the construction of roads, pipelines, and other building. Fishermen and divers may report the finding of artifacts from underwater sites. Numerous other sites have come to light through natural exposure. Torrential rains and pounding surf sometimes expose ancient remains, and, in sandy prairie regions, wind erosion may reveal bones and artifacts.

On the other hand, archaeologists may actively look for sites where they believe relics may be found, particularly in caves or at strategic locations on rivers or other bodies of water. Aerial photography has proved in recent years an important tool for archaeologists searching for the remains of ancient cultures.

FIGURE 4. Aerial photo of a portion of the Tehuacan Valley of Mexico. The short, dark parallel lines are prehistoric agricultural terrace systems which allowed water and soil to build up behind rock alignments. Aerial mapping is the only efficient way of recording these devices. (Courtesy George J. Gumerman, Department of Anthropology, Southern Illinois University at Carbondale)

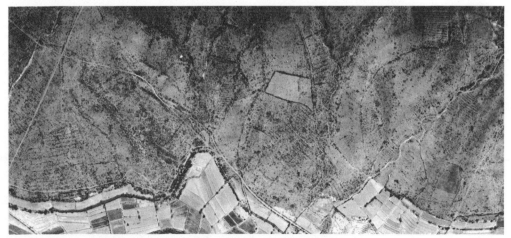

Aerial photographs effectively "chart" large regions, revealing a pattern of earthworks or other evidence not discernible at ground level. Buried structures tend to encourage differential plant growth, and the presence of archaeological materials can cause a marked difference in the color of soil.

Salvage archaeology leads to discoveries by a different route. When the building of dams or reservoirs will result in the flooding of a previously inhabited area, archaeologists often rush out to salvage what they can before the area becomes inaccessible.

Old documents or written reports may lead archaeologists to a site rich in archaeological remains. Copán, a majestic ruined Mayan city in northern Honduras, was found in 1836 when an amateur archaeologist, John Lloyd Stephens, came across an old military report that described strange stone ruins in the wilds of Guatemala. The report was brief and exceedingly dry, offering scant information, but it was sufficient to send Stephens deep into Central America. He took with him his friend Frederick Catherwood, a skilled draftsman whose precise sketches of pre-historic architecture are still admired.

The two men plunged into the heart of a country torn by a bloody three-way civil war, and they narrowly averted disaster when they encountered an aggressive band of drunken soldiers. On muleback, dodging snakes and rival armies, they crossed into northern Honduras to find Copán, a vast ruined city whose monumental buildings and elaborate sculptures exceeded Stephens' wildest expectations. And Copán was just the beginning. Stephens and Catherwood moved on into Guatemala, Chiapas, and Yucatán, finding along the way numerous other Mayan sites that had previously gone unreported. By the end of their long and productive trek through the Mesoamerican wilderness, they had explored forty-four ancient cities. In 1842, Stephens published his *Incidents of Travel in Central America, Chiapas, and Yucatán.* The book, abundantly illustrated with Catherwood's masterful sketches, captured the attention of scholars throughout the world and began a new era of New World archaeology.

Myth, legend, and rumor are other guides that can lead the archaeologist to a likely site. Many native peoples tell legends of rich prehistoric cities, and sometimes these tales turn out to be true. In 1911, Hiram Bingham was lured to Peru by tantalizing rumors of a fabulous lost city located somewhere to the northwest of Cuzco. He discovered Machu Picchu, the fabled granite city built by the Incas and abandoned more than 400 years ago.

EXCAVATION PROCEDURES

Once a site has been located and chosen for excavation, archaeologists stake it out in a grid plan, dividing the area into numbered squares. A fixed point, known as the datum point, is established on or near the site, and designated with a durable marker of steel or cement; the datum point guides workers in future excavations and provides a reference point for excavations under way.

A scale map of the area is then prepared, and preliminary test pits or trenches are dug. Ideally, photographs are taken from

FIGURE 5.   Excavation of a seventeenth-century farmhouse site near Kingston, Massachusetts, showing grid lines. (Plimoth Plantation Photo)

different vantage points at every step of the excavation. When a bone or artifact is uncovered, it is photographed, numbered, cataloged, and listed in a master register. Before it is removed, its exact position and depth are noted on the grid. All objects taken from the site are placed in durable bags and labeled with identifying numbers. Such care is mandatory: once an object is removed from the site, it can never be viewed again within the context of the site. Exact measurements and notations must be made so that none of the full evidence can be lost.

FIGURE 6. An Indian village excavation in the Snake River, Washington, showing a fairly advanced stage of digging. (Beckerman, Editorial Photocolor Archives)

Often, sites are stratified, and archaeologists assume that objects found in lower strata are older than objects found nearer the surface. This assumption is made, however, with constant reference to the possibility of disturbance. Faulting, sliding, frost heaving, and burrowing by animals can all disturb the stratigraphy of a site. Evidence of these natural forces is carefully noted.

Archaeologists are equally careful to record spatial distributions of materials found in the course of excavation. Objects found together presumably originate in the same time period, although exceptions—as in the case of preserved heirlooms or other antiquities—are known.

Ideally, the archaeologist relies on a brace of experts to aid in accurate interpretation of the site. Animal bones and plant remains are collected for expert analysis to determine types of animals and plants domesticated or collected by the site's prehistoric inhabitants. Logs, beams, bits of charcoal, and other materials are collected for use in dating the site. Casts and molds are made of perishable objects, and tracings or rubbings are made if any carvings are found in excavation. Chemists, physicists, zoologists, geologists, paleontologists, and numerous other experts may descend upon the site to contribute their varied skills—at least in theory. In practice, time and money are generally limited, and the archaeologist often finds himself doing the work of a dozen experts in related fields. Still, he takes care to preserve excavated materials so that if funds later become available he can draw upon the skills of others to expand or support his conclusions. Fieldwork comprises by far the briefest portion of an archaeologist's investigation; he may study the materials he has excavated, together with his records of excavation, for a number of seasons after he has completed his fieldwork. During this time he may turn to various consultants for aid in identification or interpretation of evidence gathered.

It is important to remember that to excavate a site is to destroy it. This is the reason for the painstaking procedures and detailed records developed in archaeology. It is only because such methods have been devised that archaeologists have been able to construct the rough history of culture outlined in the following chapter.

FURTHER READINGS

Chang, K. C. *Rethinking Archaeology*. New York: Random House, 1967.

Daniel, Glyn. *The Origins and Growth of Archaeology*. Baltimore: Penguin Books, 1967.

Dunnell, Robert C. *Systematics in Prehistory*. New York: Free Press, 1971.

Fagan, Brian M. *In the Beginning*. Boston: Little, Brown, 1972.

Heizer, Robert F. and Sherburne F. Cook. *The Application of Quantitative Methods of Archaeology*. New York: Wenner-Gren Foundation, 1960.

Heizer, Robert F. and John A. Graham. *A Guide to Field Methods in Archaeology*. Palo Alto: National Press, 1967.

Hole, Frank and Robert R. Heizer. *An Introduction to Prehistoric Archaeology*, 2nd ed. New York: Holt, Rinehart & Winston, 1969.

Kenyon, Kathleen M. *Beginning in Archaeology*. New York: Praeger, 1968.

Meggers, Betty J. *Prehistoric America*. Chicago: Aldine, 1972.

Meighan, Clement W. *Archaeology: An Introduction*. San Francisco: Chandler, 1966.

Paor, Liam de. *Archaeology: An Illustrated Introduction*. Baltimore: Pelican Books, 1969.

Rapport, Samuel and Helen Wright, (eds.). *Archaeology*. New York: Washington Square Press, 1964.

Trigger, Bruce G. *Beyond History: the Methods of Prehistory*. New York: Holt, Rinehart & Winston, 1968.

CHAPTER X

STUDIES IN
CULTURE PREHISTORY

Tools and implements, which are often the only available evidence for early man, are immensely important to the archaeologist. Prehistorians in fact have long viewed archaeological evidence in terms of a complex evolutionary system of human toolmaking. This system, introduced in 1836 by Christian J. Thomsen, divided all of human prehistory into three great ages: the Stone Age, the Bronze Age, and the Iron Age. Since Thomsen's time, of course, the system has been expanded, modified, and refined, but human toolmaking ability remains a trait of monumental interest to prehistorians since it reflects numerous other attributes that are uniquely human.

IMPLICATIONS OF HUMAN TOOLMAKING

What are the biological implications of patterned toolmaking? Certainly man's upright posture frees his hands for the manipulation of objects and, consequently, for the manufacture of tools and implements. The latter requires clear vision, good depth perception, and manual dexterity. The manufacture of regular, patterned tools also implies the knowledge and use of language, which permits the transmission of culture from one individual to another and from each generation to the next.

Apparently, tool use was increasingly important in later human development; although scientists cannot reconstruct a step-by-step chronology, most agree that habitual tool use had great social and biological implications. Many experts believe that the trend toward greater brain size may have resulted—at least in part—from the pressure to become progressively more selective in the use of tools. This larger, more complex brain played a crucial role in the evolution of speech, and speech, in turn, made possible the transmission of knowledge regarding specific patterns and traditions of toolmaking. Theoretically, at least, more complex tool traditions would have led to the acquisition of larger and more varied food supplies, which would have made possible the existence of larger social units.

Much of what we have learned about the earliest human cultures is based on the analysis of stone tools. The emphasis on stone is inevitable, for although early man used wood, bone, horn, and other materials in toolmaking. It is stone which survives best and which therefore comprises the bulk of evidence for early man.

The Technology of Tools

The earliest human tools were quite crude, and it is not always easy to determine whether a particular specimen was deliberately fashioned by man. Flint, which was often used by ancient man, is easily fractured by rapid temperature changes, glacial action, frost, and other natural means. Indeed, many of the so-called eoliths, or "dawn stones," which graced nineteenth-century collections have turned out to be derived from strata greatly predating the appearance of man on earth. While we cannot be positive that a stone was deliberately fractured, purposely fractured stones do have certain characteristics. Finding more than one such stone in the same area decreases the probability of chance factors to almost zero. Kenneth Oakley, a leading authority on the subject, describes such a fracture:

> (The) surface of a fracture due to a sharp external blow appears clean-cut, and shows a definite bulb of percussion with faint radial fissures and ripples originating at a point on the edge of the flake or flake-scar.[1]

Archaeologists do not always find it easy to determine the original functions of tools unearthed in excavation; but they make inferences on the basis of ethnographic analogy, through practical experimentation, or through analysis of the archae-

---

[1] Oakley, Kenneth, *Man the Tool-maker*. Chicago: University of Chicago Press, 1964, p. 17.

ological context from which specimens are recovered. Among the most recognizable of stone tools are *choppers* (probably used for butchering meat and scraping animal hides), *knives, hand-axes, scrapers* (which generally show marks of wear only on one side), *projectile points, burins* or *gravers,* and *drills* (boring instruments typified by a narrow, bit-like end).

BUR′ IN
a flint blade,
one end of
which has a
wide, sharp
chisel edge.

Toolmaking demands not only manual control and coordination but also a thorough knowledge of the materials used. What happens when a stone craftsman attempts to chip a stone? Depending, of course, on the materials selected for use, the stone may crumble; it may fracture along the lines of its crystalline structure, as in the case of such quartzes as jasper and chalcedony; or it may split smoothly in what is called a fracture plane, leaving visible concentric rings on the split surface at or around the point of impact. Obsidian and flint were favored by prehistoric toolmakers because they split in the latter fashion. But for the most part early man used what was available to him; if he could not easily obtain these types of stone, he made do with less suitable materials.

Chipped tools are fashioned by percussion (direct and indirect) or pressure methods. Among the direct percussion techniques are the following:

HAMMERSTONE. The worker holds a nodule of hard stone in one hand and strikes it with a rock—the hammerstone—held in his other hand.

HAMMER-AND-ANVIL. The toolmaker places the target stone on a rock, which serves as an anvil; when the target stone is struck with a hammerstone there occurs an instantaneous rebound of the anvil and, ideally, the desired fracture.

BAR METHOD. The artisan uses a hammer of wood or bone in place of the hammerstone, striking off broad, shallow flakes.

BLOCK-ON-BLOCK. Flakes are dislodged when a stone is struck against the sharp edge of a larger, stationary rock.

It might be well here to distinguish between core and flake tools. Core tools are those which result when a stone has been trimmed so that it has assumed the desired shape. Flake tools are those fashioned from one of the flakes struck from the core.

Direct percussion techniques can produce excellent, sharp-edged tools. Early man found, however, that he could reduce the impact of the blow and produce much finer work through indirect percussion. In this process, he inserts an intermediate punch between the hammerstone and the stone that is to be worked. In skilled hands, the intermediate punch yields improved implements. For even finer work, the artisan may push or pry small flakes off by pressing with an appropriate instrument. The technique is called *pressure flaking*.

FIGURE 1. Techniques of preparing stone tools. (a) Percussion with a hammerstone. (b) Percussion against a stationary anvil. (c) Bar method. (d) Pressure flaking. (Adapted from F. Clark Howell and editors of Time-Life Books, *Early Man,* New York: Time-Life, 1965.)

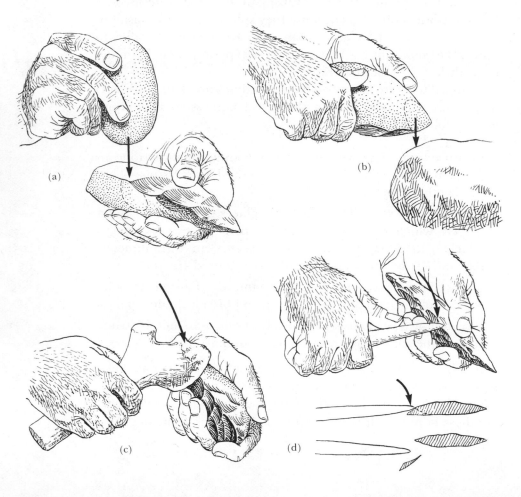

In addition to percussion and pressure methods, tools may be ground or pecked, and polished. Grinding, of course, is tedious and time-consuming, though it may be expedited if it can be done under water, which acts as a natural lubricant. Pecking is a method of pounding, and this technique is used for the same types of stone as grinding. Pecking, however, yields a rougher surface in the finished implement. Both pecking and grinding were used most often on noncrystalline and composite rocks that fracture along even lines of cleavage.

Many stone tools excavated by archaeologists originally had hafts. Some Upper Paleolithic axes have holes drilled through them for hafting; and projectile points often have distinctive notches, tangs, or stems by which they probably were attached to a spear or arrow shaft.

Culture and Human Behavior

By examining man-made objects closely, archaeologists infer their purpose, the manner in which they were made and used, and to a certain extent, the degree of intelligence necessary to make them. In essence, artifacts reflect the degree of culture or civilization possessed by the people who manufactured them.

In building a knowledge of early human populations, we are particularly concerned with artifacts found in direct association with human skeletal remains, and we will be concerned in this section primarily with the cultural evidence associated with fossil populations on which we have already focused. Thus the time-span covered in this chapter is limited to the Pleistocene.

Unfortunately, the early representatives of ancient human populations did not anticipate our eagerness to learn about them. Some populations left behind meager skeletal remains, with no cultural evidence whatsoever, while other populations are represented solely by cultural artifacts. The result is an inadequacy in the cultural record that exists despite the diligent efforts of determined archaeologists. There is actually no dearth of relics, but the abundance is hopelessly one-sided right now, consisting chiefly of stone and bone objects. Few articles of clothing, fabrics, skins, housing materials, basketry, or fashioned wood have survived. Obviously, this leaves considerable blanks in our knowl-

edge of the cultural life of early man. But as in the case of
skeletal remains, archaeologists strive constantly to narrow gaps,
and each year additional material comes to light.

A number of prehistorians have argued that the nature of
the material available for stone tools had great influence on
the types of tools produced by early populations. However, there
is abundant evidence to the contrary. One of the most remarkable
facts revealed in the study of prehistoric culture is the constancy
of tool types irrespective of materials locally available.

Another erroneous but widely held view is that the making
of stone tools and implements was a time-consuming and laborious process. The implication is that early man, unhampered

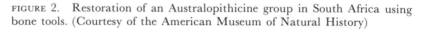

FIGURE 2. Restoration of an Australopithicine group in South Africa using
bone tools. (Courtesy of the American Museum of Natural History)

by the complexities of modern civilization, had plenty of time on his hands. This view of Paleolithic life is far from realistic; early man was totally dependent for survival on his success in hunting, trapping, and gathering wild edibles. From studies made of contemporary native peoples, archaeologists realize that this is not an easy life: individuals fight a constant battle with nature, using their total time and energies in an endless struggle to wrest sufficient food supplies from an often hostile environment. Australian groups, some of whom still have almost Paleolithic cultures, provide an excellent example, as do certain South American tribal groups, and many contemporary Eskimo groups.

Such groups should not, of course, be viewed as analogous

FIGURE 3.   Restoration of a Middle Pleistocene family using Abbevillian tools. (Courtesy of the American Museum of Natural History)

to Paleolithic peoples for at least two reasons. First, their environments are usually less than optimal, and long-term development cannot be like that of Paleolithic Europeans on fertile land in a moderate climate. In addition, elements of culture less dependent on environment (kinship, music, religion) are almost certainly changed since the Paleolithic. While Eskimos and some South American native people cannot be seen as preserved Paleolithics, a careful investigation can isolate some similarities.

Clearly, if the making of stone implements had required many hours of work, early humans would have starved to death, leaving no ancestors to populate the earth. To the contrary, the making of implements from stone is a relatively simple matter of controlling the fracture; once the basic technique is mastered, the actual making of a stone tool is a fairly rapid process. Numerous anthropologists have found that they can produce a functional stone tool in a matter of minutes.

Since stone is the most durable material used by early man, ancient cultures are classified according to stone implements recovered from sites. In culture prehistory, we use certain terminology to indicate the development of culture: the term *Paleolithic,* or *Old Stone Age,* for example, represents the time which coincides with the geological epoch *Pleistocene;* and cultural periods within the Paleolithic are named for the stone industries which occurred or evolved within that larger block of time.

The Paleolithic is commonly divided into three parts: the Lower Paleolithic (extending from the beginning of the Pleistocene to the third, or Riss, glaciation, a relatively lengthy span of time); the Middle Paleolithic (squeezed between the Riss and Wurm glaciations); and the Upper Paleolithic (beginning at the peak of the Wurm glaciation and ending with the termination of the Pleistocene). The entire time span is nearly three million years.

The Lower Paleolithic

Long before stone tools first appeared in Europe, African hominids were using crude pebble tools, each of which had a jagged cutting edge where a few flakes had been struck off. These tools, the earliest known, are called *choppers* or, because they are the most common tools found in Bed I at Olduvai Gorge, *Oldowan* tools. They also appear however at sites in South Africa, the Transvaal, Kenya, Algeria, Morocco, and Abyssinia—in fact, in most parts of the African continent.

Similar choppers were made and used by *Homo erectus* in Asia; they appear in sites in China, Burma, Indonesia, and India. Even a few early European sites, such as Swanscombe, Clacton-on-Sea, and Verteszollos, have yielded tools relatively similar to those of Africa and Asia in the early Pleistocene.

In Africa the versatile chopper gradually gave rise to the hand-ax, a pear-shaped core tool. As we have seen, a core tool is fashioned by removing flakes from a stone until the desired shape has been achieved, while flake tools are made from flakes previously removed from the core. Early man used both types, although he often favored one over the other; that is, industries often demonstrate a greater percentage of core tools than flake tools, or vice-versa.

In any case, hand-axes were fashioned so as to have a continuous jagged cutting edge all along one side; they were not hafted to handles but were held in the hand by the non-fractured side; they were all-purpose tools, used for cutting, butchering, scraping, and digging. The hand-ax had a wide geographic distribution in Africa, western Europe, and India, and specimens from widespread regions are remarkably consistent.

Archaeologists are not yet able to pinpoint the place of origin of the stone hand-ax, but it is generally believed that this versatile tool originated in Africa, spreading into Europe and India during Lower Pleistocene times. Inexplicably, the hand-ax did not extend into eastern Asia, where the chopper continued to serve as the characteristic Lower Paleolithic stone tool.

In Europe, early stone hand-axes are called *Abbevillian*, after Abbeville, a French site from which such tools were excavated. More refined hand-axes of a later period are called *Acheulean*, after the site at St. Acheul, France. An extension of the Abbevillian, the Acheulean begins in the middle of the second interglacial and extends into the Middle Paleolithic. Man obviously acquired new mastery over stone in the Acheulean stage. Hand-axes from this period tend to be flatter and more evenly flaked, with more functional cutting edges. They also exhibit

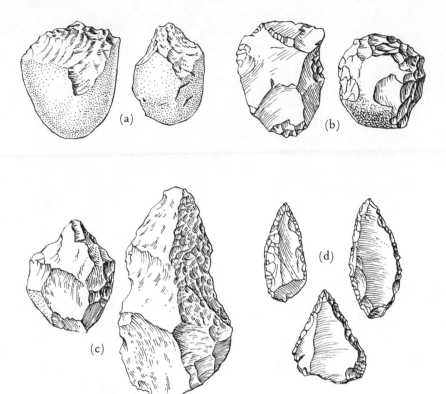

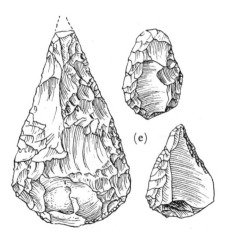

FIGURE 4. Lower Paleolithic
tools. (a) Oldowan chopping
tools. (b) Chopping tools from
Choukoutien, China. (c) Abbevillian hand-axes. (d) Acheulean hand-ax and sidescrap-
ers. (e) Levalloisian points.

greater variety: the cleaver, also bifacially worked but possessing a wide cutting edge, was introduced and its use spread.

It was during the Acheulean period that a new technique, called the *Levalloisian,* was developed for the making of flake tools by a special method of core preparation in which the core is carefully trimmed and shaped to resemble a tortoise shell. Small flakes are then removed from the perimeter of the tortoise core, and these flakes are reworked into a variety of scrapers and points. The Levalloisian technique, which was perhaps man's first attempt at mass production, spread through Europe, the Near East, southwest Asia, and Africa. And no wonder: flakes dislodged from the specially prepared striking platform were larger, more symmetrical, and more utilitarian than those removed in the old random method. Apparently, the Levalloisian technique was invented independently at a number of sites where man habitually worked with flint. Flakes made in the Levalloisian manner have been found at sites in Africa, Europe, and North America.

The people who lived in the Lower Paleolithic were not sedentary but wandered from place to place in search of game and other food. They camped on the edges of rivers and lakes but, as evidenced by extremely thin archaeological deposits, did not remain very long at any single site. There are no extensive refuse deposits and no burial areas, either of which would indicate lengthy human habitation. Most of the evidence consists of stone implements left behind on the erratic trails of prehistoric nomads. From butchered animal remains, we know that Lower Paleolithic hunters preyed on both small game and such larger animals as elephants and rhinoceros. The use of fire during this ancient period is known in Europe, at Verteszollos, and in China, at Choukoutien; but there is no evidence of its use in Africa until the latter part of the Acheulean period.

THE MIDDLE PALEOLITHIC

The Middle Paleolithic does not differ sharply in the cultural sense from the preceding period. There is a continuation of the industries described for Lower Paleolithic times, and the Acheulean and the Levalloisian are found throughout the third interglacial. Changes in these kinds of stone tools did take place, but such modifications were generally no more than a sophistication or refinement of technique. Tools from the Middle Paleolithic do tend to be smaller and more refined, with some special developments such as the crude triangular points which appear first—so far as we know—at a site near Ehringdorf, Germany. These, of course, are the earliest projectile points.

Among the early Middle Paleolithic industries is the *Tayacian*, a little-known but important stone industry limited to a few scattered sites in France and Spain. Tayacian tools tend to be crude and simple, chiefly represented by rough flakes reminiscent of the earlier period. The importance of this industry is in its association with the fragmentary cranial remains from Fontechevade. This association, as well as the early date for such modern skeletal remains, is an enigma.

The *Mousterian* is quite a different matter, for it is associated with the remains of *Homo sapiens neanderthalensis,* a population archaeologists know well through an excellent accumulation of skeletal evidence. Sites in Europe and the Near East are generally located within rock shelters or caves. Tools include small, heart-shaped hand-axes, triangular points, side scrapers, and some simple bone awls (penetrating tools). It is interesting to note that in some European sites and in sites in Palestine, the Mousterian combines with the Levalloisian, and is characterized by the production of Mousterian-like tools made from Levalloisian

FIGURE 5. Middle Paleolithic tools: Mousterian scrapers.

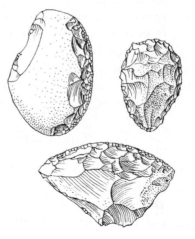

flakes. Bone is used some, but not as frequently as in Upper Paleolithic times.

During parts of the Middle Paleolithic, the weather turned extremely cold as glaciers moved across northern Europe. Neanderthal man began to hunt such cold-weather animals as reindeer and cave bears. Certainly, Neanderthal knew and used fire, and, judging from the many scrapers found among his tools, he fended off the cold with clothing made from animal skins. From skeletal remains unearthed at such sites as Krapina and MonteCirceo, archaeologists believe that at least some Neanderthals were cannibalistic.

The Neanderthals, on the other hand, were the first people known to bury their dead, though they did not do so consistently. Numerous Neanderthal bones have been found, mixed with animal remains, at the backs of habitation caves. But at other sites, graves were dug, and buried with the dead were grave offerings which included hand-axes, shells, Mousterian flints, sets of animal bones or horns and, often, blankets of wildflowers. The frequent use of grave offerings suggests that Neanderthal man had some notion of an afterlife; and while archaeologists are reluctant to speculate beyond their evidence, there are other implications of religious beliefs to be found at Neanderthal sites, specifically collections of bear skulls, often arranged in groups and surrounded by low stone walls or placed in special niches carved in the cave walls. Are these symbols of hunting magic practiced by people who depended for their survival upon success in the hunt—or relics of a prehistoric bear cult similar to those practiced in fairly recent times by American Indians? We may never know for sure, but what we can infer is that the deliberate Neanderthal burials and grave offerings provide archaeologists with their earliest evidence for human religious beliefs and practices. Further evidence of magico-religious beliefs appears more frequently in the Upper Paleolithic.

The Upper Paleolithic

Following the first peak of the Wurm glaciation in Europe and the rest of the Old World, a notable change occurred in the production of stone tools. Ancient man made his greatest cultural progress during this period. The Upper Paleolithic witnessed the replacement of Neanderthal man by *Homo sapiens sapiens,* who still made and used stone tools—but with a new and different emphasis.

Blades (long, narrow flakes struck from cores), burins (chisels produced by striking small spawls at forty-five-degree angles from the ends of flakes or blades), and bone tools reached maximum production toward the end of the Upper Paleolithic. Evidence of actual dwellings begins to appear. Semi-subterranean pit houses were used in central Europe, southern Russia, and Siberia. Such living accommodations suggest the development of a more complex social life and represent a new life-style for Upper Paleolithic peoples who looked very much as we do today. Compared with what we have seen for earlier times, where basic cultural similarity was the rule, it is interesting to note the great cultural diversification typical of the closing phases of the Paleolithic.

The single hold-over from the Middle Paleolithic is the Mousterian, characterized in the Upper Paleolithic by better technical development and several local industries. The essential tools include triangular points, side scrapers and other types of flake tools, small hand-axes, some simple bone tools, and—for the first time—rare blades and burins.

The disappearance of the Neanderthals and their culture occurred sometime during the first interstadial of the Wurm glaciation. No one knows what happened, and the only evidence we have is negative: Neanderthal burials, so prevalent before, are no longer to be found; and although certain elements of the Mousterian industry continued in later Upper Paleolithic industries, the true Mousterian ceased to exist when its founders disappeared.

At one time, many prehistorians thought invasions by other people and a massacre of the Neanderthals accounted for the transition. Now, as further evidence is discovered, it seems increasingly likely that Neanderthals simply evolved rapidly at this point. A large number of intermediate fossils is being uncovered, and these indicate that, toward the end of the Lower Paleolithic, the Neanderthals were showing very great individual variation anyway. It is still possible that more advanced people also moved in as the ice sheet withdrew and the climate became warmer.

The earliest Upper Paleolithic industry associated with the appearance of *sapiens* populations is the *Perigordian*. It has been recognized in sites dating from the first interstadial (contemporary with the Mousterian) and continues until the peak of the third advance of the Wurm glaciation. The early tool assemblage is essentially limited to southern France and includes large blades, burins, scrapers, and simple bone tools. Similar tool types have been found in Palestine, and there are some who believe that the origin of the European Perigordian—as well as of the people who produced it—should be placed somewhere in the Middle East.

As we trace the development of the Perigordian into the later phases of the Upper Paleolithic, we can see dynamic changes in basic tool types. First, the industry spread from its initial beginnings to a general European distribution. The large blades gave way to smaller blades with narrower backs, to a variety of specialized burins, and to tanged (stemmed) points that have been made from blades. Human skeletal remains are associated at a number of sites and are classified, without question, as *Homo sapiens sapiens.*

Another early and more widespread Upper Paleolithic culture was the *Aurignacian,* whose stone technology is characterized by an abundance of flake scrapers and burins. The single feature that most obviously distinguishes the Aurignacian from the Perigordian is the frequent use of bone in the former, in such implements as split-base bone points, pins, awls, gouges, and chisels. In addition, bone needles and items of personal adornment (necklaces of pierced teeth and shells decorated with bits of bone) are important elements in the Aurignacian assemblage. Aurignacian industries have been located over a wide area from Afghanistan and Iraq to France, Germany, and Spain, and their appearance in the European archaeological record seems abrupt, as if those responsible for it had migrated in from elsewhere in the Old World.

Art as we know it made its first appearance in the European Aurignacian, and Aurignacian art is impressive. Stylized profile drawings of numerous animals, together with paintings of hands,

FIGURE 6.   A more sophisticated cave painting of the Upper Paleolithic from the roof of the Altamira cave in Northern Spain showing a bison above and a galloping bear below. (The Bettmann Archive)

adorn Aurignacian cave walls. The earliest cave paintings in western Europe, including the early ones at Lascaux, are attributed to this culture. Obviously, these accurate and beautiful representations of animals served a magic or religious function; many animals are depicted with spears sticking in them, apparently to represent the success that the hunters wished for. In a great many cases, these drawings are found far inside caves which means that the artist was often required to assume awkward working positions in small spaces. On numerous occasions, more recent paintings are found to have been superimposed over older ones. For these and a variety of other reasons, it is very probable that much or all of this cave art represents more than the release of aesthetic expression. Because of the short burning time of most torches, the resultant trapped smoke, and the hidden hazards, hominids appear never to have penetrated caves much beyond the mouth for any reason except to execute these drawings. Evidence of habitation seldom goes beyond a few yards into a cave.

The *Gravettian,* ranging from southern Russia to Spain but concentrated in central Europe, was another early Upper Paleolithic culture characterized by skilled art. The Gravettians hunted the mammoth and made use of mammoth ivory for tools, weapons, and other implements. They sculpted graceful animal figurines in clay and then fired them. They also carved figurines in bone or ivory, and it was the Gravettians who created the famous "Venus" figurines.[2] Their cave paintings resemble those found in southern France.

Later than the Aurignacian and the Gravettian was the *Solutrean,* one of the more mysterious industries—and one of the most aesthetic—of the European Upper Paleolithic. The Solutrean lasted a very short time, peaking at about 18,000 B.C. Sites have been found in France, Hungary, Poland, Spain, and southern Russia, and their ancient inhabitants are noted for having produced the finest examples of stone workmanship. The technique of parallel flaking on both faces produced beautiful, highly

---

[2] These were very small female statues, most often very obese and with large pendulous breasts. While they have been found in fairly great numbers, their purpose and significance are matters of speculation.

symmetrical laurel-leaf blades and shouldered points. Unfortunately, however, no human skeletal material has ever been found
at any Solutrean site. Predmost, Brunn, and La Roc skeletal
remains are usually assigned to the Solutrean cultural period,
but no clear association between human remains and Solutrean
artifacts has yet been seen.

The culmination of Upper Paleolithic culture came in France
in the *Magdalenian* period, dating between 15,000 and 10,000
years B.C. Magdalenian industries have also been found in Germany, Hungary, and Spain. During this time, the climate was
extremely cold, and the most abundant game animal was the
reindeer.

The outstanding trend during the Magdalenian is the decline
of stone tools and their replacement with a variety of bone tools,
of which the basic tool form was a harpoon point. In fact, some
authorities have divided the Magdalenian into six developmental
stages based on the evolution of the harpoon point. The art
which had originated during the Aurignacian reached a peak
during Magdalenian times: the early animal profiles gave way
to distinctive three-dimensional polychrome representations
of the animals on which these people hunted. Incised work on
bone and antler was also spectacular, and the workmanship
devoted to these paintings and engravings far exceeds utilitarian
needs, thus providing further evidence that aesthetic values were
significantly important to Upper Paleolithic humans.

The Magdalenian industry, with its bone tools and art, does
not appear to have been duplicated elsewhere in the world. It
is associated with the human skeletal remains from Chancelade
and Obercassel, which some experts have classified as Mongoloid.
Mongoloid physical features, and tools reminiscent of those produced by modern Eskimo cultures, lead some people to hypothesize on the origin of recent circumpolar populations, but so far
this is only an interesting speculation.

During the Upper Paleolithic, African industries began to
deviate from the amazing conformity that had prevailed
throughout most of the Paleolithic, and the tool assemblages
dating from the end of the Upper Paleolithic demonstrate remarkable variation. In north Africa, two industries dominated
the Upper Paleolithic. Found in sites from Morocco to Egypt,

the *Aterian* was first thought to be Mousterian but later recognized as a variation of the Levalloisio-Mousterian. Typical tools include tanged points and spear blades up to nine inches in length. The origin of the Aterian probably lies to the south, and some experts see associations with the *Sangoan*. Sangoans were early producers of Acheulean-type core bifaces in the tropical forests of south Africa. As yet, however, there are no positive human skeletal associations.

Found in Algeria and superficially reminiscent of European industries, the *Capsian* tools are extremely small (called *microlithic*). Small blades and burins were, because of their size, most probably fitted into slots on bone or wooden handles. They were certainly too small to be used efficiently in the hand. Skeletal associations point to early *Homo sapiens sapiens* populations.

In north Africa, Egypt appears to represent an isolated cultural development. The *Sebilian* industry obviously has its roots in the African Levalloisian, but the stone tools made from Levalloisian flakes become smaller and smaller until they too can be classed as microliths. Rather than naming new tool types, we assume that the Sebilian simply represents a microlithic Levalloisian which is so far unknown in other regions of Africa. No human skeletal material has been found in association with Sebilian artifacts.

In eastern and southern Africa, the Capsian prevails in a number of sites, but there is also a continuation of the Levalloisian industry, called *Stillbay* in this area. Characterized by triangular points with bifacial retouching, but produced from Levalloisian flakes, the Stillbay is distinguished from earlier Levalloisian in the great variety of tool types produced from flakes struck from tortoise cores. Again, no human skeletal material is associated.

We know very little about the late cultural manifestations in Asia. Insufficient investigation has been undertaken, and only one industry has been well described. Nevertheless, the *Ordosian*, which occurs in northern China, remains a little-known assemblage partially reminiscent of the western Mousterian; yet the inventory includes burins and micro-blades along with typical points and scrapers. The date is fourth glacial or possibly very early post-glacial. The people responsible for the Ordosian ap-

pear to be Neanderthaloid. Certainly Asia has much to add to
our knowledge of Paleolithic prehistory, but we can only wait
for what future discoveries reveal.

A survey of tools throughout the Paleolithic of the Old World
leads us to conclude that the people who lived during this ancient
time depended on a hunting-fishing-gathering economy; there

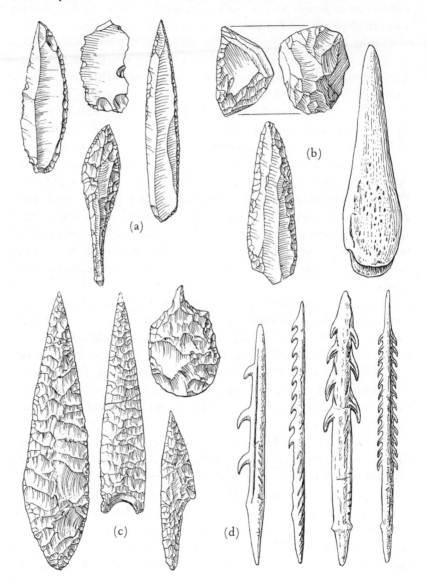

was no horticulture or 'agriculture. As for the domestication of animals, there is some evidence that the dog may have been domesticated during the late Paleolithic of Europe.

In post-Pleistocene times, ecological changes were so great and so relatively sudden that they gave rise to major cultural re-adjustments. True domestication of plants and of animals

FIGURE 7.   Upper Paleolithic tools. (a) Perigordian flint tools: backed blade knife (left), burin or graver (top center), and points. (b) Aurignacian tools: scraper, blade, and split bone point. (c) Solutrean tools: laurel leaf point, point with concave base, end scraper (with finger rest) and shouldered point. (d) Magdalenian bone harpoon point. (e) Various microliths: blade fragment (upper left), burin, lunate, trapezoid, scalene triangle, and arrowhead. (f) Aterian tanged points. (g) Stillbay tool types.

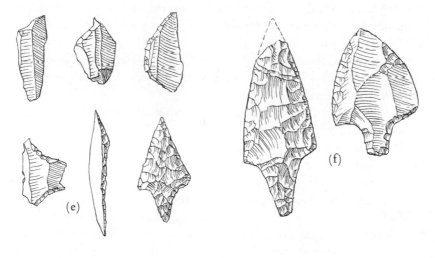

other than the dog began somewhere in western Asia in the Mesolithic, the cultural period following the Paleolithic. This process led in the course of a few centuries to the rise of economies in which hunting and fishing became subsidiary to agriculture and stock-raising; but it was the practice of both that provided a firm basis for the earliest Old World civilizations.

The Prehistoric New World

Archaeologists have been fortunate in accumulating for the Old World a relatively stable framework in which to define cultural developments, however fragmentary our current knowledge may be. For the New World, of course, since human beings arrived there late, already equipped with a material culture, our developmental sequence begins not with the crude tools of the Old World but with a number of evolved tool complexes. In our study of the Americas, we depend particularly upon the cultural remains since we have scant physical evidence of the earliest immigrants.

Human occupation of parts of North and South America has been conclusively demonstrated for as early as 13,000 years ago, and there are archaeological hints that the date might stretch back 50,000 years or more. It is reasonably certain, however, that man was in the New World by at least 30,000 to 40,000 years ago, and that he probably arrived, in two or more waves of migration, by way of a land bridge across the Bering Strait between northeast Asia and Alaska. So, following our coverage of the Old World, we shall consider only the evidence in the New World that can be attributed to the Pleistocene.

From the evidence that we have, it is clear that the earliest immigrants to the New World followed a single cultural way of life—that of big-game hunting. Paleolithic hunters followed game as it wandered freely across the Bering Strait land-bridge; and there is little or no indication of increased population density or of a shift to a more sedentary settlement pattern during the Paleolithic.

The earliest New World culture is designated as Paleo-Indian; and two distinct types of projectile points—*Sandia* and *Clovis*—compete as evidence for the earliest man-made weapons in North

America. Although they have never been found in the same site, most authorities believe, on a typological basis, that Sandia is earlier.

SANDIA.   The Sandia projectile point is restricted in its geographic distribution to the North American west and southwest. It is characterized by a stem or tang on one side at the base of the point, and it has been found with fluting (a groove running down the middle of the face of the point) or with partial fluting associated with a concave base.

CLOVIS.   This point has a wide geographical distribution, having been found in Alaska, Canada, and at a number of other sites in North, Central and South America. It has always been found at the lowest levels of the sites and is usually associated with the butchered remains of mammoths. Carbon-14 dates suggest 11,000 to 13,000 years; the last date for this projectile point is probably 9,000 years ago.

FOLSOM.   Our next clue to the cultural propensities of early man in the New World is represented by another type of projectile point designated as *Folsom*. The Folsom point also has a wide distribution but has been found most frequently west of the

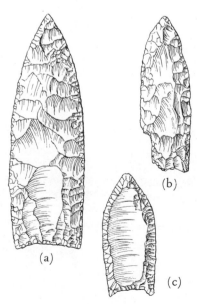

FIGURE 8.   New World projectile points. (a) Clovis. (b) Sandia. (c) Folsom.

Mississippi River, where it has been located stratigraphically above (or more recent than) the Clovis points. It is interesting to note that the animal most often associated with Folsom is not the mammoth but the bison. Carbon-14 dates place the Folsom culture between 9,000 and 10,000 years ago. The Folsom point is fluted, sometimes bifacially, and demonstrates parallel flaking in some examples.

Although the bones of Folsom man have never been found, his existence is accepted on the basis of the tools he left behind. Skeletal remains of all North American populations are rare; but many fossilized skulls and other bony portions have been offered over the years as having belonged to the most ancient New World inhabitants. All have undergone the meticulous analysis of the best scientific minds; but most have failed the rigorous geological and paleontological requirements for validity. A few have survived—and these few provide archaeologists with their insights into the physical nature of these early Americans.

In 1846, a clay deposit in a deep ravine near Natchez, Mississippi, yielded a hip bone with a long and complicated history. This pelvic bone was recovered in association with the bones of ground-sloth, mastodon, and certain species of horse and bison—all varieties that met extinction many thousands of years ago in the New World. Early dating estimates were not much better than guesses, since the geological scheme for North America was not well known at the time of this discovery. The first estimate, given by the highly esteemed English geologist Charles Lyell, dated the deposit at 100,000 years old—a date which we now know to be inaccurate. Next, an early fluorine analysis made in 1895 showed that the human hip bone was older than the ground-sloth remains, implying that the associations were not sound.

In 1948, Professor M. F. Ashley Montagu revived interest in the Natchez material when he carried portions of the bone to England for new fluorine testing, the results of which showed again that the hip bone predated the remains of the ground-sloth. Not until later was it discovered that the ground-sloth had been extinct for only 8,000 years; it was possible, after all, that the pelvic bone had been buried before that date.

In 1953, wind and erosion exposed a fragmentary human braincase near Midland, Texas. Once the bones were reassembled, they were found to represent the top and back of a skull that probably belonged to a female who was about thirty years old at the time of her death. Projectile points, grinding stones, and an incised bone were found with her. But controversy still ranges over the Midland discovery: test results range from 10,000 to 20,000 years, and because the bones were found in a "blowout" (wind-eroded) site, no geological evidence remained to subsubstantiate either date.

FIGURE 9. Skull of Tepexpan man. (Courtesy of the Smithsonian Institution)

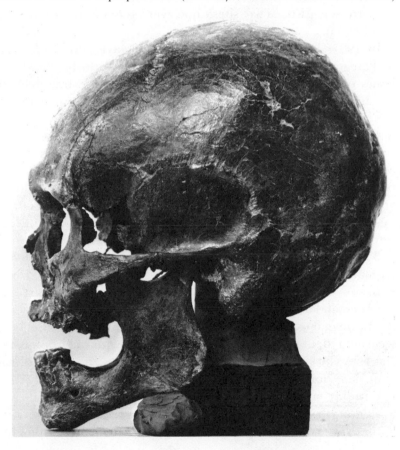

In 1947, a complete skeleton was unearthed near the tiny village of Tepexpan, in Mexico. Using an electrical detecting device, Dr. Helmut de Terra, an American geologist, and Dr. Hans Lundberg, a Canadian, found the bones at a depth of about four feet, lying in the undisturbed layers of an ancient lake near the butchered remains of two mammoths. The skeleton, on the basis of site geology, was determined to be about 11,000 years old—a date substantiated by carbon-14 tests. The bones belonged to a male who was nearly sixty years old at the time of his death. He differed physically in no way from modern inhabitants of the same region.

South American sites have also lured those who search for the New World's oldest human bones, but most of the fossils found have not withstood the test of time nor the scrutiny of modern scientists. Two sites, however, remain of interest to prehistorians.

In 1937, Dr. Junius Bird excavated a cave site, *Palli Aike,* in Pategonia, where he found numerous cultural artifacts, the bones of extinct ground-sloth and horse, and the fragmentary remains of early man. The cave was dated by the carbon-14 method at approximately 9,000 years. And located in the Lagona Santa region of Brazil is another cave, known as *Lapa de Confins.* It was here that, in 1935, a human skeleton was found under conditions that suggested great antiquity. No absolute date can be derived from the remains, but the evidence points to a time at least equivalent to that of the Palli Aike site. The Confins man looks exactly as archaeologists would expect: in skull features and body form, he is typically Amerindian.

By 10,000 B.C., then, primitive Asiatic hunters had crossed on foot into the New World, where they spread and inhabited most of North and South America. They looked very much like their descendants, the Indians who populated these regions when the European explorers appeared in the fifteenth century. There seems no doubt that they originated in Asia: their physical characteristics and their cultural artifacts are almost identical with those found in Siberia for the same time period.

With the end of glaciation, sea levels rose to obscure the path of migration into the North American continent. Inhabitants of the New World were cut off from the cultural developments of the Old and they developed their own ways of life. In time, they gave rise to the diverse Indian tribes of North America, to the Mayan temple builders of Yucatan, to the mighty Toltecs and warlike Aztecs of Mexico, and to the Incas and pre-Incas whose wealth and cultural achievements astounded the Spanish conquistadores who sailed to the Americas in search of riches.

Civilization came later to the New World than to the Old; it was not until about 500 A.D. that true cities flourished here. By that time, Teotihuacan, the short-lived but influential ceremonial center in the Valley of Mexico, supported a dense human population, probably through large-scale agriculture. In Guatemala, the Maya had approached their cultural peak, reaching impressive heights in sculpture, architecture, astronomy, mathematics, and hieroglyphic writing. In Peru and Bolivia, various peoples worked skillfully in gold and silver, produced large quantities of fine textiles and pottery, and raised mighty armies. The Inca dynasty was not founded until about 1200 A.D.—but the peoples of Peru at that time rivaled the ancient Egyptians in the splendor of their cultural achievements. They brought under cultivation vast regions of arid desert by means of intricate irrigation systems; they spanned the continent with a complex network of paved roads, perfected the process of human mummification, and united many diverse peoples and customs in building an awesome new empire.

FURTHER READINGS

Bordes, Francois. *The Old Stone Age.* New York: McGraw-Hill, 1968.

Braidwood, Robert J. *Prehistoric Men.* 7th ed. Chicago: Scott, Foreswood Cliffs: Prentice-Hall, 1970.

Chard, Chester S. *Man in Prehistory.* New York: McGraw-Hill, 1969.

Clarke, Grahame. *World Prehistory.* Cambridge: University Press, 1961.

Clark, Grahame, and Stuart Piggott. *Prehistoric Societies.* New York: Alfred A. Knopf, 1968.

Cole, Sonia. *The Prehistory of East Africa.* New York: Mentor, 1963.

Ehrich, Robert W. (ed.). *Chronologies in Old World Archaeology.* Chicago: University of Chicago Press, 1964.

Jennings, Jesse D. and Edward Norbeck (eds.). *Prehistoric Man in the New World.* Chicago: University of Chicago Press, 1964.

Macgowan, Kenneth and Joseph A. Hester, Jr. *Early Man in the New World.* Garden City: Doubleday, 1962.

National Geographic Society. *Discovering Man's Past in the Americas.* Washington, D.C.: National Geographic, 1969.

Oakley, Kenneth P. *Man the Tool-maker.* Chicago: University of Chicago Press, 1964.

Powell, T. G. E. *Prehistoric Art.* New York: Praeger, 1966.

Sanders, William T. and Joseph Marino. *New World Prehistory.* Englewood Cliffs, Prentice-Hall, 1970.

Stern, Philip Van Doren and Lillian V. Stern. *Prehistoric Europe.* New York: W. W. Norton, 1969.

Trustees of the British Museum. *Flint Implements: An Account of Stone Age Techniques and Cultures.* London: The British Museum, 1950.

Ucko, Peter J. and Andree Rosenfeld. *Paleolithic Cave Art.* New York: McGraw-Hill, 1967.

Wendorf, Fred, Alex D. Krieger, Claude C. Albritton, and T. Dale Stewart. *The Midland Discovery.* Austin: University of Texas Press, 1955.

Willey, Gordon R. *An Introduction to American Archaeology.* Englewood Cliffs: Prentice-Hall, 1966.

Willey, Gordon R., and Philip Phillips. *Method and Theory in American Archaeology.* Chicago: University of Chicago Press, 1958.

CHAPTER XI

THE DAWN OF CIVILIZATION

The end of the Paleolithic coincided with the end of Pleistocene times; and with the beginning of the Mesolithic about 12,000 years ago, great changes in climate and ecology swept the earth. The weather turned markedly warmer. In Europe, the ice-sheets retreated to the north, and so much water was released from retreating glaciers that sea levels rose considerably and inundated large previously inhabited regions Forests began to appear, and the vast open plains of Upper Paleolithic times gave way gradually to dense woodlands.

Flora and fauna of course responded to these climatic changes. The herds of buffalo, wild horses, and cattle began to disappear; the great mammoths were gone. Game animals became smaller and more scattered, and it is likely that hunting was much less successful than in the Upper Paleolithic. Not surprisingly, animal figures vanished from the walls of cave dwellings.

The Mesolithic

It is said that the Mesolithic represents a time of cultural decline, and it is true that artful avhievements in cave-painting and bone-working—so skillfully executed in Upper Paleolithic times —were largely abandoned during the Mesolithic. At the same time, however, the Mesolithic seems to have ushered in a new era of cultural diversification. Regions suitable for human habitation expanded as the glaciers retreated, and human culture grew sufficiently sophisticated to enable habitation of such climatically hostile areas as the Arctic. Man had already mastered the use of fire, devised tailored clothing, and learned to erect adequate shelters against the cold. Furthermore, the rate of

FIGURE 1.   Typical Azilian, Tardenoisian, Maglemosian implements, etc. (a) Painted pebble, Azilian, France. (b)—(e) Conventional human figures painted on cave wall, Spain. (After H. Obermaier) (f) Hunting scene showing bow and arrow, painted on cave wall, Spain. (After H. Breuil) (g) Fishhook of bone, Maglemosian, Denmark. (After K. F. Johansen, etc.) (h) Harpoon point of deer antler, perforated, double barbed, Azilian, France. (After G. and A. de Mortillet) (i) Dart point of bone, double slant base, Maglemosian, Denmark. (j) Dart point of bone with flint flake barbs, Maglemosian, Denmark. (k) Adze of antler, perforated, punctate ornamentation, Denmark. (After K. F. Johansen) (l) Endscraper of flint, subtriangular, Tardenoisian, Germany. (m) Arrow point of flint, cross-cutting type, hafted by lower edge, Tardenoisian, Germany. (n)—(p) Arrow points, semilunar and triangular, hafted by right chipped edges, Tardenoisian, Germany. (q) Incising tool or knife with bluntly chipped back, Tardenoisian, Germany. (r) Incising tool or knife with slantingly chipped point, Tardenoisian, Germany. (s)—(v) Geometric flints with two chipped margins, Tardenoisian, Germany. (w) Incising tool, double pointed, three chipped margins, Maglemosian, Denmark. (After K. F. Johansen) (Courtesy of the American Museum of Natural History)

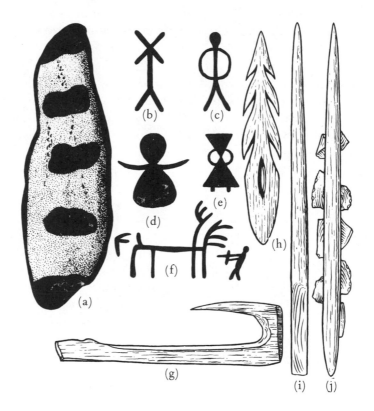

culture change and innovation appears to have increased dramatically over that which characterized the Upper Paleolithic.

Above all, the Mesolithic was a time of altered circumstances. Confronted with a changed environment, man had no choice but to find new food resources and new ways of adapting to a rapidly changing world. One important new development of the Mesolithic, occurring in Europe between 11,000 and 5000 years B.C., was an increased reliance on fish and seafood. Among the important coastal cultures of the time were the *Azilian* and the *Tardenoisian* cultures. The Azilians, a Mesolithic people occupying the same caves as the earlier Magdalenians, centered in southern France and northern Spain but extended as far as Switzerland, Belgium, and Scotland. The Azilian is sometimes called the "painted pebble culture," for they painted small pebbles with mysterious symbols, the significance of which is yet unknown.

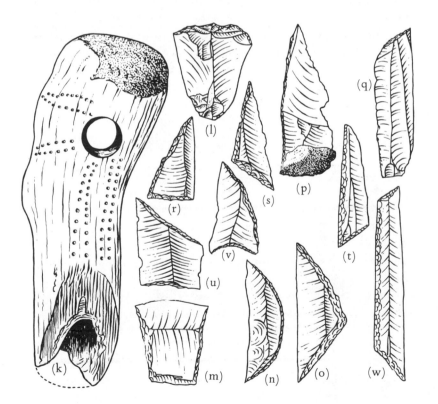

The Tardenoisian, a coastal culture with almost a pan-European distribution, is particularly noted for its microliths. Stone work did not cease with the Paleolithic, but in the Mesolithic, flakes predominated, and much smaller flakes were often imbedded in a row in a piece of wood, yielding an early type of sickle that was probably used to cut wild grasses.

Inland, at about 6000 B.C., a major new adaptation developed, centering in Scandinavia. This was the *Maglemosian* culture. Fortunately for modern archaeologists, the Maglemosians commonly lived on the borders of swamps and marshes, and near peat-bogs, where conditions for the preservation of organic materials are quite favorable. Consequently, archaeologists have been able to assemble a rich and varied cultural inventory for the Maglemosians. Their material culture included blade tools, tanged points, burins, axes, microliths, bone and amber haftings, and a great variety of arrowheads, among which were blunt points apparently used to stun small fur animals in order to avoid piercing their valuable pelts. In addition, the Maglemosians boasted various fishing devices including hooks, lines, sinkers, spears and harpoons, and seine nets. Wooden canoes, paddles, and sled runners are also known for this culture. Often, animal skins were used for boats, and were stretched over a framework much as the modern Eskimos fashion their watercraft.

What is particularly interesting about the Maglemosian culture is that its cultural inventory includes trade objects, some from as far away as the Tigris-Euphrates Valley. Archaeologists do not assume that traders journeyed between Scandinavia and Mesopotamia at this early time; rather, they feel that trading was extended over a very long span of time and localized so that each people along the trade route established trade relations only with their nearest neighbors. It is likely that desirable trade objects traveled along convenient waterways, like the Rhine and the Elbe rivers.

The northern Europeans of the Mesolithic expanded their food resources. Those who lived near the coastal waters depended heavily upon shellfish, which we know from great numbers of discarded shells found in heaps known to archaeologists as "kitchen middens." Inland, men of the Mesolithic hunted such forest animals as moose, deer, elk, beavers, wild pigs, and smaller game. Spears, and bows and arrows with microlithic points were the typical weapons.

The environmental changes of the Mesolithic also wrought great changes in man's life-ways outside of Europe. In the Middle East, around 9000 B.C., man shifted from a hunting and food-gathering system to one of intensive foraging and hunting. Now the emphasis shifted to the collection of seeds and vegetables, supplemented by hunting and fishing. Big-game hunting continued in some parts of the Old World, as well as in eastern North America, but the disappearance of the great Pleistocene game mammals eventually forced most human groups to alter their living habits. People settled in permanent locations, and life became more sedentary as vegetation again became a primary source of human sustenance.

Hallmarks of this new era were the microliths (small stone flakes set in a row along a piece of wood or bone to produce composite tools) and the introduction of milling-stones for grinding seeds. Archaeologists have charted the appearance of these implements in the Near East and in Africa, and sites in Palestine have been particularly productive. For the *Natufian* culture of Palestine, dating from around 9000 B.C., archaeologists have found that eighty percent of recovered flints are microliths; but they have also found hold-overs from the Upper Paleolithic—-backed blades, scrapers, picks,and awls—and such other stone artifacts as metates (mill-stones), pestles, hammerstones, and abundant bone fishhooks.

The Natufians lived in caves and rock-shelters when these were available and convenient; but they also constructed round stone-walled houses with storage pits sunk into the ground beneath the floors. They are the first peoples known to have stored surplus harvests against times of need. There is no evidence of cultivation, but the Natufians did collect and consume substantial quantities of seeds, including those of wild wheat and barley, as important additions to foods obtained through hunting and fishing. In addition, they devoted great care to their dead, burying them in tombs or cemeteries, and they quite clearly had a religious tradition.

In Africa, the Mesolithic complex assumed many forms in varying locales. The early Khartoum culture, dating from 5000

to 4000 B.C. along the upper Nile, was one of specialized food
collectors who lived in large settlements along the banks of the
river. They grew no crops and had not yet domesticated animals;
but their stone industry is well adapted to both hunting and
fishing, and they derived numerous food resources from the Nile.
They made pottery, too, which is a good indicator that they
lived a sedentary life.

Evidence for the Mesolithic in the New World indicates that
by 10,000 years ago Mesolithic food foragers were well established
in the drier regions of Mexico and the western United States.
Of their artifacts, the most significant is the American equivalent
to the Old World microlithic sickle, underlining the importance
of seed harvesting among the peoples of the American "desert
culture."[1] This was a widespread cultural complex, extending
from Canada through the western United States and deep into
Mexico. Archaeologists have found evidence that there existed
in this culture specialized cooking techniques, the use of basketry,
netting and matting, fur cloth, fire drills, digging sticks, wooden
clubs, and small but varied projectile points. In addition, objects
of religious significance have been recovered: medicine bags and
rattles fashioned from the hooves of deer indicate that there
was a shaman, or tribal spiritual leader. Among desert peoples
of the Americas, population was sparse and contacts limited;
thus the desert culture remained relatively isolated and virtually
unchanged for many centuries.

Clearly, the Mesolithic foraging complex of the Americas
evolved independently, but was parallel to that which occurred
in the Old World. It was a time when most peoples of the world
settled into small bands near reliable water sources, making
efficient use of accessible vegetation, small game, and fish. It
was only a matter of time until people began to use this new,
intimate knowledge of their local environments to exert some
control over nature—to reach, as it were, toward a true domestication of plants and animals.

---

[1] Some archaeologists object to the term "desert culture" on the grounds that
it is too general a reference. Its use here in no way implies that these cultures
were not individual and diverse in many ways.

The Neolithic

The term *Neolithic*, or *New Stone Age*, refers to the fact that the stone tools made and used during this period differ from those typical of the Paleolithic. The chipping technique was not lost in Neolithic times; flake tools—projectile points, scrapers, sickles—were still made and used. But Neolithic tool assemblages included as well ground-stone axes and adzes that were often drilled to accommodate a handle. Although the rubbing and grinding necessary for their production were slow, laborious tasks, the resulting tools were both durable and efficient. Neolithic rubbing stones, mortars, and pestles are common, and polished stone bowls are known from several sites in the Near East.

Such innovations reflect basic changes in man's way of life, and the Neolithic was indeed a time of crucial change, the most significant of which was the domestication of plants and animals and the resulting feasibility of permanent village life. Until Neolithic times, man had lived as a hunter and forager. He followed game when it was available or, in Mesolithic times, lingered near coastal waters for fish and other seafood, and he relied heavily upon the wild nuts, berries, fruits, and vegetables that he could collect to supplement his diet. This hunting-foraging lifestyle necessitated a nomadic or semi-nomadic existence.

Not all hunters are wanderers, of course. The Indians of the northwest coast in North Africa, for example, lived in a region so rich in game, seafoods, and wild edible plants that they were able to sustain sizable year-round villages. Such groups are exceptions, however, and certainly most Paleolithic and Mesolithic peoples roamed the land for food. Although many moved within a relatively circumscribed territory, they occupied different areas in different seasons of the year depending upon the movements of game animals and the seasonal bearing cycles of food-plants. The Neolithic would break the age-old pattern of nomadic wandering for most of the world's peoples.

The domestication of plants and animals was a gradual process that occurred independently in different parts of the world. The earliest efforts in plant cultivation were probably undertaken when hunting-foraging peoples, increasingly dependent upon wild edible plants, began to control or eliminate weeds and to drive away birds and foraging animals. True domestication did not begin, however, until seeds and roots were planted deliberately in the expectation that life-sustaining plants would eventually reappear in the same spot.

This was a revolutionary idea, and one that called for determined self-restraint. The best seeds could not be eaten; they had to be saved for planting to ensure future food supplies. Soil had to be prepared and cultivated, and pest control was usually mandatory. Still, there were great benefits to be derived from cultivating the soil and tending crops, not the least of which was a steady food supply. The idea of plant cultivation spread rapidly.

FIGURE 2.   Restoration of a Neolithic village scene from Denmark. (Courtesy of the American Museum of Natural History)

Jonathan D. Sauer argues[2] that the purpose of early plant cultivation was to produce beer rather than food. Other authorities disagree. Whatever the motivation—and the motivation must have varied with locale—the domestication of plants (and animals, too) occurred in regions where their wild forms were found: for example, the wild ancestors of wheat and barley grew in the Near East (and some still do) in lightly forested upland regions at elevations of between 2000 and 4300 feet above sea level. So far as we know, this was the first deliberate cultivation, though future discoveries may warrant revision of this supposition. The most important animals to be domesticated in Neolithic times—sheep, cattle, goats, and pigs—inhabited the same upland regions, and here sheep seem to have been the first domesticated animals. Dogs, domesticated from Mesolithic times in northern Europe, appear to have been domesticated in the Near East later than sheep, goats, and pigs. Apparently, horses were not domesticated until the Bronze Age.

Since wild forms of cattle produce very little milk, it is not likely that this was the motive for their domestication; nor were sheep domesticated for their wool since wild forms boast little of it. Evidence is abundant that the earliest purpose of animal domestication was to assure a constant supply of meat.

The domestication of plants and animals, as we have seen, made possible a new, sedentary way of life which ushered in a period of great cultural change. Of course these changes did not occur overnight: hunting must have continued long after the initial development of agriculture to provide important supplementary food; and semi-nomadic conditions must have persisted when early farmers moved on after soil resources were depleted. Nevertheless, the domestication of plants and animals led for the most part to a more stable existence which offered distinct advantages: village life provided better care for the young, sick, and elderly than they would have received in a hunting society; grain could be stored for the future; and housing, made of local materials, was more substantial and more comfortable. The material culture multiplied: possessions would have

---

[2] Braidwood, Robert J. (ed.). "Symposium: Did Man Once Live by Beer Alone?" *American Anthropologist*, Vol. 55, No. 4, pp. 515–526.

been bothersome to the nomadic, hunting-gathering peoples, but with settled village life, there was no need to worry about transportation of heavy or bulky objects. Pottery became useful, and for this reason, the finding of pottery (which travels poorly) generally means that the archaeologist can presume a fairly sedentary life for the people concerned. Looms, invented during Neolithic times, made it possible for woven clothing to replace that fashioned from animal skins; and weaving, of course, is a by-product of the domestication of plants and animals. In short, life became more secure and comfortable. Certainly human skeletal remains from Neolithic sites greatly outnumber those from earlier periods, indicating that the Neolithic was a time of rapid population growth. Settled village life, with its attendant sense of security, favored a higher birth rate, just as it prolonged life expectancy as a result of improved care.

Archaeologists have been able to recover sound evidence for early agriculture at several Old World sites. At Jarmo, a small village in northern Iraq dating from about 6750 B.C., workers uncovered charred kernels of wheat and barley. There is also evidence that the inhabitants of Jarmo had domesticated dogs, goats, and sheep. Jarmo's Neolithic population numbered about 150 people who occupied about 25 multi-roomed, rectangular houses; later dwellings had ovens and chimneys. Tools were varied, with pottery appearing in later levels of the site. Other remains indicate that the people who lived in Jarmo relied heavily upon domesticated plants and animals; only about five percent of animal bones recovered represent wild species. The site suggests as well clear evidence of a bulk carrying trade: many tools, for instance, are made of obsidian although its nearest natural source is located roughly 200 miles away, and decorative seashells found at the site must have come from the Persian Gulf. The inhabitants of Jarmo, then, were not isolated from other peoples—and this is significant. Scientists have long argued that human contacts and cultural borrowing are prerequisite to the evolution of higher systems of civilization, the development of each being stimulated by extensive cross-fertilization of ideas and borrowing of innovations. Jarmo is also significant in that, under the direction of Robert Braidwood of the University of Chicago, it was one of the first really large digs which made use of many people with special abilities. Jarmo helped to set the pattern of modern field work by including specialists from other disciplines such as geology, biology, psychology, and dentistry.

Another early agricultural site is Jericho. Located in a fertile oasis north of the Dead Sea, it is in fact one of the most ancient towns known. The lowest levels of the site date from around 7800 B.C., and successive levels indicate that a Neolithic settlement gradually developed there. Apparently, the oasis was a desirable area which had to be defended from invaders, for the Neolithic inhabitants of Jericho erected an extensive stone wall, six feet thick, with a thirty-foot stone tower. A section of the village proper dates from about 6850 B.C. Residential dwellings are rectangular rooms built of sun-dried brick and organized around a central courtyard where open-air cooking was done. Some of the buildings appear to have served as temples, and numerous dismembered skeletons have been recovered from beneath the floors of the dwellings. The people of Jericho went to some trouble in preparing the human burials: they made skillful plaster reproductions of the heads of the deceased, carefully inlaying shells for eyes.

Direct evidence of grain has not been located at Jericho, but sickle blades and metates attest to its importance as a food source. In any case, the peoples of Jericho must have been farmers; their Neolithic population—estimated at about 2000—was too large to have been sustained in this region by hunting and foraging. Although Jericho was marginal to the early centers of plant and animal domestication, there is clear evidence of trade in numerous items, including cowrie shells, turquoise, and obsidian.

Both Jericho and Jarmo are exciting sites and they have captured the attention of archaeologists around the world. In 1961, however, they were eclipsed by the discovery of an amazingly sophisticated Neolithic settlement at Çatal Hüyük, in southern Turkey. At this site, archaeologists have recovered a rich and varied cultural inventory including specialized handicrafts, wall paintings, and statuary. The town itself is a relatively extensive complex of adjoining rooms with roof-top entrances; the doorless, windowless walls of mud brick made a defensive

FIGURE 3. Community arrangements of 8000 years ago in a Neolithic city are depicted on the basis of recent excavations. This is a reconstruction of an area in the fifth of 12 building layers so far found at the Çatal Hüyük site on the Anatolian plateau of Turkey. Access to the buildings was solely from the roof, so that the exterior walls presented a solid blank face, which served effectively as a defense against both attackers and floods. Çatal Hüyük showed a surprising evolution of civilization for so early a community.

(From James Mellaart, "A Neolithic City in Turkey," *Scientific American*, April 1964, p. 95.) Copyright © 1964 by Scientific American, Inc. All rights reserved.

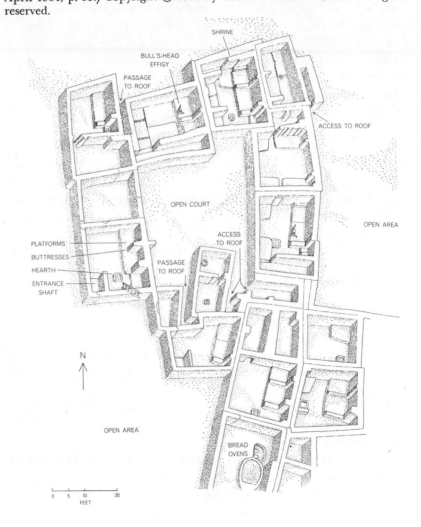

structure of the commune. The settlement, dating from 6500 to 5700 B.C., covered roughly 32 acres of fertile land, where Neolithic peoples raised crops of barley, wheat, lintels, and peas with such dazzling success that surplus yields were being produced by about 6400 B.C. E. Adamson Hoebel writes:

> One cannot help but be impressed, on the basis of what is now known from the excavations at Çatal Hüyük, at how rapidly the transition from Paleolithic hunting bands to regionally organized communities occurred, once the domestication of plants and animals—the food revolution—had taken place in the Middle East.[3]

Neolithic achievements were indeed impressive compared with those of earlier periods. Shrines, fertility figurines, and elaborate wall murals suggest a highly developed belief system among Neolithic peoples. Specialized handicrafts were beautifully executed, and trade, with its attendant exchange of ideas and innovations, was becoming extensive. Although Mesolithic hunting-gathering groups persisted in northern and western Europe until about 2500 B.C., large Neolithic settlements thrived in the Near East by 5500 B.C... and Neolithic communities spread rapidly, overland and by sea, into Crete, Sicily, Malta, southern Europe, and beyond. As they spread, early farmers encountered new environments, some of which differed greatly from those of the Near East, and special adaptations were required to meet new ecological situations.

"Slash-and-burn" (swidden) horticulture was adopted in central Europe. By this method, land is cleared by burning, crops are planted and tended for one or more seasons, and then the land is abandoned so that its fertility can be renewed. Slash-and-burn cultivation is usually accomplished on a small scale by members of settlements which seldom house more than 300 persons.

In desert regions or arid grasslands, Neolithic peoples often turned to pastoralism. Usually, they engaged in horticulture as

---

[3] Hoebel, E. Adamson, *Anthropology: the Study of Man,* 3rd ed. New York: McGraw-Hill, 1966, p. 189.

a sideline, abandoning it entirely if and when their herds grew
sufficiently large and productive.

Whatever its regional adaptations, the food-producing economy was the hallmark of the Neolithic, and it spread quickly
not only to the west but to the east as well. Early farming
communities were widespread in India, where archaeologists find
huge megalithic constructions not essentially unlike those at
Stonehenge in England. Rice and millet were cultivated in
China, where pigs, sheep, cattle, and chickens were domesticated,
as were silkworms, apparently for the loom-weaving of silk. Jade,
pottery, and ceremonial ware are common in Chinese Neolithic
sites. In southwest Asia, wheat and barley were the principal
crops; cattle, sheep, and goats were the most important domesticated animals. Pottery and weaving are also known for this
time period. In southeast Asia, the economy was based on root
and fruit crops supplemented by rice; pigs, dogs, and chickens
were domesticated. Pottery and looms were not used. Some
archaeologists believe that agriculture evolved here independently of developments in the Near East, and a few authorities
have suggested that southeast Asian plant cultivation may pre-
date that of the Near East. This view is supported by the excavation from a Thailand cave site of seeds of various cultivated
plants—peas, beans, water chestnuts—which have yielded a
carbon-14 date of some 11,700 years. Further investigation
and analysis of known sites, as well as of new ones which may
come to light, will be necessary to clarify the chronology.

THE RISE OF CIVILIZATION

Food collecting, incipient agriculture, settled farming villages
—these are the first important steps in cultural evolution
toward true civilization. By 6000 B.C., domesticated plants and
animals were common in the Near East, and within another
2000 years agriculture was widely established. The time was ripe
for a new revolution, the urban revolution. With it came the
establishment of the first human civilizations.

Archaeologists know that it was about 4000 B.C. that some
of the Neolithic farming villages began to grow into towns, and
then into cities. The difference between villages and cities, of

course, lies not in size or population density but in structure. A true city consists of both urban and nonurban populations, the latter usually living at some distance from the city proper and serving as food-producers. The urban population is then free to engage in various specialized, nonagricultural tasks and pursuits. The city itself tends to become a center for political action and spiritual power.

Clearly, the differences between a village and a city are qualitative and complex, and prehistorians have devised extensive criteria on which to base a distinction. The best known and most succinct discussion of these criteria is by V. G. Childe,[4] who carefully notes that while a productive agriculture is basic to the development of civilization, simple food surpluses cannot in themselves produce this result. The following are characteristics of early civilization as specified by Childe:

1. The population is large and organized, and capable of organized social interaction.

2. Specialization of production among workers is instituted, together with means of distribution and exchange of goods.

3. Surpluses produced by farmers and artisans are channeled into a central accumulation of goods.

4. Specialization and exchange go beyond urban boundaries in contributing to the development of trade.

5. Monumental public architecture is constructed and maintained.

6. Relatively sophisticated art forms reflect religious beliefs and aesthetic appreciation.

7. Systems of writing[5] and basic accounting facilitate organization and management.

---

[4] Childe, V. G., *The Dawn of European Civilization,* New York: Alfred A. Knopf, 1958; *What Happened in History,* Baltimore: Penguin, 1954; *Man Makes Himself,* rev. ed. New York: New American Library, 1952.

[5] Writing was present in the important early Old World urban centers and in most of the New World centers; however, archaeologists have traditionally noted that the Incas of Peru lacked even the most rudimentary writing system. Recent evidence, though, in the form of recurrent symbols on ancient textiles, suggests that the Incas may have had a system of writing after all.

8. The development of such sciences as arithmetic, geometry, and astronomy takes shape.

9. Residence replaces kinship as a means of political identification in a well-structured political order.

10. Social classes emerge, headed by a privileged ruling class of political, religious, and military functionaries responsible for the organization and administration of community affairs.

For the most part, Childe's criteria of civilization have withstood the test of time. They are misleading only if they give the impression that all early urban centers were identical. The fact is, that while certain cultural patterns may have spread from one region to another, each center maintained its own culture, language, architecture, and life-style. In numerous significant ways, each was unique.

CENTERS OF OLD WORLD CIVILIZATION

In the lower half of Mesopotamia, that geographical region which encompasses the Tigris-Euphrates Valley, there emerged the dynamic early civilization we know as Sumer. Its achievements were impressive for its time, and its history was complex.

It was about 4000 B.C. that settlers first moved into this fertile region; they were probably Iraqi highlanders who brought with them a system of developed agriculture. Soon more than a dozen walled city-states—most within sight of others—dotted the alluvial delta. Since each was anxious to expand its own territory and its productive agriculture, warfare was not uncommon.

These early settlers are known as the Ubaid people, after the archaeological site at Al Ubaid. Their most significant characteristic was their rising concern with religion, which would lead, in time, to great temple complexes and to the establishment of powerful priestly classes. But the days of the Ubaid peoples were numbered; for by 3500 B.C., the Sumerians themselves had entered the area, probably from Iran, and they quickly expanded upon patterns of living established by their predecessors. During the Uruk phase (c. 3500–3000 B.C.), they erected huge ziggurats and monumental temples that dominated the communities in which they were found. Each city-state had its own imposing temple dedicated to its primary god, whose protection extended over the land under his jurisdiction. During this time, the priestly class began to govern the economic life of the cities of southern Mesopotamia, serving both religious and administrative functions. Workers toiled on temple land, drawing seeds and tools for their labor and returning stores of grain for the use of the temple and its priests.

Not all land was held in common for the maintenance of the temple and/or the community. Numerous documents have come to light to show, for instance:

> . . . that the citizens of the city-states could buy and sell their fields and houses, not to mention all kinds of movable property.[6]

Cylinder seals were invented and used to place marks of ownership on merchandise. Nor did the temple continue to serve as the sole source of power. Continual warfare among the city-states of the region encouraged the rise of military leaders. A hereditary kingship developed, and the result was an effective balance of power. In addition, since private property made feasible an additional means of social mobility, no sector boasted absolute control over the populace. Social historians believe that the Sumerians enjoyed a relatively free and open society, which may help to account for the amazingly creative and innovative culture that developed.

Sumer produced the earliest known system of writing, found in the form of incised clay tablets. Such texts shed little light on actual religious doctrine in ancient Sumer, but they do emphasize the importance of religion and highlight the role of the priests as community organizers. The Sumerians also supported the first known schools, which were apparently organized and administered to benefit the children of wealthy or politically important families.

---

[6] Kramer, Samuel Noah, *The Sumerians: Their History, Culture, and Character.* Chicago: University of Chicago Press, 1963, p. 75.

Full civilization was attained in Sumer between 3200 and 2800 B.C. Wheel-turned pottery, copper and silver implements, and religious statuary were common by this time; agricultural productivity was at a peak; draft animals were harnessed to carts, plows, and chariots. Division of labor grew increasingly more sophisticated as priests, soldiers, and government officials became full-time professionals. Democratic town councils adjudicated intercity disputes; and matters of land allotment and natural resources fell to the head priests, as did labor assignments. In this way manpower was made available for the maintenance of walls, irrigation systems, and community buildings.

Cities grew more slowly along the banks of the Nile than in the Tigris-Euphrates Valley. Indeed, early Egyptian civilization differed in numerous important ways from that of Sumer, although its earliest origins were similar. Along the fertile Nile Valley, between 4500 and 3200 B.C., simple yet self-sufficient farming communities were established, and, perhaps due to their geographic isolation, they remained relatively unchanged for some time. Then, about 3200 B.C., North and South Egypt were unified, and there emerged the first pharoah-king of a united Egypt. The period following was one of rapid culture change.

From the beginning, the pharoah-king controlled both church and state, delegating powers and authority to loyal priests and government officials. These lesser authorities were responsible for the control of the enormous amount of manpower necessary to construct pyramids and colossal royal tombs. Laborers had no wheels or cranes; only ramps, levers, and rollers were used in the construction of vast and imposing structures.

One explanation of the Egyptians' ability to effectively organize and carry out unusually large-scale, public works projects, particularly the irrigation systems, is offered by Karl Wittfogel.[7] His thesis is that such large-scale projects are a certain indication of an autocratic, centralized despotism with a well-organized bureaucracy at its disposal. However, the existence of some large-scale projects such as the irrigation works of the Hohokam Indians in Arizona where the governmental structure was not

---

[7] See Wittfogel, Karl, *Oriental Despotism.* New Haven: Yale University Press, 1957.

centralized or bureaucratic leaves Wittfogel's thesis in considerable doubt as a general theory.

Occasionally, the king's power was threatened, both by the noblemen and by the priestly class; but the pharoah who ruled Egypt was held to be a living god, and his authority was not easily challenged. Indeed, one of the most remarkable facts to emerge from the study of ancient Egypt has been that of its cultural and social stability. Rigid conventions dictated the expression of art and religious belief, and traditional social structures and customs persisted unchanged over an immense span of time.

Some historians attribute such stability to the country's relative isolation, but there is clear evidence of frequent outside contacts. Although Egyptian influence is not noted at Sumer, a number of Sumerian cylinder seals are found in Egyptian sites. Similarly, although the Egyptian system of writing was not introduced directly from Sumer, the fact that it came so suddenly into existence in Egypt suggests that the stimulus for a written language came from there. Evidence points as well to considerable contacts between Egypt and Crete, and it is likely that the Egyptian influence had great impact in Crete.

Less is known of the ancient Indus Valley civilization, now called Harappa after one of its two principal cities. Covering an area 1200 by 700 miles, its territory far exceeds that of its Egyptian and Mesopotamian contemporaries. But its life-span was shorter: recent carbon-14 dates suggest that the Harappa culture was established about 2500 B.C.—and it collapsed at some point between 1700 and 1500 B.C. for reasons not yet understood by prehistorians. Some argue that the decline of Harappa was the result of overgrazing, lack of sufficient rainfall, or deforestation. Others believe that Aryans, nomadic cattle-herding peoples from the northwest, established themselves as the dominant power in the region.

At its peak, however, Harappa civilization was remarkable in its own way. Its primary cities, Harappa and Mohenjo-Daro (about 400 miles apart), show traces of Sumerian influence; yet that influence must have been indirect and selective, for the Harappans did not utilize the arch, first invented in Mesopo-

tamia, or the round column. Cylinder seals are found in great
number, although archaeologists are not yet able to decipher
the Harappan inscriptions on them.

The Indus Valley cities differ most noticeably from those of
Mesopotamia and Egypt in their lack of identifiable temples
or monumental sculptures and in the inferior workmanship of
tools and implements. Art is modest here, and on a much smaller
scale than is known for Sumer and Egypt.

But what the Indus Valley peoples lacked in workmanship
and art they made up for in city planning: public and private
wells abounded; streets were straight and intersected at regular
right angles; street drains solved the problems of sewage disposal,
and drains from individual residences led into the public sewers;
houses varied in size and number of rooms, indicating class
differences. But of the eighty settlements excavated so far, all
are uniform in their culture: dwellings were built of standard
sizes of bricks; a system of uniform weights and measures was
clearly established; and wheel-turned pottery is strikingly similar,
even in far-flung settlements. Obviously, the Indus Valley civilization boasted a well-developed political system. And, though
life expectancy was not impressive, careful attention was given
to community matters such as hygiene and sanitation. As in
Egypt, change was slow, at least until the pastoral peoples from
the northwest entered the region about 1500 B.C. The emergent
civilization seems to combine the features of the early Indus
Valley civilization and the culture of the Aryan pastoralists.

The traditional characteristics of civilization—true cities, a
writing system, division of labor and class stratification, state
organization, monumental public constructions, widespread
trade and communication, and the early development of sciences—began to appear in northern China about 1500 B.C. on the
alluvial plains of the Yellow River. Archaeologists know relatively little about early Chinese cultural advances, and they
question whether Chinese civilization emerged as a local development or as the result of stimuli from the Near East. However,
because the most essential criteria for civilization appeared rather
abruptly in northern China, most authorities believe that at least
some aspects of the emerging civilization resulted from the diffusion of ideas and innovations from the west.

Developments in the New World

In the Old World, then, archaeologists have identified four relatively separate centers of early civilization. The dates for these (northern China, c. 1500 B.C.; Indus Valley, c. 2500 B.C.; Egypt, c. 3200 B.C.; and Sumer, c. 3500 B.C.) imply that civilization had its origins in ancient Sumer, and that Sumerian cultural advances provided powerful stimuli for the development of other Old World civilizations. But what of the New World?

The pattern is similar. Archaeologists believe that Mesolithic foraging peoples were harvesting wild corn in the Americas more than 7000 years ago. In Mexico, at some point between 6500 and 5000 B.C., they succeeded in cultivating avocados and squashes, and over the next 2000 years, they domesticated corn, beans, chili, gourds, and other varieties of squashes. Nevertheless, they continued to rely heavily upon hunting and gathering techniques for the bulk of their diet. Then, about 3400 B.C., farming villages began to appear, and people turned increasingly to agriculture. Here, as in the Old World, settled village life had its advantages. Pottery appeared and, with a stable supply of manpower, irrigation agriculture was undertaken by 700 B.C. Less than 1500 years later, true cities flourished on solid agricultural bases.

Again, as in the Old World, early farmers adapted to meet the pressures of diverse environments. In the Mesoamerican lowlands, slash-and-burn (swidden) agriculture was practiced. Since the soil is easily exhausted when cultivated in this manner, the people who employ this method must frequently shift their fields and villages. In the highland regions, however, climatic conditions are more suitable for farming; a smaller area of cultivation can support a denser population and can provide as much as ten times more produce. At the time of European conquest, the fertile Mexican highlands supported Tenochtitlán, the Aztec capital that was five times the size of sixteenth-century London. (See Figure 4.)

The remarkably sophisticated civilizations of Mesoamerica were based on a solid agricultural foundation, the principal products of which were squashes, corn, and beans. In South America, the domesticated potato was the staple food crop,

FIGURE 4.   The Great Temple of Tenochtitlan reconstructed by Ignacio Marguina from descriptions by Spanish conquerors and existing Aztec monuments, Mexico. (Courtesy of the American Museum of Natural History)

though in rain-forest regions manioc was the staff of life. Domesticated animals did not achieve the importance they did in the
Old World until invading Europeans introduced horses, cattle,
and sheep. A few native animals—the llama and alpaca—were
used, and guinea pigs were (and still are) domesticated for food
in the Peruvian Andes. Dogs, of course, were domesticated during
Mesolithic times in the Americas; a few tribes used them for
food.

It was the Neolithic food revolution that gave rise to civilization, to cities as religious and political centers, to specialized
crafts and extensive trade, and to the complex social structures
that helped produce a new way of human life in both the Old
World and the New.

But what use is this knowledge to us? What, in fact, is the
value of archaeology? Ideally, archaeology—together with its
sister disciplines—contributes to a humanistic orientation of life.
Those who understand the past have come to realize the extent
of complexity of human society. Only man has the means to
direct the course of his own destiny; and if he is to improve
his world, he must first understand it. It is well for him to realize
that there are multiple repositories of human truth—and to be
willing to sample them all.

FURTHER READINGS

Childe, V. G. *New Light on the Most Ancient East* (4th ed.). New York:
   Norton, 1969.

Clark, Grahame. *The Mesolithic Settlement of Northern Europe.* Cambridge:
   University Press, 1936.

Clark, Grahame. *World Prehistory.* Cambridge: University Press, 1969.

Clark, Grahame, and Stuart Piggott. *Prehistoric Societies.* New York:
   Alfred A. Knopf, 1968.

Cole, S. *The Prehistory of East Africa.* New York: Menter, 1963.

Daniel, G. E. *The Megalith Builders of Western Europe.* London: Hutchin-
   son, 1958.

Ehrich, R. W. (ed.). *Chronologies in Old World Archaeology.* Chicago:
   University of Chicago Press, 1965.

Hawkes, J. and L. Woolley. *History of Mankind: Cultural and Scientific Development.* Vol. I, Parts 1 and 2, *Prehistory and the Beginnings of Civilization.* New York: Harper & Row, 1963.

Mallowan, M. E. L. *Early Mesopotamia and Iran.* New York: McGraw-Hill, 1965.

Mellaart, J. *Earliest Civilizations of the Near East.* New York: McGraw-Hill, 1966.

Wheeler, M. *Civilizations of the Indus Valley and Beyond.* New York: McGraw-Hill, 1966.

CHAPTER XII

STUDIES IN
LIVING PREHISTORY

When Thor Heyerdahl set sail in May, 1971, in his untested, fifteen-ton papyrus reed boat, he brought to popular attention a controversy that has raged among anthropologists for more than a century. While other, more traditional, scholars were content to argue the possibility of extraordinary prehistoric voyages linking the Old and the New Worlds, Heyerdahl—fonder of action than debate—set out to prove that it was possible for the ancient Egyptians to have conquered the high seas as early as 3000 b.c., landing in the Americas thousands of years before Columbus and in time to have influenced the development of the higher civilizations of Guatemala and Peru.

Heyerdahl and six companions recreated as exactly as they could the conditions that would have existed for Egyptian sailors: their fifty-foot vessel duplicated in minute detail the structure of papyrus craft as depicted in Egyptian tomb hieroglyphics; and they restricted themselves to the food supplies that would have been available at the time. They departed from the same coastal waters of Morocco that launched Columbus, hoping to ride trade winds and equatorial currents across the Atlantic to a safe landing on the Yucatan peninsula, home of the Maya. Their mission was to demonstrate by actual example that prehistoric peoples had the means to traverse uncharted oceans.

For Heyerdahl, who crossed the Pacific twenty-four years ago on the balsa-log raft *Kon-Tiki,* putting out to sea in a paper boat represents no more than a practical (though adventuresome) attempt to solve one of the most intriguing of archaeological riddles: what happened in the Americas before the arrival of Columbus? No one has yet satisfactorily explained the rise of such remarkable New World empires as those of the Toltec, Maya, and Inca, where peoples of amazing sophistication raised highly organized communities characterized by achievements often duplicating—and at times surpassing—those on the other side of the Atlantic. Nor have scientists been able to decipher the cryptic but persistent hints among these communities of pre-Columbian contacts between the Old and New Worlds.

At the heart of the mystery lies the question of human creativity. We know that the earliest Old World civilizations—the growth centers of ancient Egypt, India, China, and the Near East—were variously interrelated, and that the development of each was stimulated by extensive cross-fertilization of ideas and the borrowing of innovations. Scientists have long assumed that human contacts and cultural trading are prerequisite to the development of systems of civilization. Is it possible that the peoples of Central and South America, living in absolute isolation from the cradles of Old World civilization, raised their incredible empires in separate, unrelated development? Or must they have been shaped by influences carried to them by nameless peoples who reached New World shores so long ago that we have no hope of establishing that they existed?

Any ocean poses an awesome barrier to the spread of populations and ideas; anthropologists have traditionally rejected the notion that prehistoric peoples possessed the means to cross an unmapped sea. The isolationists argue (and very adequately) that there is no good reason why the peoples of Central and South America, having once unlocked the secret of agriculture, could not have produced their cultural marvels unaided. Man is a creative animal, given to invention in response to his needs; what he invents in one hemisphere, he can invent independently in the other under the same set of needs and circumstances.

Nevertheless, certain elements in the higher Mesoamerican civilizations are strangely and overwhelmingly reminiscent of Old World cultures, among them the very features that most intrigue Heyerdahl—sun-worship cults, hieroglyphic writing, skilled techniques of human mummification, medical procedures, and pyramids and monuments that rival those of ancient Egypt at the peak of her splendor. Nevertheless, after continuing investigation, no incontrovertible evidence has been found for contact, and many archaeologists contend that transoceanic contact is not necessary to explain cultural parallels. Cultural developments are similar between cultures where we know that there was no contact.[1]

Few professional archaeologists find Heyerdahl's unorthodox research methods acceptable. They argue that his research is inconclusive, his preparations inadequate, and his conclusions untenable. At the same time, however, they encourage their colleagues to devise, like Heyerdahl, their own means of investigating the past. Today's archaeologists represent a new breed of learn-by-doing prehistorians who readily develop unique investigative methods to fit unique problems in prehistory. Their goal is to bring the past to life: to emphasize not the bony remains and fragmentary artifacts of the dead past but the depth and excitement of living prehistory. Limited only by their imaginations, they strive to reconstruct the *living* past.

The "new archaeology" is "experimental archaeology," characterized by attempts to reconstruct the past by recreating activities or events within the limits of what is given in nature and what was, or could have been, available in an aboriginal setting. The keystone of experimental archaeology is imitative experiment.

Although the emphasis is new to archaeology, the imitative experiment itself is not. In 1934 sickle-like objects were recovered from a cave in Mount Carmel. The discovery excited great interest because if the objects in question could be positively identified as having been agricultural tools, they would provide evidence for one of the earliest appearances of the practice of true agriculture in the Near East. Robert Ascher of Cornell University notes:

> The question arose as to whether the luster on the flint edges of the "sickles" was the result of cutting wood, bone, or grass. If it could be demonstrated that the type of luster evident on the "sickles" could be the result of cutting grass, and could

---

[1] Portions of the foregoing introduction are drawn from an article by the authors, "Odyssey: the Peopling of the New World," *Mankind: the Magazine of Popular History,* Vol. II, No. 6, pp. 59–60, © Mankind Publishing Company, 1970.

not be the result of cutting bone or wood, then the practice of agriculture could be inferred.[2]

In 1935, E. C. Curwen performed experiments with parts of replicas of "sickles," closely simulating the amount and kind of wear to which such objects would be subjected. The results of his study demonstrated that bone, wood, and grass produce noticeable differences in luster, and that the type of luster produced by grass was similar to the luster on the sickles from Mount Carmel.

Such imitative experiments were taking place, then, thirty-five years ago. But today's prehistorians attempt such studies much more frequently. Although excavation remains a crucial technique in archaeology, it is now combined with other types of research in order that results can provide the most meaningful explanations of relics and artifacts that are unearthed. Numerous archaeologists stress the importance of ethnographic fieldwork as a degree requirement for graduate students in archaeology, because the background it provides enables them to study the remains of material culture in a more imaginative fashion.

Anthropologists often live for extended periods among contemporary native peoples, extracting from their research a characterization of how life must have been lived among prehistoric peoples. Others, as we have seen, track free-ranging primates or chart primate behavior in controlled situations in order to glean from such studies behavioral traits that might have been common to the earliest hominids. Still others, having excavated prehistoric sites, have chosen to camp among the reconstructed ruins in order to learn how sound ancient shelters were in variable weather, and how food might have been prepared in primitive vessels and over prehistoric hearths. Using only local materials in the making of implements and clothing, they discover how effectively the environment might have assured the comfort and survival of earlier human beings.

Often, as we have noted, insights are to be gained from scientists outside the field of prehistoric studies. For example, geolo-

---

[2] Ascher, Robert, "Experimental Archaeology," *American Anthropologist* 63:793–816, 1961.

(a)

(b)

FIGURE 1. Some contemporary primitive peoples. (a) A Tasaday family from the island of Mindanao, Philippines. The Tasaday until only very recently obtained food, clothing, and shelter with the aid of only Paleolithic-type stone implements. (UPI) (b) A Gran Pajonal Campa girl, Peru, spinning cotton. (Black Star, Emil Schulthers) (c) A woman, also from the Gran Pajonal Campa, making a basket. (Black Star, Victor, Englebert) (d) An Aboriginal woman from Ernabella Mission Station, South Australia, spinning Merino wool into yarn. (Black Star, David Moore) (e) Women of the Small Namba in New Hebrides grating taro with wooden implements. (© Kal Muller, Woodfin Camp)

(c)

(d)

(e)

gists Eiler L. Henrickson of Carleton College and George R. Rapp, Jr. of the University of Minnesota are currently investigating ways to identify the original sources of Bronze Age metal artifacts through trace-element analysis. The major component of such artifacts is copper, and Henrickson and Rapp have hypothesized that copper from diverse regions might contain different quantities or types of trace elements. Their preliminary studies indicate that the trace-element pattern of a copper sample may link it to its source, sometimes so specifically that a particular mine can be identified.

In 1972, archaeologists at Oxford University tested an ingenious method of dating ancient pottery—one based on the fact that most clay contains certain radioactive elements. Employing this new technique, investigators have discovered that a number of pieces prized by the world's most prestigious museums are fakes.

In 1971, Swedish archaeologist Paul Astrom reported success in lifting more than 200 fingerprints impressed on concealed parts of ancient earthenware—prints that survived the centuries to serve as signatures for now-nameless artisans. By comparing intricate loops, arches, and whorls, Astrom found that he could distinguish fingerprints of one group of artisans from those of their predecessors. If fingerprint patterns can indeed be used to identify races and national groups (and most authorities believe that they can), the prehistoric routes of ancient trade items might be traced many thousands of years later.

The point is this: fossil bones and cultural artifacts are invaluable for a reconstruction of the past; but if they are to provide clues that are truly revealing, they must be examined in imaginative ways. Today's prehistorians are prepared to fit their methodology to the problems at hand, devising insightful interpretations through unusual—often bizarre—research techniques. Until months before his death in 1972, L. S. B. Leakey continued to startle his more conservative colleagues by stalking wild game with his bare hands, for it was in this way that he could best reconstruct the hunting habits of early man. Not all studies in living prehistory are so energetic, but most demand imaginative new research methods. The last decade in particular has witnessed exciting new approaches to specific prehistoric problems.

Primate Art

Anthropologists interested in reconstructing the origins of human art have focused their attention on primate art—with the result that at least one orang-utan has made a name for himself in the art world.[3] Djakarta Jim, a five-year-old orang housed in the Topeka, Kansas, Zoological Park, made world headlines recently with his "one-ape" showing of original water-color paintings. One painting, entered under an assumed name, took first place in a regional art contest intended for human artists. In displaying the orang's paintings, Zoo Director Gary Clarke intends no mockery of modern art. He and others insist that primate picture-making serves a valid scientific purpose, providing fresh insights into the development of human art. Certainly Jim's artistic endeavors, performed without the rewards of food or favor customarily bestowed in animal training, represent the ultimate example of tool-use by a nonhuman primate.

Zoologists, psychologists, and animal behavioralists are also serious students of ape art. Physical anthropologists and prehis-

FIGURE 2.   Djakarta Jim supervised by a keeper uses watercolors and non-toxic oils. (Courtesy Gary Clarke)

---

[3] Portions of material presented here on primate art are drawn from an article by the authors, "Djakarta Jim: Prize-Winning Ape Artist," published by *Science Digest,* Vol. 70, No. 4, pp. 28– 33. © The Hearst Corporation, 1971.

torians are more interested in the facts of deliberate tool-use and manipulation—and in the attempt, on the part of an ambidextrous ape, to create a visual image. The earliest known study of infrahuman art was undertaken in Moscow in 1913. Mrs. Nadie Kohts conducted a three-year comparison of the artistic development of her young son Roody with that of an infant chimpanzee named Joni. Early drawings by the two subjects, consisting of simple line-scribbles, were identical in style and execution. Later efforts differed as Roody's development outdistanced the chimp's. Nevertheless, Mrs. Kohts established for the first time the fact that nonhuman primates are capable of artistic progress through time and practice. Joni's later paintings showed a marked increase in visual control, together with a deliberate intersection tendency; that is, Joni began to crisscross bold lines with shorter ones, usually at right angles.

Since the Kohts experiment, more than thirty chimpanzees, gorillas, and orangs—along with a few capuchin monkeys—have been encouraged to paint. Most have produced simple paintings without guidance or assistance, and for all of these animals—as for prize-winner Djakarta Jim—the impulse to draw or paint was self-rewarding.

In an attempt to isolate the basic fundamentals of esthetic creativity, scholars from numerous fields have examined prehistoric cave paintings, contemporary folk art, paintings and sketches made by the mentally disturbed, and infant scribbles. However, as zoologist Desmond Morris notes, none of these sources provides the sort of information necessary to characterize the most fundamental levels of human art. Even the earliest examples of prehistoric cave painting suggest a rather advanced, sophisticated, and stylized level of esthetic expression. The same is true for folk art. As yet, few scientists boast the skills needed for an objective analysis of the art of the insane or of infant scribbles which are influenced by proud or scornful parents at even the earliest stages. On the other hand, primate picture-making represents artistic effort in its simplest and most rudimentary stages. Many scholars believe that it is only from ape art that they can deduce the fundamentals of esthetic creativity and reveal the origins of human art. Working at the London Zoo with an amiable chimp named Congo, Desmond Morris studied nearly 400 pongid pictures. He concluded that ape artists demonstrate—at minimum levels—the definite elements of esthetic variation, composition control, and calligraphic development that characterize human artists. Pongid artwork also appears to have an intriguing relationship to the scribbles of very young children. The precise nature of that relationship remains to be defined, but studies in primate art appear to be promising for the light they may yet shed on the origins of human art.

Numerous primatologists have been working too on discovering the origins of human speech. At the famed Yerkes Primate Center in Atlanta, Georgia, researchers are trying to discover just how much capacity for language nonhuman primates possess. In an ongoing study, designed to span a period of four years, young orangs and chimpanzees will be taught to gain rewards by pressing lighted keys on a large keyboard of symbols. At first, a single correct response will bring the reward, but gradually the primate subjects will be expected to combine several different symbols, just as a human child must learn to form a sentence from words. Responses are computerized so that the results will be available for study in statistical form.

Mummies and Radiography

Other advances in science yield similar benefits. The development of radiography, for example, has expanded the scope of studies involving mummified human remains, which are of particular interest because preserved body tissue yields considerable information not obtainable from cultural or skeletal remains.[4] From the Egyptian mummies, for example, anthropologists have gathered a wealth of information regarding ancient disease patterns—evidence which greatly extends our knowledge of life in ancient times. But there are cultural riches, too, to be retrieved from the bodies of Egypt's royal dead: personal jewelry, gold talismans, and precious stones hidden within the mummy wrappings at the time of entombment. These are of great interest

---

[4] Portions of the material presented here on radiography of mummified remains is drawn from an article by Sharon S. McKern in *Science Digest*, Vol. 68, No. 1, pp. 8–13 © The Hearst Corporation 1970.

to archaeologists who hope to reconstruct the history of Egyptian spiritual beliefs.

The artificially preserved bodies of Egypt's richest pharoahs first captured public attention in 1922 when, after six seasons of unrewarding excavation, a young British archaeologist named Howard Carter descended into the depths of a 3300-year-old tomb and emerged to announce the single most spectacular discovery in the history of archaeology: the undisturbed tomb of Tutankhamen, with treasures and mummy intact. There had been earlier discoveries in Egypt's Valley of the Kings, but most of the mummies previously recovered had been ravaged by looters in distant times. Intent upon taking small, transportable valuables, these determined thieves ripped open coffins to get at the royal mummies, and then hacked away with knives to collect the gold, silver, and gems that were by custom tucked into the mummy wrappings. Working in desperate haste, the vandals smashed what could not be carried out and set fire to the broken coffins. Often, they left behind a trail of discarded booty—including, in one instance, a heavily-bejeweled mummy arm dropped into a corner by an ancient intruder anxious to make his escape. Modern prehistorians have found recovered mummies so badly damaged that they were useless for study.

But the discovery of Tutankhamen, intact after thirty-three centuries, raised the hope that other unravaged remains could be found. Swarms of scientists descended into the Valley to follow Carter's new methodical approach to excavation. And the new scientific procedures proved fruitful: an incredulous public watched as tomb after tomb was located and emptied of its remarkable contents, to be studied and preserved as a priceless heritage.

Now literally hundreds of mummies were available for study. But examination, involving the unwrapping and dissection of the remains, was necessarily destructive. Some mummies that had defied decomposition for more than two thousand years began to putrefy as soon as their wrappings were removed. Others crumpled to a fine powder that rose in dusty clouds when they were handled.

The task of unwrapping was in itself monumental. Each mummy is enveloped in an elaborate series of linen bandages.

The swathing for an average specimen may measure 450 yards in all; and one mummy wore 876 yards of gossamer-sheer fabric. Rings, bracelets, necklaces, and gold finger-stalls are intricately entwined within the wrappings, and dozens of gold and gem-encrusted amulets are tucked deep within them, caught up in multiple alternate layers wound crosswise and transversely. Carter found 143 costly charms distributed over 101 separate parts of Tutankhamen's mummy. In order to retrieve such valuables for study, unwrapping was necessary—and often impossible. Ancient morticians poured embalming unguents over each mummy. These sticky oils and resins hardened through time to pitch-like consistency, and modern investigators were forced to chisel away at the wrappings, without direction and with obviously unfortunate results. Prehistorians found themselves perched uncomfortably on the horns of an investigative dilemma: did they preserve and protect the remains by foregoing examination? Or did they collect facts and riches, risking destruction of the mummy through exposure and autopsy? X-ray analysis, of course, might circumvent these two equally unacceptable alternatives. But few investigators had access to complex radiographic equipment, and most museum directors were reluctant to permit the removal of mummies from their collections for even a short time.

Such obstacles were scaled with the development of small portable x-ray units, and radiography has recently emerged as a rewarding new research tool in the study of mummified remains. In 1968, for example, researchers found that the mummy long identified as Queen Makeri's baby contained instead the skeleton of a monkey. This was a simple case of mistaken identity, embarrassing to museum curators but understandable because animal remains are not often found in royal sarcophagi. But x-ray analysis works equally well in detecting forgeries. Mummy "fakes" are sold relatively frequently to unsuspecting collectors and amateur archaeologists; these turn out most often to contain the bandaged remains of animals or lumpy concoctions of wood, plaster, and wire. X-ray also discloses the presence of other objects: in one case, a mummy with an amputated forearm was found to be wearing a carefully-fitted artificial limb complete with digits.

Anthropologists have learned that while they can date a coffin by style they cannot assume that it contains its original occupant. A coffin bearing the name of a man may turn out to hold the mummy of a woman. X-ray detects from the skeletal remains facts of age and sex sufficient to verify identity, without unwrapping or disturbing the mummy itself. Ancient embalming techniques, previously known only through destructive autopsy, can now be confirmed through radiographic analysis. The Egyptian mummification process entailed the total evisceration of the body, and in early specimens, eviscerated organs were cleansed and placed into canopic jars to be entombed with the mummy. In later specimens, these organs were wrapped and restored, with sawdust or other packing material, to the appropriate body

FIGURE 3.   Side view of x-rayed Egyptian mummy shows a dense object on the lip which was a solid gold disc. Solid mass in the back of the skull indicates hot resin was poured through the nostrils after the brain was removed. Pins are modern; they hold deteriorating wrappings in place. (Photo courtesy of Eastman Kodak)

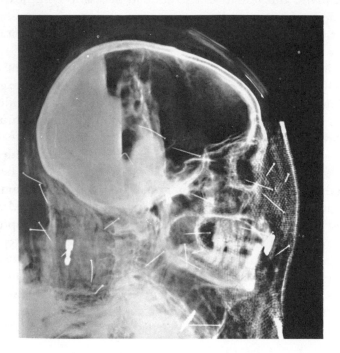

cavity. To render the corpse more life-like, mud was packed under the skin, and artificial eyes were placed over the shrunken orbits. Evidence for each of these procedures is apparent through x-ray. Indications of disease and injury are readily visible, too. Several diseases previously assumed to be modern in origin—arteriosclerosis and cirrhosis among them—have been diagnosed in mummified remains. Arthritis, silicosis, pneumonia, appendicitis, kidney disease, fractures, gallstones, and traumatic childbirth have also been diagnosed. Sometimes, x-ray isolates the actual cause of death.

For archaeologists, the most dramatic use of radiography is in the recovery of valuables incorporated into the mummy wrappings. Some specimens are literally wrapped in layers of gold and precious stones, while others boast only a few protective amulets of hammered gold. Apparently the wealth hidden within the mummy wrappings was in proportion to the rank of the individual and the affection of his survivors. Because amulets are radiopaque, they are readily detected by x-ray. Once localized, they may be retrieved by archaeologists through small, careful incisions in the wrappings, leaving the mummy otherwise undisturbed. Investigators have recovered innumerable objects in this way. Their value in sheer bullion is enormous; and as objects of art or clues to the past, they are beyond price.

Not all modern archaeological techniques are so dramatic. At every large university, prehistorians continue to perform the more tedious, mundane tasks that still comprise so large a part of the study of prehistory. For every Leakey and Heyerdahl, there are hundreds of lesser-known researchers who make invaluable contributions to the science through the constant refinement of existing techniques. In fact the most significant aspect of the "new archaeology" is its emphasis on improvement over older methods. This is crucial, for to dig is to destroy, and once an excavation has been completed, nothing remains but the reports prepared on the findings. The site cannot be restored to its original state for re-checking or re-evaluation. There is no opportunity for an independent worker to dig again in the hope of validating (or disputing) published findings. Thus the repetition of an experiment, the most basic requirement in science, cannot be achieved in archaeological excavation. Compensation must be found in meticulous excavations and accurate, detailed records. These are all that remain, in the end, of hard-sought clues to the living past.

FURTHER READINGS

Brothwell, D. R. and E. Higgs (eds.). *Science in Archaeology*. London: Thames & Hudson, Ltd., 1963.

Carter, Howard. *The Tomb of Tutankhamen*. London: Cassell & Co., 1927.

Kellogg, W. N. and L. A. Kellogg. *The Ape and the Child*. New York: McGraw-Hill, 1933.

McKern, Sharon S. *Exploring the Unknown: Mysteries in American Archaeology*. New York: Praeger, 1972.

Morris, Desmond. *The Biology of Art*. New York: Alfred A. Knopf, 1962.

INDEX